To Roxane —
I am looking forward to
happy days working with
you.

Best

Jeff

Summer
2011

# CLOSED MINDS?

# CLOSED MINDS?

## Politics and Ideology in American Universities

BRUCE L. R. SMITH

JEREMY D. MAYER

A. LEE FRITSCHLER

BROOKINGS INSTITUTION PRESS
*Washington, D.C.*

*Copyright © 2008*
THE BROOKINGS INSTITUTION
1775 Massachusetts Avenue, N.W., Washington, D.C. 20036
www.brookings.edu

*Library of Congress Cataloging-in-Publication data*
Smith, Bruce L. R.
  Closed minds? : politics and ideology in American universities / Bruce L. R. Smith, Jeremy D. Mayer, A. Lee Fritschler.
       p.       cm.
  Includes bibliographical references and index.
  Summary: "From interviews, focus groups, and a national survey, paints a comprehensive picture of today's campus political attitudes. Contrasts the current climate of disengagement with the original civic mission of American colleges and universities, and suggests how universities can reclaim and strengthen their place in the nation's political and civic life"—Provided by publisher.
  ISBN 978-0-8157-8028-1 (cloth : alk. paper)
  1. Education, Higher—Political aspects—United States. I. Mayer, Jeremy D. II. Fritschler, A. Lee, 1937– III. Title.
  LC173.S59 2008
  378.73—dc22                                              2008020085

9 8 7 6 5 4 3 2 1

The paper used in this publication meets minimum requirements of the American National Standard for Information Sciences—Permanence of Paper for Printed Library Materials: ANSI Z39.48-1992.

Typeset in Minion

Composition by Pete Lindeman, OSP Inc.
Arlington, Virginia

Printed by R. R. Donnelley
Harrisonburg, Virginia

*For*
DEJA *and* JACKSON
NAORU
AIDEN *and* PHOEBE

# Contents

Appendixes

# Acknowledgments

We gratefully acknowledge the assistance of the Lounsbery Foundation of Washington, D.C., in supporting our work. Jesse Ausubel of Rockefeller University, a member of the Lounsbery Foundation's board, originally suggested the idea for the study. We thank him and David Abshire, president of the foundation, and Maxmillian Angerholzer III, its executive director, for their encouragement and support. Rodney W. Nichols, adviser to the foundation, was a source of wise counsel and encouragement throughout the project.

Allan Silver of Columbia University helped to point the effort in the right direction and provided helpful suggestions at critical points. Catherine E. Rudder of George Mason University was a stimulating colleague and advised us on a number of difficult methodological problems. James H. Finkelstein, vice dean of the School of Public Policy, George Mason University, ran interference for us over the course of the project.

The University of Virginia's Center for Survey Research administered our national survey and came up with innovative ways to ensure a high response rate and a representative sample (as we discuss more fully in the technical appendix on sampling). In particular, Thomas Guterbock, Debby Kermer, and John Lee Holmes were crucial to the success of our survey. We thank all of our academic colleagues from around the country who took the time to complete the survey and, in a number of cases, volunteered additional comments.

Special thanks are owed to Robert E. Calvert of DePauw University, whose own work helped to give shape and direction to our effort. He read the entire manuscript with great care and offered extensive and detailed suggestions for revisions that greatly strengthened our analysis. C. Peter Magrath of the College Board and former president of the National Association of State Universities and Land-Grant Colleges (as well as three major universities over the course of his career) read the manuscript in draft and offered a detailed commentary, which was of great assistance. An anonymous Brookings reviewer gave a pointed and useful critique of certain aspects of our work.

We benefited from discussions with Richard D. Legon, president of the Association of Governing Boards of Universities and Colleges; Terry Hartle, senior vice president of the American Council on Education; Robert Andringa, former president of the Council for Christian Colleges and Universities; Anne D. Neal, president of the American Council of Trustees and Alumni; Roger Bowen, former executive director of the American Association of University Professors; Representative Gibson C. Armstrong of the Pennsylvania House of Representatives; Dustin Gingrich, staff director of the Pennsylvania Select Committee on Academic Freedom; and professors Joseph J. Karlesky of Franklin and Marshall College, Clyde Wilcox of Georgetown University, Neil Gross of Harvard University, Matthew Woessner of Penn State Harrisburg, April Kelly-Woessner of Elizabethtown College, and Michael Munger of Duke University.

To the many impressive students and dedicated college professors and administrators we interviewed, or with whom we discussed informally various aspects of the study, we give a general but heartfelt expression of our appreciation. It was a great pleasure to have the chance to talk with so many thoughtful and enjoyable colleagues. We almost wish the project could go on forever (and sometimes it seemed like it would!).

We thank our students Gayatri Ramnath and Brian Hanlon for research assistance and Elizabeth Kelly of Duke University for her assistance. Marjorie Crow typed numerous drafts of the manuscript. Robert Faherty, Mary Kwak, and their colleagues at Brookings Institution Press were especially helpful and encouraging.

# 1

## Introduction

Our aim in this study is to examine whether there is political or ideological bias in American higher education. We want to evaluate the criticisms of universities for being too left or liberal and to undertake the task in a systematic, fair-minded, and nonpartisan fashion. We know that we cannot fully answer all of the questions surrounding this topic, but we hope at least to chart the terrain sensibly. By making a convincing start, we hope that other scholars can develop the subject further. More answers will emerge as colleagues (and citizens) debate the issues, and, of course, there will be no final answers on some of the broadest questions. It is also important, as part of the inquiry, to discuss how universities *should* address what we call the civic education and citizenship issue—that is, what should colleges and universities be doing to prepare students better for effective citizenship in our democracy. This concern broadly relates to the teaching of political philosophy, values, rule of law, professional ethics, and what it means to be a citizen, matters that call for reasoned argument but do not lend themselves to scientific truth.

We represent in our study team a broad range of the political spectrum, from Republican to Democratic to a shade of Green, although it is probable that none of us would qualify as among the most fervent of partisans. If we could manage to achieve a measure of agreement among ourselves, we hoped to be able to provide research results that our fellow citizens and our academic colleagues of all political persuasions might find useful and worthy of consideration.

Because the topic is difficult, we chose to approach the task through a variety of methodologies and angles of vision. We examined carefully previous studies to identify what has been proven and not proven and what new approaches might be fruitfully pursued. We sought to avoid mere eclecticism and anecdote, although we have not been afraid to draw on the "tacit" knowledge we have gained through long experience in the trenches as teachers, administrators, and policy analysts.

The subject of faculty political attitudes and ideology has been much studied and written about, in systematic and less systematic ways, since at least the 1950s by scholars from a number of disciplines. We make no pretense that we can fully resolve the contradictions, the inconsistencies, and differing interpretations found in previous studies. Achieving convincing methods of studying the topic entails not only the challenge of gathering data but also the challenge of drawing sensible conclusions and interpretations once we have agreed on the "facts." But we are convinced, and believe that our colleagues and fellow citizens will come to share our belief, that it is possible to discuss the issues civilly and, in the process, to achieve a deeper understanding of how the universities can serve society. Our overall finding, it is only fair to tell the reader up-front, is that we do not find evidence of rampant bias in the universities or of liberal bias in the conventional meaning of the term. We find evidence of an "antipolitical" bias in much of what the modern research universities do. That is to say, most professors, like most Americans, have an aversion to politics and find ways to avoid thinking seriously about politics and political issues. There is a tendency to take refuge in forms of specialized and "objective" knowledge, which is thought to be a more lofty intellectual endeavor than trying to cope with the muddy normative issues of politics. There may also be a kind of reflexive utopianism in the thinking—or non-thinking—that professors bring to political matters. Professors are not always aware of the political and philosophical assumptions concealed in their thinking. In this sense, we argue, the universities are not permeated with politics; in fact, they do not have enough political awareness or the right kind of political engagement.

The alleged negative effects of too much politics are not in evidence when one looks at the universities. Professors, even conservative professors, do not generally think that they are discriminated against in hiring (according to the responses to our survey questionnaire). Nor do they believe that they are biased in the classroom. This is perhaps not surprising since nobody likes to think he or she behaves unprofessionally. If professors were the only ones to think that they are not biased in the classroom, we might be inclined to worry that they are uncritical and not conscious of their own faults. But we found that students also do not believe that their professors are biased to any significant degree, although conservative students are more likely to think their professors are somewhat more biased than liberal students do. Moreover, a state legislative inquiry—the most extensive of its kind in the nation—found, as we detail in chapter 7, that bias is "rare" in the state's public colleges and universities. Taken together, the weight of the evidence seems convincing to us.

Then why has there been such concern about political bias, and why do some Americans continue to believe strongly that professors are biased? We answer this question in several ways, first by showing how various activists have used the idea of bias as a political tactic. According to activists and interest groups on the political right, radicals have taken over the universities and use them as a base to launch attacks on mainstream values. And activists and interest groups that we identify as politically left have created their own bogeyman in depicting a right-wing conspiracy to subvert academic freedom and bring universities to heel. These individuals and groups have needed each other to rally their own forces. But this rhetorical combat has come to reflect a kind of shadowboxing among activists, but there are real differences in cultural perspectives.

We start the study by setting the modern American university in its proper historical context. That is, we briefly trace the evolution of the American university from a predominant role as transmitter of cultural values to teachers, ministers, and other professional classes to the emergence of the modern research university in the period after the Civil War and the early part of the twentieth century. The modern university has its origins in (a) the evolution of some of the older colonial and postcolonial colleges, (b) the institutions created under the land grant legislation adopted during the Civil War and subsequent federal legislation, and (c) the entirely new institutions made possible by the vast new wealth and philanthropy of the Gilded Age. Americans borrowed from German conceptions to form the new entity of the research university. We also cover the emergence of tenure as a protection against presidents and trustees who widely and freely fired professors for speaking out on topics such as socialism, unionism, and pacifism. And we sketch the many changes affecting the universities as the country moved first to an era of mass higher education after World War II and then to the eclectic and global university of today.

The universe of postsecondary education in the United States is a complex one, including 4,200 two- and four-year degree-granting institutions, of which 1,700 are public and 2,500 are private (in addition, some 2,150 more nondegree-granting schools also qualify for federal student aid). Of the 1,700 public institutions, 1,100 are two-year colleges, which enroll half of all freshmen. Of the 2,500 independent private institutions, some 1,600 are four-year, not-for-profit colleges (and an additional 300 are four-year, for-profit institutions). About 20 percent of undergraduates are enrolled in private institutions. An interesting feature of our system is that we have 900 religiously affiliated institutions enrolling about 1.5 million of the 15 million undergraduate students in all of postsecondary education. A few of the religiously affiliated institutions are universities, but most are four-year colleges. The religiously affiliated schools are largely Christian, of which about 225 are Roman Catholic, more than 100 are bible colleges, more than 150 are seminaries, about 150 other schools combine faith and civic missions, and 150 others have become more secular and are scarcely distinguishable from the nonreligious colleges. Congress has exempted these religious institutions from the application of nondiscrimination laws regarding the hiring of faculty members, so such schools are allowed to hire only Christians, only Jews (or no Jews), or only members of their own particular denomination.

Our concern in this study is primarily with the PhD-granting universities that are research intensive—that is, the universities receiving most of the federal research funds and granting the largest share of the graduate and four-year undergraduate degrees. In some sense, these institutions serve as the flagship institutions of the entire higher education system. The most elite of the more than 200 institutions granting the doctoral degree are the sixty-four universities belonging to the Association of American Universities (AAU).

Our work includes a national survey conducted in 2007 from a unique random sample provided by the Center for Survey Research of the University of Virginia and distributed via e-mail and the World Wide Web. We include our survey instrument and our focus group design as part of the methodological appendix. While our random sample includes in its universe all undergraduate institutions in the country, we focus primarily on the research-intensive universities, especially those in the AAU, plus a number of other, less research-intensive universities (and to a degree our analysis also applies to the select four-year liberal arts colleges). Seventeen of the AAU universities are listed among the top twenty universities in the world, according to a recent survey (and thirty-five are in the top fifty). Since the charge is that the elite universities are dominated by a liberal and secular ideology, we look mainly at those institutions. Also, since it is primarily at these institutions that faculty receive their graduate degrees, bias at these institutions, if it does exist, would have an impact beyond their campuses. As it turns out, the assumption that the research universities harbor the most liberal faculty members is wrong since recent studies have shown that the select liberal arts colleges and the less research-intensive universities have a slightly higher percentage of the more liberal professors on their faculties than do the major research universities.

The major research universities attract the most publicity, often unfavorable, about episodes of alleged bias, but this may reflect the fact that there is *more,* rather than less, contention and debate on these elite campuses than on the other campuses. The intense media attention that has focused on the major universities may reflect in some part the perspectives and the "master narrative" brought by the media to their scrutiny of the universities. Populist critics who attack universities often find the elite schools the more tempting targets. The fact that universities are uncomfortable with bad publicity is understandable and certainly part of the reason why they are chary about genuine political debate. The nuances of an academic debate do not always translate into the rough and tumble of real politics.

The vocabulary for discussing the issues that concern us is itself worthy of study, because words such as *bias, political,* and *ideology,* not to mention the terms *liberal* or *conservative,* create confusion and often obscure meaning. Anything political connotes *partisan* to many Americans who dislike politics to begin with, and the term *bias* creates an impression that universities engage in improper partisan activities. But if *political* is understood to refer to our shared understandings and institutions and to the public good, the public philosophy implied by the American Constitution, including the rights and obligations of citizenship, the relevance of the framers' civic republican tradition for the contemporary scene, and other broad issues of common concern—as we think it should—then clearly political debate belongs in the universities and, indeed, should be encouraged and considered a vital part of what universities are *for.* And to have a view, viewpoint, approach, or interpretation of an event—and to bring such views to one's classroom—is not to impose bias on one's students, but to teach. Students expect their professors to profess, to expound on the subject, and are savvy enough to know when they are being stimulated, their minds are being stretched, or when, and if, they are being bamboozled. In chapter 8, we take up and develop these themes further.

Focusing on the major universities, however, leaves out of our consideration most of the institutions that self-identify as conservative or religious. A special kind of ideological and religious orientation exists on such campuses and gives them a clear sense of purpose that is rarely found in the large heterogeneous research universities. For example, Brigham Young University, which according to the Carnegie Corporation classification system is among the nation's important research universities, gives preference to Mormons in hiring in accord with the university's mission. We do not suggest that there is anything improper with a religious institution preferring an avowedly religious individual for its faculty, but a complete picture of faculty bias in the nation's universities would have to include this consideration. It is little known outside of the academy, and sometimes even within it, that higher education is one of the few remaining job markets where an applicant can be turned away from a job for being an atheist or for being (or not being) Jewish, even though universities now operate within a complicated framework of affirmative action laws and regulations that outlaw other kinds of discrimination.[1]

Another aspect of this study is the curriculum. If higher education has begun to reflect the cultural disputes in the broader society (or has played a part in igniting those disputes), the divide between universities that teach science as a secular discipline and those few that teach creationism or intelligent design is a stark example. Whether secular universities can or should teach courses about the role of religion in society, and how or whether they can do so without advocating particular religions, is a serious issue that should be debated inside and outside the universities. This is a matter that merits further research and reflection, but we have made only passing reference to the topic here. As in other aspects of our study, we hope to stimulate debate, discussion, and research on the many issues we touch on but cannot fully resolve.

For the purposes of this study, we focus on three areas where, presumably, if bias of a political nature is to be found, it will show up most importantly. Hence we focus mainly on three areas: classroom behavior, hiring and personnel decisions, and the general intellectual climate at the elite institutions, knowing full well how difficult it is to get an accurate perspective on these issues. Definitive answers, especially findings that would meet the highest standards of scientific rigor, are very difficult to come by, and we are often forced to settle for assessments and judgments of a more qualitative nature. Despite the difficulties and uncertainties, we think our findings, preliminary and provisional though they may be, are more than suggestive, and, indeed, we gain confidence in our conclusions because they are supported by a number of quite different methods of analysis. We therefore are confident that we have called attention to issues of importance and presented some clear findings.

Overall, to our surprise, we found that, far from being saturated in politics, the universities generally have all but ignored what used to be called civics and civic education. Universities *should be* the home of lively and civilized political debate, and all too often, for a host of reasons, professors ignore political debate and have little or no interest in the basics of the constitutional order, in political philosophy, and in the ethical dimensions of the professions or of democratic society. We believe that these topics should be a part of every undergraduate curriculum.

Thus we believe that universities should in some sense return to a role that they played more than a century ago, namely, that of educating students for citizenship in our democratic society. We make no pretense that this will be an easy task or that we know exactly how the universities should revise their undergraduate and professional school curricula to accommodate and encourage a new focus on the values of civic awareness and democratic citizenship. But we offer various suggestions to this effect in chapter 9. The obstacles to achieving such a goal will be formidable, for students and professors have struck a comfortable bargain in which students pursue vocationalism and professors pursue their specialized research interests, while both neglect important elements of a liberal education.

Many vital issues confront the modern university, but political bias is not one of them, if by this we mean that professors are engaged in an effort to indoctrinate their students according to some political ideology. Nor do we find a suffocating uniformity that pervades all departments, schools, and programs across the complex, sprawling, and heterogeneous modern university. Departments, schools, and programs are more likely to pursue their own specialized paths, down the many byways of knowledge and buffeted by the many distractions that pull students and professors into their distinct specialties and subspecialties. We are trying to refocus attention on what is common in the educational experience and how the universities can help to prepare their students for democratic citizenship. We hope our readers will find our arguments worthy of their consideration.

# 2

## Higher Education
## and the "Culture Wars"

Have America's universities shifted pervasively to the political (or to the cultural) left and become captive to a narrow ideology? In the past thirty years, critics, many of them conservatives, have thought so. The assertion is that the typical American university has been dominated by ideologues outside the mainstream or at any rate hostile to traditional values, with the corollary that faculty members and administrators tend to foster a "politically correct" campus environment.[1] At a time when the left in American politics apparently had lost its political moorings and the right seemed ascendant, the universities were said to be a last bastion of leftist thinking or sometimes were merely depicted as being absorbed in a narrow, self-obsessed internal debate that was largely divorced from real-world politics.

Yet American higher education has been viewed as a world model for its independence from government, business, and other outside institutions, for its transparency, and for its fostering of open debate and discussion. If these characteristics are being eroded, it behooves those of us in the higher education community to think about making timely changes. It is a fair guess that most in higher education today consider independence and transparency to be values of the highest importance and deem "service" to society—at least short-run service—to be a lesser goal, although some feel that the universities are far too eager to pander to commercial and government interests. To lose control over hiring and promoting faculty, granting tenure, and defining curricula and requirements for evaluating students to outside bodies, including national, state, and local government or corporate influences, would alarm educators, who would feel that the loss of autonomy betokens a university system less able to serve society effectively in the longer run.

Richard Hofstadter in his classic study *Anti-Intellectualism in American Life* cites four main sources of anti-intellectualism in American life: certain aspects of our religious life, including periodic bursts of spiritual fervor; a preoccupation with practicality in our business culture and practices; a radical egalitarianism in the ever-present populist tendencies in our politics; and a misplaced utopianism and overemphasis on egalitarianism in what Progressive educational reformers thought was conducive to "democracy" in our educational practices.[2] Given "mass" higher education, we see in the universities today some of the same tensions and debates about educational practices that face America's public schools. America has yet to reconcile comfortably our aspirations for a thriving high culture, which is elitist by nature, with the egalitarian impulses of our popular culture.[3] In this book we seek to explore these and related concerns, and we try to account for why the debate over the universities has heated up so dramatically in recent years. The debates have taken many odd turns and twists, and strange bedfellows have been much in evidence. Attention to what the argument was all about will help us to understand the alignments and coalitions at work.

## The Conservative Revolt and the "Culture Wars"

We can date the conservative critique of the universities from the work of Allan Bloom. Bloom was neither the first nor the most systematic conservative critic of the modern research university. At least within the discipline of political science, Herbert Storing in a 1962 collection, *Essays on the Scientific Study of Politics*, challenged the prevailing premises of the "value-neutral" behavioral study of politics.[4] Yet Bloom, a political philosopher from the University of Chicago, was clearly the paterfamilias of the more recent conservative critics of higher education, touching off a debate extending well beyond the confines of the academy. Storing's work was noticed, like most scholarly books, by only a very narrow circle of colleagues in his discipline. Bloom, a prominent member of the "Straussian" school of thought, published *The Closing of the American Mind* in 1987, which shortly became a national bestseller, selling more than one million copies.[5]

Although Bloom made references to actual conditions on a few campuses, his book was not an empirical work. It was, rather, an engaging and stimulating foray into intellectual history. The book's popularity with conservatives was surprising, however, inasmuch as the targets of his wrath included many notions that had become pet themes of contemporary conservatives. Nor was Bloom a conservative in the sense of traditional conservative figures such as Edmund Burke or American conservative thinkers such as Russell Kirk. Bloom, without the benefit of a consistent conservative position, freely criticized Enlightenment as well as post-Enlightenment thought, modernity in general, American materialism, individualism, capitalism and the culture that resulted from the free market, scientism and the scientific outlook, popular culture, rock music (which he especially loathed), and a host of sacred cows and popular causes of all kinds. While he was broadly in the tradition of conservatives as diverse as Edward Shils and Leo Strauss, his attacks on the market and on science, which had become rare in more recent conservative thought, made him an unusual hero for conservatives. He generally cast the university as properly being in an adversarial role toward society, and in this respect he belonged with the cultural left and with avant-garde social critics. He wanted the universities to play the role of social critic and to disparage mainstream American values, which he considered materialistic and shallowly utilitarian. His ideal was that of a university devoted to a traditional liberal education, meaning primarily classical studies. In this sense he was a traditionalist in his pedagogy, a cultural conservative, and a defender of the Western canon against postmodernism. Bloom scarcely mentioned the sciences and the engineering disciplines and paid no attention whatsoever to the role of the professional schools in the universities. He thus encapsulated the splits in the conservative critique, opposing the idea that the universities should be "useful" (favored by populists on the right) and advocating an emphasis on the classics (favored by traditionalists and cultural elitists, many of whom were also political liberals).

While Bloom's book was attracting widespread attention, a debate over the "literary canon" roiled English departments in the universities and spilled over into the wider public dispute that was now set in motion. A minor furor was precipitated by an article appearing in 1988 in the *Chronicle of Higher Education* by Christopher Clausen, chair of the English Department at Pennsylvania State University.[6] In the article, entitled "It Is Not Elitist to Place Major Literature at the Center of the English Curriculum," Clausen made a vigorous, if conventional, defense of the traditional Western canon. What, one might ask, if it *were* elitist? As an aside, in any case, he opined that he would "bet that [Alice Walker's] *The Color Purple* is taught in more English courses today than all of Shakespeare's plays combined."[7] This offhand remark, which turned out to be grossly incorrect when the Modern Language Association examined curricula at a large number of universities, was quoted in columns of the *Washington Post,* the *New York Times,* and the *Wall Street Journal* as proof of the deplorable growth of "political correctness" on America's campuses. The dispute had nothing to do with politics in the usual sense; it was a cultural issue or an issue of academic politics.[8] The squabbles within English departments were simply a return to the "normal" state of affairs for the field, which has never had a central paradigm (except for the temporary period just before and after World War II, when the New Criticism gave English professors, at some universities at least, a sense of unified professionalism).

University of Virginia sociologist James D. Hunter in 1991 gave general expression (and the label) to the debate when he published *Culture Wars: The Struggle to Define America,* in which he cast the debate over the universities in the wider framework of a clash of cultural perspectives in American society.[9] He saw a battle under way between, on the one side, those whom he called the traditionalists or those with an "orthodox" outlook, who were committed to "an external, definable, and transcendent authority," and, on the other side, the progressives, who were defined by their adherence to the spirit of the modern age, a more rationalist outlook.[10]

The orthodox traditionalists were not to be dismissed as mere reactionaries. They were sustained by a deep moral vision—a commitment to the continuity of the best in the nation's traditions—and guided by enduring principles. The progressives, for their part, also had a compelling moral vision and commitment to a noble end. Their goal was nothing less than "the further emancipation of the human spirit and the creation of an inclusive and tolerant world."[11]

The terms of the resulting debate that raged on the campuses and in the media were confused and confusing. Symposia, conferences, campus events, and professional gatherings took up the challenge of defining what the clash of cultural perspectives meant for the universities or for the nation. The views ranged from celebrating the changes in the curriculum to deploring them and from urging a new social engagement to counseling a retreat from the messy external world to the inner citadels of the academy and pure scholarship. The contributors to the debates were sometimes overtly polemical but more often scholarly in tone. Nearly all commentators, wherever located in Hunter's typology of cultural warriors, agreed that the "mass" nature of higher education was a striking new phenomenon for the system, if not for the elite institutions that did not absorb large new numbers of students. The greatly expanded access to higher education and the more diverse student bodies had, however, inevitably produced changes everywhere in the curriculum, in faculties, and in university operations.

The campus debates eventually began to produce, among a mainstream core of faculty members, a degree of intellectual exhaustion with the subject and a rough consensus on a few principles. These might be stated as follows: cultural conflicts were to be lived with and accommodated. Differences were to be debated, respected, but not harped upon endlessly, with an implication that beyond a certain point enough would have been said and everybody could get back to work. But academics can never agree wholly or come up with the last word on any argument (this is the bane but also the glory of the species *homo academicus*). Gerald Graff, in *Beyond the Culture Wars*, took the view that the cultural conflicts in the universities were simply the inevitable result of a long period of "expanding the departmental and curricular playing field."[12] The conflicts that "have accumulated as the academy has diversified have become so deep, antagonistic, and openly political that it has become impossible to prevent them from becoming visible to outsiders."[13] But the way to handle this problem, in his view, was simply to make the conflicts grist for the intellectual mills—that is, to include discussion and debate of the issues in the curriculum: "The academic curriculum has become a prominent arena of cultural conflict because it is a microcosm, as it should be, of the clash of attitudes and values in America as a whole."[14]

That was one solution to the problem of adapting to, and perhaps insulating the universities from, the populist impulses in the national life. Another solution was simply to distance oneself from the culture wars altogether and retreat into one's scholarly work. To Mark Lilla, it was important to "disconnect" from the culture wars, which were the consequence of the universities becoming mass institutions. There are, he insisted, "dangers in letting oneself be drawn too deeply into these debates. . . . So let this be the last symposium on the culture wars. Let us turn back to our work, back to speaking to the happy few still capable of discussing the arts, literature, and ideas in a language that will forever remain alien to that of populist democratic politics."[15] (Lilla did not heed his own injunction, however, rejoining the battle with a significant new contribution.)

To Stanford historian Thomas Bender, in a careful scholarly analysis of American academic culture over the past fifty years, the important point was simply that "the ambitious, white, male, Europe-oriented professional culture of major research universities that had taken its style and intellectual agenda from the 1950s could not sustain itself through the last quarter of the twentieth century."[16] In the place of the 1950s academic culture, there had arisen "a more varied and thus more complicated academic culture that found it difficult to speak with one voice."[17] To speak of the culture wars in journalistic shorthand was not, to Bender and many others, a helpful way to understand the complex and subtle reality taking place in the universities. We agree with his assessment, and we try in this book to supply a compelling analysis of what has happened in the universities. In particular, we explore, and challenge, the conventional notion that the universities were "taken over" by a gang of politically correct radicals after the 1960s who practiced "identity politics" and subverted the quest for truth. The 1960s certainly brought changes to the academic culture of the 1950s, but the academic culture that emerged after World War II was unusual in many ways and not the unproblematic "golden age" as it was sometimes portrayed. Leftist politics were said to have permeated the entire university, or at least certain departments, once the radicals came to dominance. We argue in subsequent chapters that, far from being saturated in politics, the universities are mostly not sufficiently engaged in political debate, in the correct sense of that term. One may find a certain reflexive utopianism and an inward-looking "sand box" politics focusing on curriculum and intellectual orientations that displace and pass for the discussion of real issues of politics, political economy, religious liberty, constitutionalism, republicanism, and citizenship obligations. We take up this theme in more detail shortly.

A host of other observers has warned that reducing the debate to catch terms, with more emotive than substantive content, plays into the hands of critics of the academy.[18] Yale's C. Vann Woodward found much common ground and common sense among his faculty colleagues but conceded that there will always be a small, if noisy, minority on the left as on the right who "must realistically be assumed to be poised to seize the posture of obstructionists."[19] Woodward might have added that the faculty extremists have gained access to the media and have often managed to project themselves to the credulous, or to be caricatured in journalistic reports, as standard-bearers for the intellectual class. By exerting themselves, however, the sensible faculty middle ground could prevail and keep the intellectual climate in the academy civil, thoughtful, and free, according to Woodward and other moderates. Woodward was a classic example of a faculty centrist who commanded wide respect from his scholarly colleagues and did not fit conveniently into the conventional categories of "liberal" and "conservative." A moderate Democrat and a political liberal, he was also a cultural conservative, an inveterate foe of campus radicals and the new left, a strong upholder of academic standards and critic of affirmative action in admissions and faculty hiring. He cofounded the International Council on the Future of the University, together with University of Chicago sociologist Edward Shils, Columbia University philosopher Charles Frankel, German historian Thomas Nipperdey, Dutch political scientist Hans Daalder, and other American, Canadian, and West European scholars, to fight campus radicals and government regulations threatening the freedom of inquiry at U.S., U.K., German, and Italian universities. The men and women involved in this project ranged from the center left to the center right in their politics, but all were social or cultural conservatives of some sort who strongly disliked what they saw as threats to academic integrity coming from militant feminists, Marxists, self-styled revolutionaries, and almost any cause even remotely linked to the new left. Although many of the Americans were Democrats, they were appalled by riots at the Democratic National Convention in Chicago in 1968 (less by the alleged police brutality than by the protesters who they believed precipitated the police actions). Although few of these professors had been political activists, they now became generally disillusioned with politics and became less engaged with national political issues. The International Council on the Future of the University maintained a small office in midtown Manhattan, held an international conference biannually, issued country reports, commissioned studies, and admonished government regulators. It began to lose its momentum and unity of purpose as the threat from campus radicals and from government policies on affirmative action seemed to recede in America and the student revolutionaries in Europe were caught and imprisoned.[20] The organization fell into limbo after 1978, when escaped convicts murdered Charles Frankel, its president and chief fundraiser, in his Westchester County home.

As we detail in a later chapter, a truce settled upon American campuses in the 1970s after the tumults of the 1960s. This truce was marked by many small compromises, both an opening up of discourse in some respects and a narrowing of the range of issues debated (as reflected in the culture war debates of the 1990s, which focused on issues of race, gender, and sexuality as these affected the campuses). A general political quiescence and less politically engaged atmosphere settled on the campuses, as students pursued their career goals and faculty members pursued their specialized research interests. One could almost say that a kind of informal compact was struck among key university constituencies: students got self-expression and empowerment in university-sanctioned student organizations and advanced their career goals through early specialization, faculty got the opportunity to go their separate ways in their own research specialties and subspecialties, and administrators aggrandized their authority in the name of promoting social goals such as diversity and more effectively managing the new complexities of the educational enterprise. What suffered, as we argue in subsequent chapters of this book, was the goal of a shared educational experience, a common liberal education, and preparation in the broadest sense for citizenship in our democratic society. Of course, it is difficult to generalize about an enterprise of such complexity and diversity as our higher education system. In many ways the leading schools were apt to do a better job of fostering the goals of a broadly liberal education for students, but they also should be held to a higher standard, since the example of the elite schools ripples through the sector as a whole and helps to set the overall tone and direction.

Literary scholar Andrew Delbanco of Columbia University offered another interpretation for what he perceived as the strangely detached mood on many campuses. The neuralgic mood among some colleagues might be, he thought, the result of a generally liberal faculty feeling estranged from the politics of the Reagan and first Bush eras, and he speculated that this mood might dissipate with a Democratic president in the White House.[21] President Bill Clinton, though he had been a University of Arkansas constitutional law professor before becoming governor and then president, disappointed liberal campus constituencies with his "don't ask, don't tell" military recruitment policy and soon became embroiled in battles with Republicans who took over both houses of Congress midway through his first term. The cautious triangulation strategies and leadership style that Clinton pursued did little to stir any engagement of the campuses with political causes or to alter the fundamental realities of government relations with the universities.

Conservatives, meanwhile, were heartened by a number of developments, including court decisions striking down broadly worded campus speech codes, California's and Texas's dropping of race-based affirmative action admissions policies for their public colleges and universities, and, more generally, favorable trends in social indicators such as crime rates, divorce, and illegitimate births. The Republican retaking of Congress in 1994 boosted conservative morale after the loss of the presidency to Bill Clinton. Some conservatives declared that the culture wars were over, with the conservative side winning. Other conservative critics conceded that the culture wars were at least "in abeyance."[22]

In 1998 Alan Wolfe of Boston College published a study, *One Nation, After All,* which cast doubt on the whole notion of the culture war in the first place and, in any case, officially pronounced its demise.[23] Based on extensive interviews of middle-class Americans in eight cities across the nation, Wolfe concluded that most Americans reject ideological extremes of the left or right and share a set of core values: "The people who have spoken in this book . . . understand that what makes us one nation morally is an insistence on a set of values capacious enough to be inclusive but demanding enough to uphold standards of personal responsibility."[24] The culture wars of the 1990s, it seemed, were nothing more than an internal squabble "being fought primarily by intellectuals, not by most Americans themselves."[25] Much the same point was made more recently by Morris Fiorina, Samuel Abrams, and Jeremy Pope in their 2005 book, *Culture War? The Myth of a Polarized America.* Even on most of the contentious social issues of the day, it was partisan elites, not the mass public, who were bitterly divided and unable to reach compromises.[26] The battles, sometimes stylized and almost choreographed, among activist elites are discussed at length in several of our chapters, most notably in chapters 6 and 7. In the latter chapter we document how a dramatic campaign to show political bias in Pennsylvania's colleges and universities turned out to be much ado about little. The episode offered a clear demonstration that politics, in the form of an official inquiry by the state legislature, did not threaten the academic freedom of the state's public colleges and universities. Indeed, the inquiry, which was conducted in a fair, procedurally correct, and professional fashion by politicians from both parties, turned up evidence that the claims of political bias were overblown and contrived and avoided the partisan donnybrook that the extreme partisans on both sides of the dispute, along with the sensation-hungry media, ardently wanted for their own reasons. To satisfy the critics, university officials at most campuses pledged to adopt new grievance procedures whereby students could complain if they felt their professors were engaged in political indoctrination in the classroom.

## The Universities, the War on Terror, and Accountability

The September 11, 2001, attacks on the World Trade Center and the Pentagon, the resulting war on terror, and the war in Iraq could hardly avoid having an impact on the nation's campuses. A new mood and a new chapter in the relationship of higher education to society emerged, and a part of this new mood was a heightened concern with political bias in the universities. A number of campus incidents that attracted wide publicity can be traced directly to the new climate. On the eve of the war in Iraq an assistant professor of anthropology at Columbia University said at a campus forum that he hoped for "a thousand Mogadishus" so that imperialist America would learn a lesson. The president of Columbia, Lee Bollinger, was besieged with 20,000 e-mails and innumerable phone calls that blocked his phone system for days. Bollinger said he disagreed strongly with the professor's statement but defended the faculty member's right to speak his mind. The university had to relocate the professor in question to a new campus apartment after he received death threats.

Another figure who became a prominent symbol of the problem of a one-sided faculty was an obscure journalism professor at the University of Colorado in Boulder. The professor, Ward Churchill, set off a storm of protest when he published an article in which he blamed U.S. policy, not the terrorists, for the 9/11 attacks. He then made the matter worse when he sought subsequently to exonerate some categories of office workers, such as chefs or Xerox operators, from guilt and complicity in U.S. policy, but not others, in an absurd exercise in casuistry. Churchill became the poster boy for conservatives newly enraged by campus leftists, particularly when he called the victims "little Eichmanns." David Horowitz, a conservative activist and gadfly critic of the universities who appears in our story at a number of points, accurately credits Churchill's article and subsequent remarks as fueling his own organization's growth and launching his own popularity as a social critic. When asked in a 2005 interview to account for his rise to prominence as a critic of universities, Horowitz replied, "Two words: Ward Churchill."

At Duke University, a professor's website was shut down temporarily by the university when he called for military retaliation against terrorists and then was reopened by university authorities confronted with a storm of furious protest from the faculty and from off-campus watchdog groups.

Incidents involving Middle Eastern studies, where Israeli and Palestinian perspectives came increasingly into conflict, sharpened existing tensions on a number of campuses, sometimes catching the attention of the news media and sometimes being handled quietly by university officials. At Columbia, once again an object of intense news scrutiny because of its prominence and its location in New York City, an assistant professor in the Middle Eastern Language and Culture Department lost his temper with a student when she mildly queried his account of atrocities committed by Israeli troops against Palestinian civilians and ordered her to leave the classroom. The incident set off a dispute that festered for months and eventually led the university to conduct a formal investigation.

In another highly publicized incident that grew into a national cause célèbre, the arts and science faculty of Harvard University voted, by a narrow margin, to express a lack of confidence in President Lawrence W. Summers after he suggested at a conference that gender differences in the distribution of higher math skills might provide a partial explanation for why fewer women are found among the top elite in science and math. Summers earlier had angered faculty liberals when he stopped an effort to have the university divest itself of all investments in Israel. Summers was eventually forced to resign in June 2006 after only five years as Harvard's president, ending a melodrama that at times produced a press feeding frenzy.

The restrictions that the USA PATRIOT Act of 2002 placed on student and faculty visas, on ways to account for potentially dangerous chemical and biological substances that could be used by terrorists, and on access to e-mails for law enforcement purposes—as well as the act's reporting requirements—chafed, creating new sources of friction between universities and the federal government. Stem cell policies and global warming issues constitute further areas of disagreement that appear to pit the scientific community, or at least some parts of it, against government policymakers.

When President George W. Bush endorsed the teaching of "intelligent design" in the public schools (even though he said that local school boards and not the federal government should determine public school curricula), his words for many in the scientific and academic communities represented a populist pandering to evangelicals, created a negative effect, and to some even amounted to a Republican "war on science."[27]

## New Studies and Criticisms of the Universities

In this context of critical appraisal of universities, a series of studies has presented new evidence alleging that faculties have shifted dramatically to the political or cultural left. Voter registration lists have been used to uncover registrations as high as 9:1 Democrats over Republicans in certain West Coast universities; political giving for Democrats and Republicans by faculty members has shown a Democratic preponderance as high as 8:1 in some law faculties (but a 50:50 ratio in another law faculty); and other indicators of liberal dominance have been found.[28] A major survey of Canadian and U.S. faculty members, students, and administrators found indications of possible discrimination in hiring and tenure decisions against Christians, political conservatives, and women in elite colleges and universities (a claim we examine in detail in chapter 9).[29] The expounding of personal political views by professors in the classroom even when their remarks are not related to the subject of the course was alleged in a survey of student opinion conducted for the American Council for Trustees and Alumnae (ACTA) in the month prior to the 2004 presidential election.[30]

The new studies, or "second-wave" studies as Neil Gross of Harvard and Solon Simmons of George Mason University call them, were less "social scientific investigations" than previous studies of faculty political attitudes and "were closer to being thinly disguised works of political advocacy intended to back up the charge of 'liberal bias' in academe."[31] The new studies have helped to produce a more critical climate for the universities. The 1990s culture war debates resembled a large faculty meeting, with colleagues disputing extramurally on a rather esoteric level. The newer criticisms, disseminated widely via blogs and talk radio, were aimed at, and did achieve, a more pervasive public impact. In this new climate the respected journal *The Economist,* in an otherwise laudatory account of American higher education, issued this dire diagnosis and warning in 2005:

> America's academic paradise harbors plenty of serpents. A political correctness that has plagued Mr. Summers is just one example of a deeper pattern: America's growing inclination to abandon the very principles that have made it a world leader . . . universities are no longer as devoted to free inquiry as they ought to be. The persecution of Mr. Summers for his sin of intellectual rumination is symptomatic of a wider problem. At a time when America's big political parties are deeply divided over profound questions on the meaning of "life" to the ethics of preemptive war, university professors are overwhelmingly on the side of one political party. Only about 10 percent of tenured professors say they vote Republican. The liberal majority has repeatedly shown that it is willing to crush dissent on anything from speech codes to the choice of subjects worth studying.[32]

This opinion, coming from a respected journal, exposed a problem that the universities had not confronted earlier. Whereas past critics focused on internal pedagogical disputes and spoke often in the modulated, if not always wholly respectful, tones of the academy, the tone as well as the audience of the second-wave criticisms suggested flaws so fundamental that they could not be corrected by internal reform (at least not by the faculties and administrators). Outside intervention by government watchdogs or metrics of accountability from more aggressive trustees now are proposed as remedies.

The remedies have often been vague because they are uncertain as to their targets; the observer has been left to reason backward from the solution to infer the supposed problem. In this book we are more concerned with diagnosis than with remedies, although we have some ideas about what we think needs to be done to make the universities more effective institutions of learning. We do not shrink from prescription when we think it is merited, but our primary aim is to present a reasoned analysis of what the actual problems are with the universities as they seek to deal with complex social, political, and cultural trends. If the diagnosis is right, the correct medicine can follow. The wrong medicine will make the patient worse.

One remedy is the idea of an "academic bill of rights," the invention of David Horowitz, the former radical now turned conservative, whom we mentioned above. This idea of the academic bill of rights, which we discuss in greater detail below, calls for state legislatures somehow to "suggest" or to "urge" public colleges and universities (for Horowitz says he does not want state government or the federal government to legislate directly) to protect students from indoctrination by liberal professors. Students need to be included, says Horowitz, in the doctrine of academic freedom, which at present largely protects the rights of professors to freedom of speech. From this core notion spring other ideas, for example, students in their course evaluations might be given the opportunity to register complaints about professors who inject politics into the classroom. And since "viewpoint diversity" is key to a lively intellectual climate on campus, special efforts need to be undertaken, it is argued, to ensure that conservatives are hired and represented on faculties.

The academic hiring process is a special target of numerous critics. It is assumed that university departments go out of their way to hire only liberals. Since liberals are heavily represented on faculties (as our own national survey, reported in chapter 5, shows that they clearly are), this must be because, say the critics, these liberal birds flock together and take pains to cull out nonconformists and dissidents. In chapter 9, we take up the issue of academic hiring and examine whether such discrimination does or does not exist. The academic pipeline for doctoral students who become future college teachers is complex: the stages include the initial choice of a major at the undergraduate level, the mentoring a student receives from his or her professors, the choice between graduate and professional school or immediate entry into the job market, commitment to and completion of a doctoral course of study based, in part, on encouragement and support from professors, the initial placement in an academic setting, or the choice of think tank or nonacademic employment, the receipt of promotion and tenure, publication of one's work, and elevation to the highest ranks and honorifics in the field, special endowed professorships, and leadership posts in the profession. Discrimination, if it exists, could occur at any or all of these stages of the career.

To answer the questions statistically or even suggestively based on credible analysis is very difficult because data are inadequate and research to date casts only partial and intermittent light on pieces of the puzzle. Obviously, human agency plays a part at every stage as well: students exercise choice over their career and the next steps in their life. There is some evidence to suggest that conservative students tend to choose a vocational major in contrast to liberal students' initial choice of a major and that liberal students may receive more mentoring as undergraduates.[33] It is also quite possible that students with a conservative bent choose law school or business school over graduate school or immediately enter the labor market.[34] Undergraduate students in general, and those at the elite institutions especially, do not feel disgruntled with schools or with their experiences. Students who do earn a doctorate may go to a think tank or other nonacademic employment, or they may end up at a less-prestigious or sectarian college where they feel more comfortable or more welcomed. Appointments at the more senior levels, when a professor moves up the career ladder to a more prestigious school or when someone does or does not get a coveted professorship, are notoriously difficult to appraise from the outside (and sometimes even insiders cannot pinpoint what factors were decisive in selecting a particular individual for a post). It is hard to get clear answers to such questions of potential discrimination in the academic career path, but we try to evaluate various claims in chapter 9. We also provide an explanation of how the academic hiring process has changed, and changed dramatically, in the years since two of the present authors entered graduate school and the academic profession some fifty years ago. We asked professors in our survey whether they thought that religious or political bias had affected their own academic career. Surprisingly, perhaps, we found that most conservative professors, even the strong conservatives, did not feel that they had experienced such bias in their own career and institution. The main bias that we can detect in appointments at the prestigious universities is in the direction of "safe" professionals, that is, the individuals with strong research credentials who will be tenurable and productive scholars and researchers. These individuals may be mildly liberal, as this category is defined in survey questionnaires, but they tend to be politically disengaged and uninterested, whether in the philosophical, practical, or civic aspects of politics. This is partly what we mean when we argue that there are not enough politics, political discussion, and debate in the universities.

Another nostrum pushed by critics of the contemporary university is the call for metrics to measure educational outcomes and thus presumably to ensure accountability. Secretary of Education Margaret Spellings appeared to make an explicit linkage between the kinds of accountability requirements that are expected of the public schools under the No Child Left Behind Act of 2002 and what should be required for colleges and universities. The recommendations of a commission she appointed to study higher education echoed the many reform panels set up to deal with the public schools—for example, the commission advocated the review of graduation rates, student performance on standardized tests, attendance rates, job placements, and the like. The Spellings Commission seems to have gone out of its way to pick data that, on first reading, cast U.S.

higher education in an unfavorable light. The report states, for example, that the United States is in fourteenth place in the world in college graduation rates. The reference is to graduation rate data for the Organization for Economic Cooperation and Development (OECD) countries, according to which the U.S. rates are average to below average (the first attachment to the Spellings Commission report). The reason why the United States is not closer to Iceland and other leaders in the OECD metric is that our participation rate is much higher than that of most other industrial nations, with some 70 percent of the relevant age cohort attending colleges or universities. The proportion of high school graduates going on to higher education in the United States has risen from about half to nearly three-quarters in the last thirty years. Therefore, we have a more open admissions strategy, with a consequent dropping out of some students in contrast to other OECD nations. For this and other reasons, graduation rates are not a good measure of educational quality.[35] High graduation rates could be a mark of low college participation or of lax standards. More broadly, treating higher education with the same metrics as the public schools strikingly illustrates how the "mass" dimension has affected the context of public debate.

The Spellings report, furthermore, ignored a second OECD measure of success in which the United States ranks second highest among the nations studied. That is the "attainment rate," a measure of the proportion of an age group that actually holds a baccalaureate degree from a postsecondary institution. Here the United States ranks second in the OECD metrics behind only Norway. If one combines degrees from universities and from community colleges, the United States still ranks second, with only Canada ranked higher. A more commonly used set of data, not employed by the Spellings Commission, is the Shanghai rankings. This method of ranking research universities uses a methodology that counts the peer-reviewed articles by faculty in scholarly journals and the number of Nobel and other prizes earned. It is an independent survey that does not rely on information provided by the universities themselves. Thirty-seven of the first fifty, fifty-five of the first 100, and seven of the first ten universities ranked are U.S. institutions. Encouraging though this measure might seem, it is based largely on faculty achievement and prestige among peer groups. Such measures do not tell us how well American colleges and universities are performing as transmitters of our civic culture and traditions.

Our aim in this study is different from such quantitative disputations: in particular, we seek to examine more narrowly the alleged politicization of America's colleges and universities. We take the issues raised by recent studies seriously and try to address them as fairly as we can. We make no pretense that we can fully resolve all of the major questions, but we are convinced that the issues can be aired vigorously and civilly and that out of such debate some tentative answers can be achieved. Our findings surprised us in some important ways and in other ways reaffirmed what we thought before going into the project. Writing this book was an adventure, and, like anything worth doing, it was hard work. We hope the reader will share our enthusiasm for the subject.

# 3

## Emergence of the U.S. Research University

In this chapter we look at how the universities were created in the country, their missions at the start and how those missions evolved, and how some of the past complexities foreshadow themes that we discuss in later chapters. This history is necessary because the past is always prologue and because we cannot understand the present ambivalence in the universities toward political education and civic engagement without seeing how the Progressive tradition promoted the values of expertise and scientific knowledge while disparaging politics. The Progressive movement was schizophrenic in that it both fostered the public service responsibilities of the newly established professions and subverted the idea of service to society and civic engagement. Professionalism became redefined and reoriented into more commercial channels as the universities competed with each other for students and pushed graduates into the expanding industrial economy. The original enthusiasm for shaping public policy soon ran up against the distasteful realities of politics, political controversies, and political machines. The universities, in keeping with the strand of Progressivism that reflected faith in the experts rather than in "the people," found ways to train their graduates in scientific and business management for private companies, as managers of the public schools, public health systems, city governments, railroad commissions, or the bodies that regulated and promoted commercial developments. The great Victorian educational reformers who founded and ran the new universities liked the idea of their professors serving society, but not if those same individuals stirred up political controversies and angered powerful donors and trustees. Academic freedom, to the presidents, meant teaching an expert body of knowledge in the classroom, not engaging in political debate that aroused controversy and confronted the business interests that supported the universities. So long as professors engaged in science and the pursuit of truth, and steered clear of controversy, the universities would flourish and grow in size and significance.

## *The Colonial Legacy*

America's colleges and universities evolved in three overlapping periods. The first period stretched from the colonial and revolutionary eras through the Civil War, when the colleges (there were no universities in our sense at that time) were principally serving as *transmitters of culture*. The colleges' functions included preparation for civic life in the new democracy, with a related role as vocational trainers for the teaching profession, the ministry, and the law. The curriculum, modeled on the British system, consisted largely of studying the classics, the history of Rome and Greece, Latin and Greek, and, eventually, natural philosophy (or science). The framers considered this kind of curriculum appropriate for the class of citizens who would run affairs in the new republic. The virtues of the educated class were essential to the civic republican tradition that underlay the constitutional order.

The original colleges were denominational in affiliation, from the founding of Harvard College in 1636 and extending into the nineteenth century (at which point a second wave of colleges, secular in nature, such as Amherst College in 1829, came into existence). The colonial colleges were founded by Protestant denominations, most notably, Episcopalian, Congregational, and Presbyterian. They usually had an explicit mission of instilling moral and Christian virtues and building the character of the students. Indeed, it was not until World War II that America's elite institutions were fully secularized and de-Christianized.[1] Gaining new knowledge through the conduct of research was not a goal of the early colleges. Such nonacademic institutions as the Royal Society in London and the American Philosophical Society in Philadelphia, the latter founded by Benjamin Franklin, were the more important institutions in the birth of modern science. Not until later, notably in the 1870s, did the hard sciences become a significant part of America's university curricula.[2]

Many of the leaders of the American Revolution and the Constitution's drafters attended one or another of the fifteen colleges existing at the time of the nation's founding. John Jay and Alexander Hamilton attended King's College (Columbia) in New York City. George Washington and Thomas Jefferson studied at the College of William and Mary. James Madison attended the College of New Jersey (Princeton), where he might have encountered Alexander Hamilton had the latter not been denied admission. Benjamin Franklin, a self-taught genius, founded the University of Pennsylvania. Benjamin Rush, a graduate of the College of New Jersey and one of the colonies' first physicians, founded Dickinson College and later Franklin and Marshall College. Other prominent Pennsylvanians studied in England, which was considered a highly desirable path to success in life before the Revolution, helping the sons of wealthy merchants to establish a career in trade.

The early colleges were not significant institutions in American society at the time of the Revolution or afterward. Still, during their student days some of the founding fathers—Madison and Jefferson certainly—picked up the ideas of liberty and limited government that shaped their political thinking. They were exposed to the works of John Locke, David Hume, Adam Smith, and other leading figures of the British and Scottish Enlightenment, and these ideas were influential in shaping the institutions of the new nation. Alexander Hamilton's voluminous reading in the works of great thinkers and in the history of the classical period shaped his contributions to the Federalist Papers and his work on the New York State Constitution. None of these men, however, was or considered himself to be a scholar, although Franklin, who was a world-class scientist, George Mason, a successful entrepreneur and political philosopher, and Dr. Benjamin Rush should be deemed outstanding intellects and exempt from this generalization. The founders saw themselves less as original thinkers than as members of a "republic of letters," in Jefferson's phrase, as men broadly learned in history and philosophy. They deemed themselves able to understand the currents of politics and to apply the lessons of the past to the practical problems of the present.[3] Knowledge of worldly affairs—both the theory and the practice of government—was to them self-evidently a critical part of education.

Jefferson, during his presidency, pushed the idea of creating a national university that would be less religious than the existing colleges. By being more secular and philosophical, the new kind of university would better prepare the country's youth for leadership in America's republican order. The idea went nowhere because Federalist leaders did not believe that creating a university was among the enumerated powers assigned to the new federal government. Nor was it, in their view, a "necessary and proper" measure to implement a specifically enumerated federal power. Jefferson's political opponents did not share the vision of republicanism that he sought for the new nation.[4] Jefferson's "wall of separation" between church and state was more absolute, and his preference for a miracle-free Unitarianism was not favored by other framers.

During his presidency, Madison tried, and failed, to create a national university modeled along Jeffersonian lines. He met with opposition from critics in Congress who believed that creating a national university would require a constitutional amendment. Later, John Quincy Adams also tried, and failed, to persuade Congress to create a university in the nation's capital as part of his program of internal improvements. In Madison's case, opposition to potential political activities by the proposed university was a factor among some politicians who, somewhat in the fashion of contemporary critics, disliked the idea that students might be indoctrinated by their teachers. Federalist critics believed that the broad spirit of liberty among the people (at least the natural leaders of society) was a better guarantee of liberty, along with the Constitution's institutional design, than the education of a new class of leaders.[5]

In 1819 the U.S. Supreme Court, in a decision written by Chief Justice John Marshall, rebuffed an effort to create a more utilitarian kind of university, in this case an attempt to alter the charter of the old Dartmouth College so as to serve the citizens of New Hampshire. Marshall's opinion upheld the sanctity of contract and expanded the protections of private institutions in rebuffing the effort to change Dartmouth's charter ("It is only a small college, but there are those who love it," said Daniel Webster).[6]

Dr. Benjamin Rush was one of the framers who thought most seriously about the educational needs of the new nation. He argued for a radical departure from British ideas when he proposed the chartering of Dickinson College in 1783. He called for the teaching of modern languages rather than Latin and Greek and insisted that the sciences, and in particular chemistry, be included in the curriculum of the new college, the aim being to promote industry. Rush was generally critical of Federalist ideas, which he considered unsuitable for a new American kind of college, but he did not dispute the main Federalist premise that education was not a governmental responsibility. Education assuredly belonged to the domain of private philanthropic activity. Nor did he dispute that religious faith should be a critical part of the educational mission.[7]

Jefferson, after his presidency, turned his attention to the creation of the University of Virginia, which became the nation's first publicly supported university. This state school was the prototype of Jefferson's vision of the "republican" university. The republican university would be secular and nondenominational in character, would provide instruction in the languages and history of Greece and Rome, would include the practical sciences, and would teach an understanding of the Constitution—and it would seek out the best students of Virginia. His dream was realized during his lifetime, as he attended the inauguration banquet in 1824, along with Madison and Lafayette. The land grant universities, when they were founded after the Morrill Act of 1862 and the end of the Civil War, would draw on the founding principles of the University of Virginia, but laying more stress on the practical arts and mechanics.

Despite the efforts of those who saw education as vital, the colleges and universities were never significant social institutions in the period before the Civil War. As primarily teaching institutions, they drew on only a local or regional student clientele and did not even attract much attention in their local communities. They hosted few public events, celebrity speeches, theatricals, or athletic events that might have engaged the interest of the wider public. The colleges, moreover, played no role whatsoever in the great intellectual, cultural, and political currents of the time. The Second Great Awakening (the protestant revivals) of the 1820s and 1830s, the transcendentalist movement, Jacksonianism, the creation of the American novelistic tradition, and a public readership drawn to the writings of Washington Irving and James Fenimore Cooper and then of Nathanial Hawthorne, Herman Melville, and others, the rise of abolitionism, and the creation of the Republican Party in the 1850s all had their origins outside of the colleges and universities. It is difficult to quarrel with James Pierson's conclusion that, up to the period of the Civil War, "academic institutions had but a marginal place in American life."[8]

## The Emergence of the Research University

The second major period in American higher education extended roughly from the close of the Civil War to World War II. It was during the early part of this period—from 1870 to the first decades of the twentieth century—that the modern research university emerged. Laurence Veysey, in *The Emergence of the American University*, traces how the American university took shape from 1890 to 1910.[9] Several factors are key here: first, the land grant system, authorized by the Morrill Act of 1862, in which Congress set aside federal lands to be given to the states for the purpose of establishing institutions of learning devoted to the agricultural and mechanical arts, laid the basis for land grant colleges in Ohio, Wisconsin, Illinois, Michigan, Minnesota, Iowa, Nebraska, California, and other western states.[10] Subsequent federal legislation provided formula funds to the colleges for research on seeds, plant diseases, agricultural improvements, and a host of service activities in support of farmers at the agricultural schools and land grant–affiliated research institutes. Federal support through the land grant system also assisted some of the new private universities set up by private philanthropy after the Civil War (Cornell benefited greatly from land grant support).

Second, the great wealth accumulated in the Gilded Age, and the Gospel of Wealth concept that prompted large-scale charitable contributions, led to the founding of wholly new private universities and research centers that included Johns Hopkins, the University of Chicago, Vanderbilt, Stanford, Cornell, the nucleus that became Carnegie-Mellon, and the Rockefeller Institute for Medical Research, which later became Rockefeller University. Finally, great growth occurred in a number (but not all) of the older colonial and postcolonial schools (for example, Harvard, Yale, Columbia, Princeton), which represented a response to the competition provided by the new private universities and the emerging state land grant universities. Specifically, the older colleges created graduate schools and specialized laboratories devoted to research. Harvard's creation of the Jefferson Physical Laboratory in 1870, the first American university facility devoted exclusively to research and teaching in a scientific discipline, predated the creation of the research-oriented Johns Hopkins University.[11] The older colleges also expanded their undergraduate student populations. Thus the research university did not "grow out of" the colleges in any simple sense. The undergraduate divisions and the graduate divisions existed in uneasy equilibrium, creating many of the special complexities that are still part of the universities today. The overall result of these factors was an enormous expansion in the higher education system. As Burton J. Bledstein observes, "The growth of American universities was unprecedented in Western civilization. . . . In two generations, enrollment in institutions of higher education jumped from 52,000 in 1870 to 238,000 in 1900 to 1,101,000 in 1930. The number of institutions increased from 563 in 1870 to 977 in 1900 to 1,409 in 1930."[12]

The universities assumed their form and their characteristic modes of operation during the 1870–1910 period. The organizational patterns forged then have persisted with surprisingly little structural change, although the scale of operations has increased dramatically, to the present day. Here we mean the decentralized structures, with various schools reporting to a more or less centralized hierarchy headed by a president and board. The academic departments within the schools, like the government bureaus within the large executive agencies, were (and still are) the chief operating units of the university. That is, they deliver the educational services of teaching and research. The departments were, and have largely remained, organized along the lines of disciplinary specialties, with faculty members serving as self-governing professional subcommunities. The subcommunities were dedicated chiefly to the advancement of their respective scholarly fields, and teaching activities were organized around scientific progress in the fields. Advanced training and conferral of the doctoral degree joined the baccalaureate as central to the university's mission.

Along with the approximate doubling in the number of America's colleges and universities and the more than tripling in student enrollments from the Civil War to 1890 came a clash of the traditional and reformist educational ideas. Reformist educators first began after the Civil War to challenge seriously the traditionalists who favored the concept of "mental discipline." The traditional college curriculum was, as we have noted, dedicated to the teaching and transmission of cultural values. The organizing idea of the old system was that the students should study a fixed set of courses, memorize and recite their lessons, study ancient languages, and observe discipline and rigid rules of dress and decorum (teachers often lived in the student quarters and acted as proctors). Students would thus acquire the strength of character and mental toughness needed to thrive in their chosen profession. Students would, as a byproduct or sometimes as a central goal of their education, become good Christians and good citizens. The reformers advocated for the teaching of Darwin and evolutionary theories, and they generally sought to loosen or curb ties between the colleges and religious orders. Their goals included the elimination of compulsory chapel. They tried to make the curriculum more practical by deemphasizing rote learning. The reformers also tried to hire faculty who were experts in their field and who would do research as well as teach. But the reformers, unlike the traditionalists, initially lacked a unifying idea beyond the notion that universities should somehow be more "useful" to society. This concept was not self-explanatory.

At the newly founded Cornell University, for example, utility to society initially meant that all students would make handicrafts for sale to the public. Founder Ezra Cornell, in the four years from the founding of his university until his death, would wander the campus to check that students were performing their manual labor. A more active democratic citizenship also became a major goal for Cornell, which could be adapted from older ideas and educational practices.

At Harvard, under President Charles W. Eliot, utility was defined largely in terms of curriculum reforms. In particular, Eliot sought to adopt an elective system so that students could choose their own course of study. Ideally, one would like to have universities able to teach anyone almost anything.

The Victorian reformers who created the modern American university finally found their unifying concept in the idea of research and the centrality of the research mission. The founding of Johns Hopkins University in 1876 was an important milestone, although older schools—Yale, for example, being the first to have a doctoral program—had already launched programs of research and advanced training.

The universities' enrollments grew to some 350,000 students by 1910, and a number of the leading universities by then had more than 5,000 students apiece if one counted enrollment in undergraduate, professional, and doctoral programs.

The universities also enjoyed more prestige and had differentiated and distanced themselves from the smaller liberal arts colleges by the turn of the century. Growth was a general aim, and a validating principle, of all of the universities. University presidents avidly sought philanthropic largesse to expand their programs. University presidents were also generally anxious to see that faculty members did not attract unfavorable publicity to their institution. Although self-governance by autonomous subunits was the ideal, university presidents and the industrial donors who dominated the boards of trustees in practice exercised strong control over their faculties, an important topic to which we soon return.

The creation of Johns Hopkins in 1876 was based on an American adaptation of the model of the University of Berlin, which was founded in 1810 by Wilhelm von Humboldt. The university, as von Humboldt saw it, was not to engage in the process of transmitting the known truths and society's deeply rooted cultural values to new generations of students; rather, it was to pursue new truths through gaining new knowledge. Students were to participate as a kind of junior partner to the professor in the research process. There was a heavy overlay of German idealism in the Humboldtian system, however, which American educators never fully understood and clearly did not emulate.

As the enthusiasm for German ideas cooled, Americans framed their own model of the modern research university. The idea of graduate study remained a key element, but the idea was not uniformly adopted. For example, Harvard (or at least President Eliot), when it followed the Johns Hopkins model of research by creating a Graduate School of Arts and Sciences of its own, did not fully embrace the "knowledge for knowledge's sake" concept. Nor did Eliot believe that the research mission could or should be the dominant focus for the university. Other Ivy League institutions rapidly incorporated their own versions of the new ideas, although they followed the general pattern. Stanford University was established in 1891 with research as a major goal (and the University of California soon emulated the Stanford research orientation despite being a state university). The University of Chicago, underwritten by John D.

Rockefeller in 1892, favored research accomplishment as the basis for faculty appointment and promotion. The land grant universities promoted research with a strong admixture of research applications and public service.

The academic innovations were carried out by a group of entrepreneurial university presidents, including Charles Eliot of Harvard, Daniel Coit Gilman of Johns Hopkins, James Angell of the University of Michigan, Andrew White of Cornell, William Rainey Harper of Chicago, Woodrow Wilson of Princeton, and David Starr Jordan of Stanford. These men became almost as famous as the captains of industry of that age.

A class of what we would today call "public intellectuals" emerged from the faculty ranks, becoming, if not quite household names, public figures—men such as John Dewey in philosophy, Thorsten Veblen in economics, and Charles Beard and James Harvey Robinson in history. The thinkers who achieved public note were not, however, limited to academics but also included prominent muckraking journalists and members of the Progressive era "think tanks" such as the Bureau of Municipal Research in New York City and the Brookings Institution in Washington.

Although the research model provided a core concept, the "operational code"[13] of the American university was actually an amalgam, a syncretism of old and new elements that produced considerable internal tension. The universities did not abandon the notion that they were transmitters of culture, especially the values of Western civilization. The ideas that the universities should serve social needs somehow defined, that they owe to society service and useful knowledge, and that they should train people to be good citizens in our democratic and capitalist society blended with the pure knowledge mission (although the ideals of citizenship tended to lose out to both the "knowledge for knowledge's sake" and the more practical applied research missions). The blending of functions produced tensions and internal contradictions in the university ideal. The fact that the interests of the various university stakeholders were often in conflict did not, in fact, prove to be disabling. The American university was a truly American invention, a pragmatic working accommodation as much as was the nation itself.

Although they competed fiercely among themselves for students, for prominent faculty members, and for honors, public recognition, and philanthropic support, the universities were essentially the same kind of educational enterprise. The state-supported public universities modeled themselves on the private universities in structure and function, even if they differed in financing. Each university, public or private, was run by a class of administrators, headed by a president and a set of deans and subordinate officers. Each was internally divided into individual colleges and departments, representing the professors or a field of study; in each institution the curriculum and the research to be performed were largely the province of the faculty members. The individual departments chose their own members and ran (or aspired to run) their own internal affairs, but also recognized that they had to depend on their respective deans for financial resources. The deans, in turn, depended on support from the public and on private philanthropy. Each university had an overall board of trustees or directors who exercised fiduciary responsibility, which helped to buffer the university in its relations with the wider community.

The universities, in short, resembled private corporations in having a chain of command, central overhead functions, and internal specialized divisions, but differences emerged. The top administrators never enjoyed the full command powers of their corporate counterparts, and they in fact gradually lost power during the first decades of the twentieth century, only to recover a more dominant role in the later decades of the century. The professors were to carve out a critical decisionmaking role in what to teach, whom to hire, and what fields and subjects to study.

The independence of the faculty was in theory strengthened by the idea of "academic freedom," but this took many years to become a reality. Academic freedom has had periods of backsliding from the ideal (an ideal that has never been unambiguous or without its problematic aspects).[14] The authoritative statement of the doctrine of academic freedom came with the founding of the American Association of University Professors (AAUP) in 1915. The doctrine held that so long as professors were speaking within their area of professional competence, they could not be denied the right to speak and to investigate freely. This was the theory. The reality could be quite different.

Academic freedom did not fare well in the crises of 1893–94 and 1910, when the majority of faculty members sided with university presidents who had dismissed faculty for speaking out publicly (outside the classroom) on controversial issues. World War I brought a number of high-profile academic freedom cases, including the departure of Professors Charles Beard and Joel Elias Spingarn from Columbia University and Professor Scott Nearing from the University of Pennsylvania. The muckraking journalist Upton Sinclair in 1922 assailed the universities for numerous arbitrary firings in *The Goose-Step: A Study of American Education.*[15] Sinclair's portrait of the universities showed how far they still were from the modern citadels they now have become. Sinclair's study, though certainly tendentious in good muckraking style, remains astonishing in its breadth even in comparison to serious modern studies, as he covered a huge array of colleges and universities of all types and sizes, including Harvard, Beloit, North Dakota State, Brown, and all points in between. At almost every type of institution, even at the leading schools of the day, professors faced potential firing for political activism, even though in theory universities deemed themselves to have a public service obligation. Sinclair quoted the dean of Muskingum College as saying that the faculty member's relationship to the college president "should be that of the soldier to the general, it should be the attitude that he can do no wrong."[16] It should not surprise us that this institution fired a professor for teaching "a critical attitude" to his students.[17] Control of political expression was only part of a much larger surveillance of every aspect of faculty lives: professors were fired for divorcing, for having an affair, for attending church too little or too much, for being discovered to have black heritage: "In general, you may be fired if you depart in any way from the beaten track of propriety."[18]

Yet Sinclair's study makes clear that the administration was usually doing the bidding of more powerful overseers, a reminder again of how much patterns of governance have evolved (but pressure from donors is hardly unique even today). When a dean at the University of Toledo criticized the country's involvement in World War I, he was immediately fired by the trustees.[19] A president who differed with his trustees over a public issue such as silver coinage could get into hot water, as happened with President Andrews of Brown University.[20] As sociologist E. A. Ross, who was finally fired by Stanford in 1910 after many stormy years of irritating Mrs. Leland Stanford with his outspoken views on coolie labor, asserted in 1914 apropos of control that the universities exercised over many aspects of faculty lives,

> Academic asphyxiation is much more common than is generally realized. . . . The dismissal of professors by no means gives the clue to the frequency of the gag in academic life. We forget the many who take their medicine and make no fuss. . . . When a sizable donation is trembling in the balance, when an institution has been generously remembered in the will of some conservative gentlemen who take an annoying interest in the details of its life, how the governing board of the institution caters to the prejudices of the potential donor and how intolerable and unpardonable appear untimely professorial utterances or teachings which put the gift in peril![21]

Harold Laski, from the perspective of a British academic teaching temporarily at an American institution, made this observation about American professors in 1922: "Many men deliberately adopt reactionary views to secure promotion. . . . Many more never express opinions lest the penalty be extracted. . . .

Those who do are penalized when the change of promotion comes."[22] Sinclair certainly shows that, in practice, faculty members in America lacked effective protection for their academic and professional freedoms. Even as late as the 1930s, the idea that a professor should not be fired for his political views or activities required much debate and energetic defense by such leading educators as Robert Maynard Hutchins, president of the University of Chicago.[23]

The departments of the Progressive era universities were organized around disciplines that had formalized rules for research, publication, and their norms of professional behavior. The departments at the individual schools were incorporated into national associations, mostly during the last two decades of the nineteenth century. The departments did not fully come into their own as power centers until much later, but to greater or lesser degrees they operated with autonomy, subject to the direction of the powerful presidential figures who ran the universities. The national associations usually sponsored a journal that published leading contributions to the field, thus strengthening the field's identity and helping to protect its status within the university. A short list of such associations would include the American Historical Association (1884), the American Economic Association (1885), the American Physical Society (1899), the American Political Science Association (1903), the American Association for the Advancement of Science (1903, an umbrella organization representing a cluster of scientific fields and publisher of the still-influential *Science*), and the American Sociological Association (1905). Before the fields became formalized into distinct disciplines, they were subfields and then offshoots of other disciplines. An ambitious professor might feel blocked within one department and hive off to form a new one. But by 1910 the fields had hardened into a pattern, and no new field could easily be formed. Existing departments would co-opt rebels and zealously guard their turf within the university. The departmental structures have changed remarkably little over the intervening century, although, of course, many fields have changed dramatically in content, especially in the information and life sciences.

The most notable addition to the prevailing structure of departmental dominance has been the rise of the applied science institutes that have drawn together several scientific disciplines.[24] The independent cross-disciplinary institutes, departments, centers, and "studies" programs apart from the applied sciences, which appeared from the 1970s to the 1990s, probably have had a lesser impact on university structures. The ethnic studies programs were common reflections of ideological currents of the culture wars.[25] English departments have been the home of many ethnic studies programs. It has proved difficult for the interdisciplinary efforts and programs to break the hold of the departmental structures. But they have at least given clusters of like-minded faculty members a base within a larger department.

## Politics and Faculty Political Attitudes

Critics, and even defenders of the universities, sometimes argue that intellectuals are by nature inclined to be critics of society. Thus they are "liberals" in modern parlance. The notion that the universities were aligned with "liberal" political causes or tendencies does not describe the nineteenth-century university experience. Nor is it instructive to use the contemporary idiom, for liberal in the nineteenth-century usage meant the classical liberal (for example, John Stuart Mill) who favored freeing the market from paternalistic government regulation. Only with Progressivism late in the century did faculty attitudes begin to shift toward what we would currently regard as liberal causes, and even here we should be cautious in interpreting what is meant by a liberal. University liberals in 1884, for example, were mugwumps—that is, they were Republicans who refused to support James Blaine for president because they regarded him as corrupt. Hence they sat on both sides of the fence (their "wump" on one side and their "mug" on the other, that is, they waffled and equivocated). The universities did not jettison their role as transmitters of the values of the past. Being useful to society, expanding knowledge, and transmitting a cultural heritage were all seen as part of the university mission.

The political attitudes of faculty, administrators, and students for most of the nineteenth century, even as the university took shape late in the century, ranged from extremely conservative to apathetic to mildly mugwumpish. Humanist professors after the Civil War tended to be politically apathetic, to disdain popular impulses, and to be suspicious of democracy. Scientists generally had no interest in politics or social causes, except to want insulation from religious zealots who lambasted them for teaching the new doctrine of evolution.

University presidents were mostly Republicans, although some displayed mugwump tendencies. Andrew White of Cornell, for example, was an outspoken Republican who defended the Grant administration during its scandals and who voted for Blaine even though he conceded that Cleveland was the better man. Most Columbia professors in 1900 supported McKinley, as did President Nicholas Murray Butler. Butler even used the administrative services of his office, albeit furtively, to aid the McKinley campaign. A "liberal" of the day was President Charles Eliot of Harvard, who generally acted as a mugwump. He drifted toward the Democrats, leading to his overt support for Woodrow Wilson in 1912.

Early in his presidency Eliot launched a campaign to puncture the myth that Harvard was only for "the sons of the rich" and sought to recruit middle-class and working-class students for Harvard. But this had less to do with social justice or the desire to promote egalitarianism than the desire to ensure that enrollment would continue to rise. Harvard recruited women for Radcliffe College, not from any feminist motives but from a desire to expand enrollment. By 1910 women accounted for 40 percent of total student enrollment in higher education, a figure that continuously grew in the ensuing century. Today women are a majority of undergraduates.

Trustees of private universities, usually wealthy businessmen, were sometimes quirky in their outlook, but one seldom found "liberal" causes by today's standards among their benefactions. The captains of industry donated professorships and laboratories and sometimes created whole universities, but one did not find trustees rushing to create centers for the study and promotion of populism, labor union organization, poverty abatement, trust busting, and railroad regulation.

Trustees generally preferred that professors, in or out of class, avoid commenting on controversial issues of the day. The most enlightened trustees took the view that if political issues could or should not be avoided entirely, comment should be undertaken by the most experienced and enlightened men on the faculty. Witness the following resolution adopted by Johns Hopkins University trustees in 1894:

> [We] regard the discussion of current political, economic, financial, and social questions before the students of this University as of such importance that all lessons should be given only by the ablest and wisest persons whose service the University command. . . . The Trustees are of the opinion that no instruction should be given in these subjects unless it can be given by persons of experience, who are well-acquainted with the history and principles of political and social progress. . . . The Trustees recommend great caution in the selection and engagement of other teachers.[26]

But probably most conservative of all the stakeholders of the early universities were the students. In the East and in the land grant institutions of the Midwest, college students "recorded an overwhelming preference for the Republicans."[27] There was some leaning toward the Democrats during the Grover Cleveland era, but the appearance of William Jennings Bryan on the scene in 1896 "brought a frightened return to the fold."[28]

In 1908 Harvard students self-identified their political party affiliation as Republican, 308; Democratic, 40; Independent, 18; mugwump, 2; Socialist, 2;

no preference, 18; not answering, 24.[29] The most serious rival to the Republicans among students in the Middle West was not the Democrats. A straw vote at the University of Chicago in 1892 had the Prohibitionists, perhaps out of motives of flippancy on the part of the students, narrowly defeating the Republicans, while the Democrats trailed far behind. Although a mild Progressivism eventually manifested itself on some campuses, Veysey concludes, "Support for the Populists or other movements further to the left was extremely rare."[30] While these numbers may surprise a modern reader, those attending universities in this era tended to come from the wealthiest strata of American society during a period in which wealth tracked rather closely with partisanship outside of the American South.

The case of faculty political attitudes in the social sciences, as the Progressive movement gathered strength, is a more complex matter. However, most faculty members in the newly developing social sciences and in the schools of law generally did not see themselves as politically engaged and certainly not as advocates for radical social change. The reformers who embraced the notion of "useful" knowledge generally believed in neutral expertise, in improving the efficiency of government, and in serving the needs of an expanding economy rather than in altering power relations or in organizing political action. Some of the new generation of American scholars who had studied in Germany were predisposed to be critical of orthodoxies deriving from British and Scottish Enlightenment thought. It was natural for them to want fresh thinking on public problems and not merely to adopt constitutional doctrine from the framers. They sought ways to be relevant to governors, state legislators, and other public officials.

As a center of Progressivism, Wisconsin became the first state to experiment with a partnership between the state government and the public university. The idea, begun in the early 1890s, came to be known as the "Wisconsin idea." The concept envisioned an arrangement that other states could eventually follow, under which the university would provide information, statistical analyses, and technical expertise to the governor and state legislature. The purpose was to devise effective policies to solve problems and to adopt nonpartisan legislation to that end. It was envisaged that the university would also train new generations of experts who would serve as judges, commissioners, and managers to mediate between conflicting interests, such as, for example, between business and labor. Thus politics would be sidestepped, and experts would be the prominent officials who carried out the preferred solutions (preferred by scientific experts, not by the politicians or "the people").

The effort failed, however, because state, business, and political leaders began to suspect that a hidden political agenda lay beneath the rhetoric of nonpartisanship. The tendency for professors to frame issues in an academic fashion also did not fit with the practical realities of the legislative process. As a result, the experiment found few imitators in other states, although many universities founded training programs for public servants, public administrators, labor relations arbitrators, and social service workers—sometimes within the political science or economics department and sometimes as a separate program or school. The Wisconsin idea was not wholly without an impact across the nation. The seeds of civic engagement were certainly planted by the Wisconsin idea, and the experiment helped to keep alive the earlier tradition of educating students in the responsibilities of citizenship.

Several general points should be noted about the political attitudes of faculty members under Progressivism: first, since Progressivism found no clear expression in a single political party, university professors did not attach themselves to one party rather than another. In Wisconsin, the Progressive Party led by the Robert La Follettes (father and son) was the main vehicle for reform. Theodore Roosevelt and the Republican Party in New York constituted the major Progressive force in the state, battling urban corruption and seeking to implement civil service reform.

Second, Progressivism was understood to be nonpartisan and to represent "expert" solutions to public problems. Building political alliances was not the goal of the academic reformers. There was an underlying nativist streak in Progressivism (though not nearly so pronounced as with Populism). A growing suspicion of the new immigration and of the teeming urban masses made the Democratic political machine, as mobilizer of the new immigrants, alien to many academic intellectuals who broadly preached the "cult of efficiency."[31] The Progressive admiration for expertise easily became transmuted into the meritocratic ideal, which became a dominant goal of American universities after World War II.

Of course, there were intellectuals who criticized American society during the Progressive era. Certainly many academic reformers found fault with much of the established dogma and with the excesses of the Gilded Age. John Dewey attacked the ideas of David Hume and other Enlightenment thinkers as he vigorously advocated educational reform. Charles Beard attacked the founding fathers as members of the property-owning class who were out to protect their own economic interests. James Harvey Robinson criticized the traditional narrative historians who glorified the past and glossed over the problems of slavery and other injustices. Thorsten Veblen assailed the "conspicuous consumption" of the leisured classes. All of these figures were certainly reformers, and they helped to shape the climate of opinion within their disciplines, their universities, and the wider public arena. They spoke out even when they could get into trouble and risked being fired by their universities. They were influential figures in shaping an American liberalism that was broadly critical of American institutions and of the shortcomings of the American liberal tradition. The American professoriate thus began, under Progressivism, to be receptive to liberal causes and to be more liberal than society at large.

Lionel Trilling in *The Liberal Imagination* was the linear descendant of these figures when he posited in 1946 that liberalism was the dominant frame of mind in America. He defined the role of the critic as that of ensuring that liberalism is "aware of the weak or wrong expressions of itself."[32] Veblen, Beard, Dewey, Robinson, and other reformist social scientists and historians of their generation, however, probably never matched the public influence of the muckraking journalists and reformist politicians of the Progressive era.

Among the academic reform thinkers of the Progressive era, Thorsten Veblen took the most direct aim at the institutions of higher education. In *The Higher Learning in America*, Veblen criticized the universities as exhibiting the qualities of conspicuous consumption, much like the rest of the economy.[33] Donors gave too many buildings, which began to proliferate on the campuses. Business values predominated, and university officials were timid in the face of corporate power. Universities strove to compete like corporate entities; growth was equated with quality, and success was defined in crass materialist terms; a crassness of taste prevailed throughout higher education in Veblen's analysis. But Veblen was realistic enough to see how the interests of the faculty were served by many of the trends he deplored. He might be a contemporary leftist by some criteria, but he also would appear conservative to many contemporary leftists who deplore corporatism.

He was notably short on solutions, despite the scope and strength of his indictment of the universities. Veblen wanted philanthropy without the philanthropist. It did not occur to him to seek additional government support for research, apparently presuming that government patronage might be even worse than private patronage in terms of the strings attached and the potential threats to faculty autonomy. His only idea for reform was to abolish the boards of trustees as a means of reducing the influence of business leaders on university activities. While sometimes endorsing a watered-down version of his ideas on university reform, his colleagues were noticeably cool in their reception to *The Higher Learning in America*. Faculty members, as well as administrators, wanted the support of wealthy businessmen to fund their academic and research programs and looked upon Veblen as the skunk at the garden party.

Significantly, Veblen's main line of attack was not that the universities were indifferent to social justice or that professors were inattentive to activist causes. Instead, he deplored what he saw as an overemphasis on the utilitarian in the mission of the universities, a preoccupation that diverted academic energies away from what should be the universities' true mission. To Veblen the university's mission was the search for knowledge for knowledge's sake, not vocationalism and not social reform. Engaging politically, advocating the cause of social justice, and making sure that the egalitarian spirit reigned within the university itself, as was the goal of the post-1960s reformers, were not his causes, but they were less objectionable to him than placing the universities at the service of the captains of industry.

## *The New Deal and World War II*

University faculty members became involved more directly with liberal causes in the New Deal era. Although survey research findings are scant on faculty political attitudes for the 1930s, professors were more liberal than other occupational groups. It is probable that faculty, along with much of the rest of the country, shifted significantly toward the Democratic Party. Faculty liberalism generally increased, and ideological debates were common in the universities in the 1930s. The influx of scholars fleeing from Nazism and Italian fascism, many of whom were prominent Social Democrats and leftist in their political outlook, contributed to the shift in the intellectual climate on many American campuses. The new consciousness clashed with the political passivity and also with the reformist Christian values that once permeated American higher education.

The universities and faculty members experienced economic hardships during the depression, and this naturally enough contributed to the embrace of New Deal goals by many professors. Rexford Tugwell and Raymond Moley, an economist from Columbia University, were influential members of President Roosevelt's Brains Trust and became exemplars of the activist social scientist. Scientists, whose leadership had been strongly Republican and politically conservative in the past, under the leadership of Karl Compton, president of the Massachusetts Institute of Technology, made overtures to New Deal leaders. The scientific community, whose leaders previously had resisted the idea of seeking federal research support, sought new ties with the federal government for that purpose.[34]

During World War II, the nation's intellectual resources were fully mobilized.[35] To an extent not matched by the Axis forces, America and her allies drew scientists, operations researchers, linguists, historians, and others from the universities into the war effort. A new generation of area studies experts also served in wartime strategic intelligence, research, and administrative posts. The postwar tone was set by the scientists, especially by the physicists who were lionized for their contributions to radar, communications, and development of the atomic bomb. Physicists dominated the postwar advisory mechanisms set up to bring expertise to the federal government and especially to the defense agencies. The nation moved from peacetime to demobilization and then to the Korean War and to the semipermanent mobilization of the cold war era. Large-scale federal support for basic research in the nation's universities became a reality, initially to compensate for the diversion of academic scientists into the war effort and then to serve the national defense, the economy, and public health on a permanent footing.[36]

During the demobilization following World War II, some 10 million soldiers returned to civilian life, and under the GI Bill of Rights some 2 million of them sought to attend college. The GI Bill (and a similar program following the Korean War) helped to swell the ranks of those attending colleges and universities. Then, with the National Defense Education Act of 1958, following the launch of the two Soviet sputniks, the nation was precipitated into the era of mass higher education. From some 4 percent of the age cohort eighteen to twenty-four in 1910, college attendance rose to more than one-third. By 2005 nearly 70 percent of young Americans received some form of postsecondary education, a higher mobilization rate for postsecondary education than any other nation. About a third of the college-age population today earns a first degree (bachelor's or the equivalent), and a third of that number continues on to an advanced degree. The majority of today's undergraduate students, by a small but growing margin, are female, about a third of all students come from racial minorities, and more than 40 percent of the students are age twenty-five or older.[37]

The greater part of the growth took place in two-year and four-year colleges. Enrollment in the elite universities grew less dramatically. The same universities that belonged to the Association of American Universities (AAU) in its founding years (with some subtractions and additions) make up its membership today. The AAU membership overlaps closely with the list of institutions classed as research-intensive universities by the Carnegie Corporation of New York City, and these lists include the institutions receiving the lion's share of federal dollars for research and development. The top universities seek to establish their distinctive "brands" and compete vigorously with each other, but with surprisingly little of what economists call "product differentiation."[38]

The "public face" of the postwar American research university was that of scientific and technological prowess. America's economic prosperity, advances in health care, and military strength seemed to grow out of the technological cornucopia that was rooted in the research universities. The intellectual tone of even nonscientific disciplines reflected an admiration for, and a desire to imitate the rigor and precision of, the hard sciences.[39] The story of how academic culture first shifted to absorb the scientific ideal and then shifted away from what many academics saw as an excessive preoccupation with the ideal of scientific objectivity is told in the following chapter. In the conventional wisdom, science (the value-free inquiry of the 1950–65 period) displaced politics (the looser, ideologically driven debates that characterized many disciplines in the 1930s), only to have the universities subverted once again by the Vietnam era and post-1960s radicals who politicized the humanities and social sciences and made inroads into the sciences. We tell a more complicated story in the following chapters, in which we show how various factors have combined to make genuine political debate rare on most of America's campuses and education for effective democratic citizenship rarer still.

# 4

## Transformations of Academic Culture after World War II

The period after World War II, from 1945 to the student disturbances of 1968–72, has been called the golden age of higher education in the
United States.[1] Not since the Civil War, after which the sixty-seven land grant
colleges were created, and the last decades of the nineteenth century, when the
American research university fully emerged, could one point to changes of
such magnitude for higher education. The post–World War II changes
included an enormous expansion of the student body and the strengthening
of research capacities and of graduate education. There were dramatic
increases in both public and private support for university programs for basic
and applied research. The increased research support for the universities was
an important contributor to economic development, better health, and a
strong national defense. In sum, total federal government expenditures for
higher education between 1950 and 1970 increased from $2.2 billion to $23.4
billion.[2] Enrollments eventually grew from about 30 percent of all secondary
school graduates to over 60 percent.

Numbers and statistics alone do not tell the whole story of the research
universities after World War II. Changes in the academic culture are equally,
perhaps even more, important. These changes encompassed, in effect, dual
revolutions in the ethos guiding the universities. The first revolution professionalized, modernized, and secularized the universities, with the hard sciences
in the ascendancy. The sciences represented the public face of the academy, and

the scientific model, embodying the Enlightenment spirit, shaped the entire academic culture.

A second transformation occurred after the Vietnam War era and produced a more complex and eclectic academic culture, which did not repudiate the Enlightenment values of science but which, in the postmodern terminology, "problematized" the meaning of the Enlightenment. Along with this came an altered, or at least more nuanced, mission or set of missions for the universities.

Much of the postwar university expansion, and the bulk of the research support, took place, as noted, in the sciences and in engineering. The effort built from the base of American self-sufficiency that had developed gradually across the sciences before and during the interwar period. The postwar generation of U.S. scientific leaders was largely American trained, although some fields were significantly influenced by the émigré scientists and scholars who had fled from fascism in Europe.[3] The sciences and the engineering fields that grew so dramatically gave an overall tone to America's universities. Indeed, the research university acquired a broader social significance as it became the symbol of America's technological leadership in the world during the quarter century following World War II.

The social sciences participated in the general expansion of university research and contributed to the enhanced public appreciation of higher education.[4] American "high culture" earned broad respect throughout the Western world (and our "pop culture" was pervasive). International and area studies programs were particular beneficiaries of increased public and private support as America assumed the status of a world leader. The cold war imposed vast new international responsibilities on the nation that inevitably meant the fuller mobilization of the nation's intellectual resources.

A rough consensus emerged among American opinion leaders in the postwar period, in accord with the broad ideas laid out in Vannevar Bush's 1945 report *Science: The Endless Frontier* and the three-volume John Steelman report of 1948.[5] Both reports addressed the same issues and urged society and the research community to strike a tacit bargain in which society would greatly enhance its support for science, research, and higher education. In return, it was assumed that the nation's scientists and engineers would deliver broad benefits to society, including the basic research underlying advanced technologies, stronger economic development in general, new cures for disease, and a stronger military posture.[6]

The formula of support for basic research based on the expectation that short- and long-run benefits to society would follow apparently worked well for almost a generation, as judged by the pragmatic results. For the quarter century following the war, unlike the economic distress following World War I, America suffered only a brief dip in economic growth (between 1945 and 1947) and otherwise enjoyed uninterrupted growth and prosperity. For the American research university, the strategy of assuming an important role in producing useful knowledge, training foreign students who became leaders in their own countries, strengthening the nation's economy through high-tech offshoots led by former faculty members, and contributing to the national defense through Pentagon-funded research proved to be highly successful, at least in the short run. For the longer term, the heightened expectations, along with the increased public attention and visibility, contributed to the difficulties facing the universities, including increased vulnerability to the vicissitudes of research funding and pressures for immediate payoffs from university work. The universities found themselves in something of the dilemma foreseen by Veblen: they wanted patronage but found it difficult to live with the patrons.

The extraordinary expansion in the quarter century after World War II smoothed over many underlying tensions and potential conflicts in the higher education system. The serious issues that were for the moment sidestepped included tensions between the rival claims of applied and basic research; disputes over the true payoff that could be expected from research; the appropriate role, if any, for the universities in large-scale targeted national research programs; the relative priorities of undergraduate and graduate education; frictions between the "have" and "have not" universities and the resulting disputes over the allocation of research funds among different regions of the country; the lack of integration between policies for training and education as against those for research support; compliance costs and unfunded mandates resulting from government social regulations; the disparities and imbalances in public support among different fields; and the question of whether the federal government has a responsibility for the institutional health of the universities apart from its role as purchaser of specific research services. Many critical policy choices could be deferred so long as all parties benefited from the general expansion of the university system. For decades almost all of higher education did benefit, including two-year community colleges, four-year state colleges, the liberal arts colleges, public and publicly assisted universities, and private universities (the less research intensive as well as the more research intensive).

## The Research Ethos

During the initial postwar period, as the emphasis on research increased, there were certain noteworthy accompanying developments. Specialization and departmental autonomy increased, which led to lighter teaching loads, the ceding of some authority from presidents and central administrators to departments, and the quest for the "star" professor to raise an institution's standing and ranking, all of which helped to shape the aspirations of the many players in the system. For the universities as a whole, there was a pattern of what Thomas Bender calls a "leveling up."[7] By 1970 or so, research and advanced training were "no longer dominated by a select few institutions—Chicago and the Ivies. Distinction was as likely to be found in major public institutions (Berkeley, Ann Arbor, Madison) as private ones."[8]

Faculty values—the desire to pursue research opportunities, to recruit better colleagues, to seek out talented students, to achieve autonomy—largely drove the system. The values of the faculty established the standards by which universities gained prestige and status. The scholarly disciplines and their learned societies were "the central constituencies of the academic culture" for "these groups could confer a reputation for excellence."[9] The individual disciplines thus wrested some of the authority away from the leaders who previously held sway in the major universities. The rather imperial figures of the past, who resembled the captains of industry of their day, were largely replaced by leaders with more limited roles in directing their complex, sprawling, and decentralized institutions.

The professoriate became increasingly self-conscious as it consolidated its prerogatives. Some subfields devoted considerable energy to the study of the sociology or the history of the academic profession itself. The values, the political attitudes, and the organization of the academic profession were studied in detail. This body of knowledge has provided us (and other authors) with important background data, from which we draw liberally in the present study.[10]

James B. Conant, president of Harvard University from 1933 to 1953, believing that the role of science had become of central importance, established a program to study the history and sociology of science in the late 1940s.[11] Professors gained in prestige, pay, and status. Their advocates, including friendly politicians and university presidents, celebrated their achievements and heralded the importance of research in achieving a broad range of social goals. The contributions of knowledge to economic development and longer life expectancy became a mantra for university presidents in appealing to state legislators and federal funding authorities for research support. Professors were happy enough to accept the benefits of expanded research funding, but many continued to view themselves as a beleaguered minority, not fully appreciated by a materialist society. Some criticized the universities for having too much social engagement, and these colleagues stepped up their criticisms as the universities became involved in a variety of social controversies from pollution to the Vietnam War effort.

## The Secular and Cosmopolitan Value System

These changes, taken together, signified the emergence of a new cosmopolitan ethos for the American research university. This commitment to rationalist values constituted the academic revolution of the postwar era, as Christopher Jencks and David Riesman termed it in their 1968 book.[12] The American university had become de-Christianized, secular in outlook, internationalist, and less dependent on a regional or geographically limited student clientele. While it became more geared to social needs, the university was at the same time, paradoxically, more driven by its own internal norms. Thus the universities were less reflective of the values of the outside community even as they became more useful to society in multiple ways. Professors (and intellectuals generally) were respected and influential figures, as Edward Shils noted, while at the same time becoming targets for social critics and for those who feared modernity and defended a more traditional ethic.[13]

Jewish intellectuals, who had previously suffered discrimination in America's elite universities, joined faculties in large numbers after World War II. By 1960 Jewish scholars comprised 17 percent of faculty members of the major research universities, while being 3 percent of the U.S. population (and they constituted more than 17 percent in certain fields and regions).[14] The presence of Jewish scholars at many universities contributed to the generally cosmopolitan, secular, and politically liberal outlook of the professorate. Jewish students, who had been discriminated against in the Ivy League since the 1920 revision in admissions policies by Harvard, Yale, and Princeton, began to grow in numbers at these institutions as well.[15]

International studies programs flourished, and an influx of foreign students added to the diversity of the student body. By gender, race, class, and ethnicity, both the faculties and the student bodies of America's universities became more diverse.

The changes in academic values in higher education's golden age are critical for understanding the contemporary university and fathoming the criticisms directed against the universities. The new academic ethos, not merely the growth in enrollment or the proliferation of academic programs, distinguishes this first postwar chapter in higher education. Harvard in 1947 produced the Red Book, the report *General Education in a Free Society*, which envisaged a "general" rather than a "liberal" education. This became the blueprint for an undergraduate curriculum suitable for the postwar era. An emphasis on science and on the major humanist texts of European civilization, but not in the form of a uniform core curriculum, was deemed to be the appropriate model. The central thrust was that of a practical university that would broadly serve society and America's diverse democracy.

About the same time, a Presidential Commission on Higher Education issued a multivolume report, *Higher Education for a Democracy*, which reinforced the notion that an expanded higher education sector must be "directly relevant to the demands of contemporary society."[16] By this, the authors meant (though not without some dissent within their own ranks) a racially inclusive higher education sector. The educational sector would be responsive to the needs of a diverse society and would feature a curriculum in theory broadly committed to the Western Enlightenment tradition and to democratic citizenship.[17]

A commitment to modern science and the scientific outlook was, however, the core concept of the postwar university. The pursuit of scientific truth defined the internal norms of the academic enterprise. The bulk of federal research funds went to the sciences and engineering. The university presented itself to society as the home of basic scientific advances, and these advances would make possible useful applied research in industry and in government laboratories. The application of practical knowledge to the solution of society's problems was thus advanced as the university's raison d'être, a revival of sorts of the Wisconsin idea of the 1890s.

Science was instrumental to postwar prosperity and to a new knowledge-based economy. Books such as David Potter's *People of Plenty* and John Kenneth Galbraith's *The Affluent Society* caught the spirit of the postwar era but were by no means celebratory of it.[18] Expansion, dynamic economic growth, optimism, military strength, and progress toward a better future could be within reach, but we would have to learn to deal with the problems of abundance. Potter and Galbraith pointed to shortcomings that did not receive enough debate in the general complacency and self-congratulatory mood of the day. The economic experience seemed to be the reverse of the stagnation, weakness, cultural despair, and disorder that followed World War I. And the preeminence of the American research university, at once the cause and the effect of America's scientific and technological leadership, lay at the heart of it all.

It was not merely that the science and engineering fields were of world-class stature, but that the Enlightenment values underlying the progress of modern science suffused the entire academic culture. Science was not a "constructed" human activity, contingent on and reflective of cultural nuance, as it came to be viewed in some later studies on the sociology of science. Rather, science provided a set of universalistic norms, objective criteria for truth seeking, which joined the entire worldwide community of scholars in a common enterprise. The norms of science elevated the social sciences from descriptive disciplines to more rigorous fields of study, producing in the process a heightened sense of professionalism and promoting theoretical as well as applied advances. It was little wonder that rapid advances were self-reinforcing, thereby igniting the strong desire to emulate the natural sciences.[19] Foundation support for academic social science increased dramatically, initially going to a small number of elite universities but then broadening to a wider tier of institutions.[20] The National Science Foundation widened its definition of the "sciences" it could support to include the social sciences, despite some apprehension among natural scientists that doing so might undermine congressional support for basic science by introducing a "political" element into the picture. The social sciences, some scientists at the time feared, were likely to be seen as inherently subjective and thus unavoidably political in orientation and outlook. Natural scientists in the 1950s were less liberal than their social science counterparts, as they were in the 1920s when physicist George Ellery Hale, a political conservative, was the leader of the National Academy of Sciences and perhaps the most prominent spokesman for the scientific community.

Ironically, although scientists as a whole tended to be less liberal (as measured in the emerging opinion surveys that we discuss later), they often engaged in more genuine political debates than their colleagues in other disciplines. Academic scientists figured prominently in the nuclear freeze movement, the Pugwash conferences that engaged American, West European, and Soviet scientists in arms control debates, and the human rights dialogues with physicist Andre Sakharov of the USSR that contributed to the Helsinki Declaration of 1975. The scientists seemed able to separate their professional work from their role as citizens more easily than their colleagues in the supposedly value-laden disciplines and to feel no compunction about speaking out on issues of national importance. The "peace" scientists battled unapologetically with the "defense" scientists in academic and nonacademic forums. It was also from within the ranks of science that the most challenging critique of scientism and the scientific method arose in Thomas Kuhn's *The Structure of Scientific Revolutions*, a study that was conceived and carried out within the Harvard Program on Science and Society founded by James Conant after the war.[21]

## The Scientific Model Ascendant

The social scientists, as they professionalized their fields of inquiry, became less engaged with genuine political debate and less concerned with educating students in the rights and obligations of citizenship. Why this happened relates to their desire to escape from the McCarthy attacks on "liberals" and "communist sympathizers," but also to the internal logic of the professionalization they experienced. The social sciences were able to deflect McCarthyite criticism to some degree by subscribing to the norms of scientific, objective, and thus "value-free" inquiry to the extent that professional social scientists sought to eschew ideology, overt partisanship, and normative concerns. In short, as they raised the level of scientific rigor in their fields, they could separate scholarship from politics. They could, in other words, emulate their colleagues in the natural sciences (never quite appreciating that many scientists did not adopt a primitive epistemology nor abdicate their citizenship when they became scientists). Social scientists not only turned their backs on the kind of loose scholarship that often prevailed in the 1930s, they abandoned the passionate antitotalitarian battles of the 1930s, which were now rendered largely moot. A residual anticommunism remained, along with a general commitment to democracy, but these were more in the nature of inarticulate premises than fully reasoned (or argued) doctrines.

In political science, for example, as the behavioral revolution took hold in the 1950s, the field sought twin goals: to become more scientific and to promote broadly the cause of democracy.[22] The twin goals, moreover, were often presumed to be mutually reinforcing. The more the discipline could achieve a scientific understanding of politics, the more it would presumably strengthen democracy at home and pave the way for progress toward democracy abroad. The shortcomings of this simplified formula have elicited much critical commentary, both relating to the methodological defects and to the evasion of large normative concerns. Although political science had an implicit faith in democracy, explicating and debating that belief was never a prominent professional goal or route to advancement within the profession. Normative political theory withered and became a marginalized subfield (although it enjoyed a modest revival in the 1980s). The idea that political science should have any responsibility for the moral and civic education of students weakened in the postwar surge toward greater professionalism.[23]

The "modernization" subfield was another example of empirical social science that embodied a secular and mildly ameliorative outlook (and, implicitly, an ideology that could be described as liberal in that government assistance was assumed to be a necessary and effective means of promoting modernization). This subfield directed scholarly attention to the international arena and the problems of underdevelopment. Drawing on the tools of both economics and political science, experts aspired to help Third World nations to overcome backwardness, to achieve economic development, and to embrace a secular and modern outlook. In the process, it was assumed implicitly and even explicitly that economic advance would pave the way for the growth of democratic and capitalist institutions and insulate nations in the Third World from the lure of communism. Later, when the universities were supposedly becoming more liberal and displaying liberal bias, the field shifted to embrace a more avowedly private market approach. Faith in the market, like the earlier faith in government aid, was often an inarticulate major premise the implications of which were inadequately debated.

Even when this rationalist approach failed to shelter political scientists from controversy, the advocates of the scientific study of politics could take solace from what they viewed as only temporary setbacks. University of Chicago political scientist David Easton found in McCarthyism a rationale for the development of a more scientific and objective discipline. The scientific approach would provide a "protective posture for scholars."[24] One could defeat McCarthyism by giving it no target to attack. The job of political scientists was in any case to discover laws of political behavior and, as good scientists, to leave politics to the politicians.[25] This strategy, however, emptied out the political content from political science and contributed to the retreat from civic engagement that increasingly characterized the discipline. Thomas Bender sums up the point in broad terms:

> Whereas the Red Book [Harvard Report of 1946] had asked scholars to investigate and teach "the place of human aspirations and ideals in the total scheme of things," the post-war disciplines, emulating the inward-looking and donnish analytical movement, eschewed such a civic role. In retrospect it appears that the disciplines were redefined over the course of the last half century following the war; from the means to an end they increasingly became an end in themselves, the possession of the scholars who constructed them. To a greater or lesser degree, academics sought some distance from civics. The increasingly professionalized disciplines were embarrassed by moralism and sentiment; they were openly or implicitly drawn to the model of science as a vision of professional maturity.[26]

Economists, for their part, followed almost exactly the path sketched by Bender; they stepped back from the kind of ideological engagement that had been part of the discipline in the 1930s. The academic economists and experts in the government forged a broad consensus around a more analytical, rigorous understanding of economic phenomena and the behavior of markets. Businessmen, who had often been anti-intellectual in tone, had lost much of their clout within the profession with the advent of the depression and suffered a weakening of their traditional authority. They became discredited to a degree, and the academic economists assumed the leadership within the profession. The economists, and the new economics they practiced, became institutionalized in the federal government with the Employment Act of 1946, which created the Council of Economic Advisers to the President.[27] Economic intervention to promote price stability, to foster employment targets, and to stimulate growth was considered acceptable and, of course, political preferences and values were implicitly involved, but debates were conducted in technical language and at a level of sophistication that largely shut off participation by nonspecialists. Economic disputes were grounded in esoteric technical understanding. As the field became increasingly scientific, economists spoke to their specialized peers in a language not readily accessible to laymen (or to undergraduate students). Instead of preparing students to understand economic issues as future citizens, economists, even at colleges devoted to undergraduate teaching, sought to prepare their students to become professional specialists.[28]

Sociologists, too, sought to be more scientific. In the process the field displayed what the Harvard report *General Education in a Free Society* called "one of the subtlest and most prevalent effects of specialization," namely, the tendency of specialized fields "to be conceived and taught with an eye . . . to their internal logic rather than their larger usefulness to students."[29] At the elite universities, sociologists became more enamored with their aspirations toward verifiable knowledge and theory than with the applied aspects of their field. The sociologists, like the political scientists and the economists, moved away from the larger issues of power, class conflict, and social transformation that were prominently featured in the "pre-scientific" interwar and postwar period until about the early 1950s.[30] Harvard's Talcott Parsons reflected the dominant mood when he argued in a 1959 American Sociological Association address that sociology's major thrust as a discipline should be and is "primarily dedicated to advancement and transmission of empirical knowledge" and only "secondarily to the communication of that knowledge to non-members."[31] A corollary was that political activism and engagement with broad social issues or the more applied subfields within the discipline were downplayed and subordinated as professional concerns.

In the sociology of science, which became a major subfield within the discipline, Robert K. Merton of Columbia University drew attention to the scientific profession itself as a field of study. In a series of pioneering studies, he laid out the norms and reward structures that explained how science as a social system operated.[32] His theories both reflected and shaped the outlook of science as a universalistic human enterprise guided by recognizable canons of truth-seeking, priority claims, and self-regulation. Merton's conception of science's role in society was related to the ideological temper of the times. His earliest formulation, on the eve of war in 1940, stressed the close links between science and democracy. Merton then saw science in broad terms as a bulwark against fascism and communism. The value dimensions of his theory were unmistakable. Later, he moved away from that orientation and toward a more fully elaborated "scientific" theory of science as a social system. How, or whether, science could flourish under Nazism or communism and whether adverse social consequences could accompany technical progress were not taken up in his mature theories.

Seymour Martin Lipset proposed a suggestive analysis of how sociology cohered as a discipline and as a profession in the postwar period. The profession's scholarly aspirations and its thrust toward social reform were balanced and held in check by a kind of informal compact between the acolytes and the elders, in which the students and young professionals were taught the tools and methods of science as the preconditions for any future social activism.[33] In order to lay the basis for the reform of capitalism, the younger scholars were persuaded to undergo rigorous training in statistics, survey methodologies, and other tools. Thus the younger sociologists would defer to their elders for the moment and compartmentalize their activist tendencies in order to acquire the trappings of professionalism. This compact broke apart with the Vietnam War, when the younger generation of sociologists began to view their elders, and such reigning paradigms as structuralism-functionalism, as inimical to the sweeping social changes that the younger members deemed to be urgent.[34] The discipline, according to Lipset, fell into a state of disarray from which it has yet to recover.

Daniel Bell saw the whole postwar period we are describing here as a reflection of the "end to ideology" in scholarship and in postwar American thought generally.[35] Bell regarded this development as healthy and a pragmatic accommodation to reality inasmuch as the "big issues" were no longer seriously in dispute. In 1949 in *The Vital Center*, historian Arthur Schlesinger Jr. articulated a similar vision, which was a mildly progressive, liberal internationalist outlook that to him framed his discipline's intellectual mission in the cold war era.[36] Others disputed this vision and argued that Americans should break away from such a narrow view of their own past and the present. To the extent that historians have tended to view conservatives as fringe groups somewhat removed from the American mainstream, they have suffered from a failure of historical imagination.[37] Those observers have missed the complex and deep-rooted conservative traditions in America.

Louis Hartz took a different view in *The Liberal Tradition in America* by urging that a dominant Lockean ideology in American thought crippled our ability to experiment with nonliberal approaches to problems and constrained American thinking into narrow channels.[38] Because we did not have a feudal tradition to break from, America did not develop either the socialist traditions of Europe or Europe's truly conservative ideologies. The absence of true conservatism or radicalism has thus impoverished the American political dialogue. This blinkering of the imagination, in Hartz's view, has made it difficult for Americans to grasp the deeper meaning of events and to understand their own and world politics. Whether we accept fully this argument, an ideological layer or set of principles clearly was implicit in much of the "value-free" inquiries of the first generation of postwar scholars. But these principles, or any implicit consensus, were to be shattered in the next phase. There were much less of a liberal consensus and a decided fracturing of any common principles, whether methodological or political.

Thus around the time that the conventional wisdom began to view the universities as suffering from a suffocating uniformity of thought, faculties were becoming more polarized, as were Americans generally. This has complicated the task of describing the political ideologies of faculty members. American professors were clearly liberal in a certain (Lockean) sense in the 1950s, even if they did not explicitly acknowledge politics in their scholarly work or engage each other in political debate outside the classroom. They were often mildly reformist in outlook and broadly favored government intervention to remedy economic ills at home. They were internationalists in foreign affairs. In the post-Vietnam period they became less "liberal" in various ways (for example, less confident that government can solve economic problems, more distrustful of international intervention, more suspicious of bureaucracy and regulation). In place of the earlier mild liberalism, many professors adopted a more radical stance on issues such as race, gender, and sexual orientation. The spectrum of opinion became wider, not narrower. There was less of a common dialogue, however, as many fields deconstructed into narrower and narrower subspecialties.

## The Seeds of Change: Modernism and Postmodernism

From the end of World War II to the student disturbances of the Vietnam War era, with a moderately liberal Truman administration replaced by the moderately conservative Eisenhower presidency and, in turn, by the reformism of John Kennedy and Lyndon Johnson, the political attitudes of faculty ranged from apolitical to moderately liberal to a more pronounced liberalism. There were considerable variations among departments, schools, and the various fields of inquiry.[39] A mild pluralism, emphasizing the rival interests of different groups and the resolution of conflicts by bargaining among leadership elites, was a key premise of the faculty's broad political outlook (as it was for American politicians and Americans generally). The cultural outlook of most faculty members and other social elites was secular, but life styles were often conservative. Faculties were hierarchical, and younger faculty members deferred to their seniors. The dominant outlook in the postwar American university was never monolithic, however, even in the period when there was a broad consensus within many fields. The complicated modern university, with its numerous programs, divisions, and schools and its location in different regional and community settings, was riven by numerous fault lines. Beneath the surface, the reigning rationalist outlook was being challenged by internal critics even as it was being consolidated.

The seeds of the later "culture wars" could be found as early as the 1950s. Viewpoints that challenged the orthodoxies and replaced the older scholarly traditions were present within virtually every scholarly field, even if they were for the moment minority viewpoints.

The challenges came, on the one hand, from the traditionalists who were never quite persuaded that their particular fields should strive to imitate the hard sciences and, on the other, from more radical voices. Lionel Trilling in literature, who was both a traditionalist and a radical, found much wanting among his peers and in the dominant modes of American thought and culture.[40] Richard Hofstadter in history saw flaws in the outlook of the Progressive historians, stressing the complexity of social and political life that historians in the Progressive tradition (which included many of his contemporaries) had missed. History was not any simple march of progress, and he urged his colleagues to reckon with the tragic dimensions of human affairs.[41]

There was, in fact, an ethic that viewed academic culture as rooted ineluctably in moral dilemmas and conflicting human purposes. Scholars who held this view strongly doubted that research could provide a unifying moral authority for academic culture, a point of view especially congenial to scholars in the humanistic fields and to social scientists who considered themselves rooted in the humanist tradition. Others deplored the pedantry and the lack of concern for communicating with nonexperts that marked much of the modern scholarship. Julie Reuben depicted the trend toward secularism and specialization as having paved the way toward a mere formalism in philosophy and some other disciplines, a formalism that has tended to separate method from substance.[42]

In the arts and the humanities the postwar academic culture and style of scholarship had its most ambiguous effects. Typified in the New Criticism, scholars were encouraged to move away from a loose literary and biographical approach and toward closer textual scrutiny.[43] The New Criticism was a pedagogical and critical invention that paralleled the rise of modernism as a literary movement. Modernist writers, such as Eliot, Pound, Joyce, Yeats, Auden, Wolff, Stein, Hansum, Faulkner, and others, embodied an allusive complexity in their verse or prose, and the New Criticism provided a tool for understanding their work. But the New Criticism had its critics from the start, including both traditionalists and the newer postmodernist generation of literary scholars. Concentrating on the text alone seemed much too narrow an approach to the scholars who saw history and literature as integrated cultural phenomena. The "Old Moderns," in Denis Donoghue's phrase, also aroused the ire of liberal critics because of their alleged conservatism and affinity with reactionary causes, including nativist and anti-Semitic tendencies.[44] The New Criticism gave the profession of literary scholars a sense of professional identity from about 1940 to 1965, but in the end this proved to be a temporary and aberrant period. The New Criticism, moreover, probably never was as dominant as both its critics and supporters believed.[45] The divisions that afterward beset English departments seemed to represent a return to the normal disorderly state of affairs and probably should be welcomed rather than deplored. We leave such issues, however, for our colleagues in the humanities to resolve (or to live with, as the case may be).

Humanists, further, have been broadly split over the nature and place of liberal education in the modern curriculum. Some humanists have welcomed the broadening of the traditional canon to include new ethnic writers, new types of literary expression, and a broader and more inclusive definition of culture. Others have taken a protective posture toward the classic works of the Western tradition, fearing a potential dissolution of standards and seeing threats to traditional cultural values in the search for new forms of cultural expression.[46] Nor were "Western values" or the "Enlightenment tradition" self-defining concepts in any simple sense. Anglophone and Francophone Enlightenment traditions exhibited subtle but significant differences.[47] These conflicting orientations presaged the deep divide of the 1970s and 1980s when the two positions hardened into hostile and antagonistic academic ideologies.

In the arts, the seeds of the culture wars were even more clearly visible from an early point. In the 1950s Jack Kerouac's *On the Road* and the Beat poetry of Allen Ginsberg pointed toward a postmodern mode of artistic expression. A savage review of *On the Road* by Norm Podhoretz, editor of *Commentary* and later a leading neoconservative, could be regarded as a first shot in the culture wars that later erupted in the universities.[48] The materials for a firestorm clearly were present, but it took the galvanizing impact of the Vietnam War to ignite those combustible ingredients.

## The Cultural Turn of the 1960s

Much has been written about the 1960s and a resulting "cultural turn" in American academic life.[49] The fracturing of traditional academic hierarchies, the changes in the cultural domain that ruptured humanistic traditions, and the controversies that overwhelmed the social sciences have drawn the attention of countless commentators. Pundits from all parts of the political spectrum have joined the fray. The 1960s were undoubtedly a profound turning point in the development of the universities, but the "lessons" are not so easy to draw. Two of the present authors participated directly in the upheavals of the late 1960s in different university settings (our younger colleague, only six months old at the time of these events, can scarcely believe the stories we tell). The two "seniors" on our team were affected in profoundly different ways by the 1960s experience. One of us became disillusioned with the blend of expertise and service to state power—the best and brightest syndrome—which he believed had contributed to America's misguided involvement in the Vietnam War. He shared in some measure the loss of faith in America's elite institutions, including the universities as they then were constituted, that many others of the 1960s generation experienced. The other one of us was shocked by the upheavals, by the assaults on established hierarchies and institutional traditions, and turned instead in a sharply conservative direction.

If the 1960s events radicalized some faculty and university administrators, they also produced a conservative pushback that has continued to this day. Our quest to understand what really happened in the 1960s and 1970s has been sparked by our diverse personal involvement. This contrast in perspectives has done much to provide the motivation and the intellectual challenge for the present study. We have sought to understand how the more polarized campus environments after the Vietnam War both reflected and helped to precipitate the polarized political climate of the nation generally.

The campus disputes are linked to, but also operate in, a context and according to an internal logic separate from the wider political trends. The riots at the 1968 Democratic National Convention in Chicago were partly a continuation of the antiwar campaigns on the nation's campuses. In a major strategic blunder, the Democratic Party appeared to embrace the countercultural demonstrators as agents of needed change, fixing in the public mind the image of the Democrats as a party receptive to the cultural upheavals and anarchic forces unleashed by he campus riots. Republicans for a generation ran against the Democrats as the party of the countercultural radicals contemptuous of mainstream American values. For the next forty years, only two conservative-to-moderate Democratic Southern governors—Jimmy Carter of Georgia and Bill Clinton of Arkansas—managed to win the presidency, Carter in the aftermath of the Watergate scandal and constitutional crisis and Clinton the beneficiary of independent candidate H. Ross Perot, who siphoned off 19 percent of the popular vote (taking votes principally from George H. W. Bush). The Democrats went further, undermining their own 1968 nominee Hubert Humphrey by supporting him only weakly. They convened the McGovern-Fraser Commission to "democratize" the party nominating process by moving to change the rules so as, among other things, to encourage presidential primaries rather than relying on caucuses, urban machines, and the party bosses operating in "smoke-filled rooms." These favorite bogeymen of the Progressive reformers were to be replaced by the people, and especially by young people, minorities, women, and others hitherto disenfranchised or only inadequately represented. The new system "worked" in that it produced George McGovern, the candidate of the left wing of the party, as the 1972 nominee. But the nomination reinforced the notion that the Democrats were the party of identity politics and "single-issue" interest groups and movements. Liberalism came to mean something different in this context from what older liberals believed. A *New Yorker* cartoon of the time summed up America's attitude toward the word and its newer connotations. A mâitre d' cautions his waiters, "Now be sure to say that we provide generous, not 'liberal,' portions."

The same reform impulses were in evidence on the campuses, with the old-boy networks substituting for the party bosses as the targets to be assailed. The dominant white Protestant male hierarchies were to be dismantled. Hiring practices were to be opened up, minority candidates were to be encouraged, and "democracy" in general was to be brought to the universities. And if utopia could not be realized in the real world of politics (which the campus reformers seemed willing to cede to conservatives), it could be approximated on the campuses in the form of a new egalitarian and meritocratic order. As to what was taught and thought in the new scheme of things, the God's-eye view that pervaded many disciplines, in which uniform and universal truths were sought, was to be replaced by a more subjective discourse that recognized all knowledge as "constructed" through the perspectives and interests of the observer. The "theory wars" and the "identity debate," two closely related developments, became emblematic of the intellectual history of the last quarter of the twentieth century.[50]

These debates, carried on in transdisciplinary "studies" programs and institutes and within social science and humanities departments, reflected the contributions of the 1960s by exposing the shortcomings of the universalist and rationalist outlook of the previous generation of scholars. The new focus was to be on previously neglected issues of groups and group consciousness as an important dimension of human affairs and to include attention to "the human body, language, class, gender, and, above all, the solidarities and confinements associated with ethnicity and race."[51] The new debates accommodated the rigorism of the 1950s in many respects in being complex and abstruse, and even outdid earlier scholars in the obscurity and prolixity of many of their formulations. What had been political with the 1960s radicals became increasingly transmuted into a kind of intellectual scholasticism, and their energies were directed away from concern with the larger body politic and toward their academic fiefdoms. Peace on campus, moreover, was maintained by carrying on an intellectual dialogue with one's like-minded friends and ignoring colleagues in rival camps. Although some of the new academic issues, such as race and feminism, had political origins and implications, the wider political dimension became a lesser concern in the new mode of discourse.

All of the new developments were thought to have some connection to the 1960s. But if conservatives and liberals agree on one point about the 1960s, it is that this period has been over interpreted. As a concept with explanatory power, the term "the sixties" "has become a historiographic monster . . . said to explain almost everything that needs to be explained about the subsequent quarter-century."[52] Like the newer breed of historians who are suspicious of "meta-narratives" (there is no longer an American story, only the story of African Americans, Chicanos, workers, women, other social groups, and so on), we should therefore be cautious about saying what the 1960s have meant for the universities. David A. Hollinger cogently argues that the 1970s and 1980s have dealt with the 1960s to be sure, but that the main elements have been a complex and contradictory amalgam of effects. The work of Thomas Kuhn plus the racial equality movement, feminism, and French poststructuralism (especially the writings of Michel Foucault) all helped to shape these effects. Hollinger is correct when he insists that this blend does not point in one clear direction.

Yet for our specific concerns, the legacy of the 1960s does seem fairly clear, even if there are variations among individual schools and across institutional categories (for example, liberal arts colleges versus the large complex research universities). Campuses once agitated by political issues became more politically quiescent. Students no longer subject to the draft returned to career pursuits like the students of the 1950s. Faculty members increasingly took to their specialized research concerns and put aside direct political engagement once the Vietnam War ended. A more miscellaneous collection of political conflicts, controversies, and scandals, involving an array of new political actors and forces, took over the nation's attention. National politics became an increasingly more distant concern to most academics. Faculty members, never much interested in the time-consuming duties of self-governance or in attending to their collective affairs, were willing to cede back to university administrators and bureaucrats, who swelled in numbers, the authority to police the boundaries of the new "studies" programs and interdisciplinary institutes and to enforce the new federal regulations stemming from affirmative action policies, human subjects review requirements, cost accounting for research grants, and other mandates. To come together on common governance issues or curricular concerns would involve actually having to engage in dialogue with and compromise with colleagues who disagree with you. Thus there was on campus not political uniformity but difference, and toleration among warring factions only by virtue of avoiding direct engagement. Faculty members were like most Americans generally in their distaste for politics and contention. An informal truce would thus prevail to keep peace on campus so long as the potentially warring factions kept their distance. Faculty members were recruited not on broad ideological or political grounds, but on whether they were good researchers in the 1950s scientific mode or in the post-1960s constructivist school. Disinterest in politics was a positive attribute because this would help to maintain the implicit truce between the right and left that had been forged in the campus culture wars. The problem was not to keep professors from talking incessantly about politics; it was to get them to talk about politics at all.

## The Columbia Student Uprisings: A Mini Case Study

It might be helpful to give a glimpse of what *did* happen at one campus in 1968, a case that we know firsthand and one that has been widely seen as having precipitated other student protests across the country. The Berkeley Free Speech Movement of 1964 was a localized incident, a minor disruption of campus life that did not produce similar events on other campuses.[53] The Students for a Democratic Society (SDS) was a small, noisy minority at Berkeley and a few university campuses, but did not have much of a following on most campuses until the 1967–68 academic year.[54] A few radical professors encouraged the militant students at Columbia, but few of the radicals were influential faculty members. Columbia, like most elite universities, was still governed largely by traditional faculty hierarchies made up of mildly liberal but mostly socially conservative white males (with a few distinguished female professors scattered through the ranks). Many of the influential faculty members had served in one capacity or another in the World War II war effort and were strongly patriotic. Many were critical of the Vietnam War effort but were even more critical of disruptive tactics that would harm the university or impair social cohesion more broadly. The Tet offensive in March 1968 raised the faculty's political awareness dramatically, as did an internal flap involving the university's unwise arrangement to test a so-called "anticancer" cigarette developed by an entrepreneur (and potentially share in profits if it was marketed).

The colleagues who were either moderately or strongly liberal politically were almost invariably old left and New Dealers and were mostly repulsed by their new left colleagues (mostly in the graduate student and junior faculty ranks). The Watts riots of 1965 and the racial disturbances that devastated Detroit in 1967 had no links with campus radicals and had surprisingly little impact at Columbia or most other campuses. Only after the Tet offensive and Senator Eugene McCarthy's strong showing in the New Hampshire primary did the peace movement gather real momentum on the Columbia campus.

The campus atmosphere was tense, but it did not seem on the verge of an explosion. Administrators were worried, however, that the school year was too long and that exams were not scheduled until June (and, indeed, after the crisis the authorities did change the school calendar, shortening spring term so that there would be no lengthy period for "spring frolics" between the onset of spring and the pressures attending final exams and graduation). The student disturbances that temporarily shut down Columbia in April 1968 came about as a result of a string of happenstances. The incident that indirectly set off Columbia's campus disturbances was a university decision to build a gymnasium in Morningside Park, a facility that would be shared with the local community.[55] A small group of SDS protesters (the SDS numbered perhaps fifty at Columbia at the time out of a student body of approximately 17,000) had been trying to generate interest among their fellow students in Columbia's plans to build a gym in neighboring Morningside Heights but had not made much of an impact. Construction was about to begin at the gym site, and most community leaders had gone on record in support of the plan. The SDS decided on their boldest move to date: they would stage a sit-in, or rather a lie-in, at the construction side.

The protesters were stymied in their efforts to halt construction by lying down in front of the bulldozer. Somewhat demoralized, they wandered back to campus. After milling around and chanting for a time, someone suggested that they march to Hamilton Hall, a classroom and administrative building that housed the office of the acting dean of Columbia College, Henry S. Coleman. The students, without any preconceived plan, pushed into Dean Coleman's office and, becoming emboldened, remained there and decided to hold the dean prisoner.

An emergency faculty meeting was called, not by the university administration but by an ad hoc group of faculty members, to discuss how the university should respond. This group of professors, though well intentioned, produced confusion with the meeting, and did much in the ensuing days to complicate the university's efforts to cope with the situation. By providing a forum for a small faction of radical professors to harass the university administration, the ad hoc faculty caucus legitimated the student actions. The caucus demonstrated an astonishing political naiveté and ineptitude, although they soon acquired a certain cunning in manipulating the media (who flocked in growing numbers to the campus). Calls for radical reforms in university governance, an end to defense research, eviction of the Reserve Officers' Training Corps (ROTC) from campus, amnesty for the student radicals, an end to the draft, and a host of other demands were issued from the ad hoc group's steering committee in the ensuing days.[56] The campus atmosphere rapidly polarized. One of the present authors, then a Columbia assistant professor, recalls saying to a senior colleague, "I think it's time for a moderate solution," to which the latter replied, "I think it's time for an *immoderate* solution." A leader of the ad hoc faculty caucus remarked to the same author on another occasion, not reading his interlocutor's political leanings quite correctly in the heat of the moment, "We've got to grab the administration by the balls and make them accept amnesty [for the protesters]." A quip of the day was that the "moderate" right was in favor of drawing and quartering, dropping the H bomb, and *then* expelling the protesters. The "moderate" left was for burning down the university and marching on city hall.

The events might have been halted in their tracks at the first dramatic meeting. For, in the midst of the overheated debate, Dean Coleman suddenly walked into the room, having been released by his captors. He urged calm, tried to persuade the ad hoc faculty group not to take any action in the heat of the moment, and called on those in attendance to wait until the university administration could convene a formal meeting of the faculty the following day. The faculty ignored him. The SDS students, meanwhile, led by Mark Rudd, a Columbia College senior, continued to occupy Hamilton Hall and were about to settle down for the evening when their plans were suddenly altered. African American students who had joined the protest (they were not SDS members) decided that this was their show and evicted the SDS students.

After their eviction, the SDS group wandered off in a state of fatigue and demoralization. Once again, on the spur of the moment, they conceived a new idea: occupy Low Library, the university's main administrative building. The group of students pushed their way past guards and proceeded to occupy the university's main administrative headquarters on the first floor, while the university police, now reinforced, occupied the basement and blocked further access to the building (or departure from the building, except through the first floor windows). In the middle of the night, the SDS "leader" Mark Rudd and others got cold feet and urged their fellow students to leave the building. Arguing in Leninist fashion that the time was not ripe for revolution, Rudd said that the larger SDS cause had to be kept in mind and that they should not jeopardize the cause by precipitous action. A vote was called for, and Rudd lost the vote by a narrow margin (by word of mouth among Columbia faculty the vote was something like 24-19). The student rebellion that paralyzed the university for a month and rippled across the nation's campuses was thus set into motion.

The changes affecting Columbia after the events of 1968 and the similar crisis that followed the Cambodian invasion of 1970 are not easily summarized, and we make no effort to do so in any thorough fashion. A serious and protracted job crisis in academe also occurred in the early 1970s. This, plus the growing number and complexity of federal regulations and a host of other developments, makes it difficult to separate out the 1960s effects from the others. At Columbia, a kind of thermador reaction set in: the traditional faculty hierarchy reasserted itself to a degree and, for the next decade and beyond, retained the top leadership posts of the university. These included the vice presidencies, the provost's office, and the major deanships. Anyone who was a radical was effectively blocked from assuming a major administrative post, even though the most militant faculty did enjoy leverage in shaping what the academic leaders did.

A new university senate was created, featuring the tripartite estates of administration, faculty, and students. Some faculty members called instead for a faculty senate, objecting on the grounds of separation of powers that the administrators first drew up proposals to present to themselves as recommendations to the senate and, when acted on, were thence passed on as proposals to themselves in their capacities as the executives. An army of secondary administrators and bureaucrats grew up to administer the new research programs, compliance offices, government relations, development campaigns, affirmative action mandates, financial aid offices, student services, and special projects of all kinds. In the process, an already complex administration was further complicated, the university having a complex structure stemming from the days when deans and faculties carved out autonomous clusters of authority in the waning days of Nicholas Murray Butler's once formidable presidency. The lesser bureaucracy gradually acquired an institutional power that top administrators had to listen to and defer to and, to some degree, encroached on what had been faculty prerogatives.

While countercultural radicals did not "take over" Columbia in any sense, the new (old) leaders were political realists and had to compromise with the faculty left in order to restore a semblance of peace and calm to the campus. The campus left thus won some battles: classified research was banned on campus (a measure supported by many on the faculty right as well), the ROTC was kicked off campus, faculty members were to report outside consulting arrangements, university legal services for the poor were protected, the university investment portfolio was scrutinized, and a few lesser victories were gained.

As the Vietnam War ended, the Organization of Petroleum Exporting Countries raised the price of oil and roiled the global economy, the Supreme Court handed down the *Roe* v. *Wade* decision, and President Nixon resigned from office, national politics changed dramatically, and the political debates on Columbia's polarized campus soon lost the antiwar and countercultural focus, diminished in intensity, and all but vanished. The activist energies on campus were displaced into scholarly preoccupations and more inward-looking concerns. Political peace of a sort reigned on campus, sustained through a combination of traditional political disinterest, a return to professional preoccupations, and a tacit alliance to steer clear of controversy among the antagonists who had battled at the barricades during the 1968–70 student protests. A new (partly traditional, partly novel) and more complicated campus took shape, or perhaps took no clear shape, as the many subcommunities and baronies pursued their miscellaneous and diverse goals.

An occasional (unsuccessful) effort would emerge to alter Columbia's traditional core curriculum. A fragile coalition of scientists (who objected to a too heavy concentration on the required humanities and social science courses), radical humanists (who were critical of the "dead white maleness" and the absence of postmodern and postcolonial texts in the core), and discipline-minded social scientists (who wanted more student choice and more room for elective courses in the major) stood uneasily as champions of change. Against them stood a more unified group of scientists with a humanist bent (a majority of the scientists), nonradical humanists (a majority of the humanists), and social scientists who were more humanistically inclined and defended the core as it stood. The traditionalists invariably trounced their opponents. In important respects, therefore, Columbia did not change, but it was not immune from the trends and wider developments in America. Columbia's preoccupations were not political; for the most part colleagues pursued their own scholarly interests. To the extent that issues like those raised in the identity debates stirred fierce debate, this debate turned inward to issues of appointments, academic programs, admissions, and so on. The Columbia concern with large social issues, such as C. Wright Mill's "power elite" studies of the 1950s or Francis Fox Piven's and Richard Cloward's 1960s studies of welfare reform or David Caplowitz's studies of the problems of the poor in Harlem, gave way to academic debates over postcolonial theory and French structuralism and poststructuralism, as reflected, for example, in the work of Edward Said on Orientalism in the 1970s and 1980s. To the extent that Columbia acquired a reputation for faculty radicalism, it rested largely with Said and a group of like-minded colleagues in Middle East studies who identified strongly with the Palestinian cause and bitterly opposed Israeli policy toward Gaza and the West Bank (and U.S. policy toward Israel). Said and his colleagues were strongly opposed within the Columbia community, but the pronouncements and actions of his group drew the attention of Jewish watchdog groups and papers like the *New York Sun,* both of which continued to look for opportunities to unmask radicalism at the university. David Horowitz, the conservative critic whom we feature in later chapters, was a Columbia College graduate and, perhaps naturally inclined to focus his attention on his alma mater, identified nine Columbia professors, most of whom were connected to Middle East studies, as among the 101 most "dangerous" professors in America.[57]

## Conclusions

The post–Vietnam War era university was what exactly? The changes amounted to a kind of revolution, yet one that had very different impacts across the various disciplines, schools, programs, and activities of even one university, not to speak of the thousands of colleges and universities across the country.

Thomas Bender's overall assessment seems apt for Columbia and for the other major research universities. In the net, he suggests, the "ambitious, white, male, Europe-oriented professional culture of major research universities that had taken its style and intellectual agenda from the 1950s could not sustain itself through the last quarter of the twentieth century."[58] In place of the initial postwar professional culture based on science there arose "a more varied and thus more complicated academic culture that found it difficult to speak with one voice."[59]

Certainly Bender was right in noting that universities found it difficult to speak with an authoritative voice or to define for the public (or themselves) how their missions might have changed. This new and more complicated academic culture defies simple characterization. There were, and still are, strong elements of the rationalist 1950s academic ethos, with the faculty driven by the metrics of research, publication, and the approbation of their scholarly peers. Enlightenment values have not disappeared, but they have been challenged, "deconstructed," and "problematized" by the new breed of scholars who cut their teeth on the identity debates.

The sciences, once the dominant force on campus and the public face of the universities, have lost some of their authority and hence their natural leadership role in the scheme of things. The engineering disciplines, except when they have become virtually indistinguishable from the basic sciences, have suffered from something of a blue-collar aura and have begun to have difficulty attracting the best American-born students. Foreign students have gravitated naturally to the quantitative fields, where they suffer no disadvantage vis-à-vis native-born English speakers. But research in the sciences and engineering is booming, and these fields were the first to recover their bearings, funding levels, and overall intellectual vitality after the Vietnam era crisis.[60] In such disciplines as history, cultural anthropology, literature, and art history the new approaches and conceptions redefined the boundaries of inquiry and brought new insights so long as they did not go too far in their demands to remove the restrictions and what they called the "enclosures" of the previous paradigms.

The wider political setting in which the universities operate has undergone profound change. Politicians of a populist bent, such as Ronald Reagan in his 1966 race for the California governorship, found that attacking campus radicals struck a responsive chord with voters, and he was quick to exploit the theme. Reagan picked up the theme even before the campus protests had attracted widespread national publicity, and other politicians, especially Republicans but also "blue dog" Democrats, were quick to follow. In a 1966 speech at the Cow Palace in San Francisco, candidate Reagan declared, "There has been a leadership and a morality and decency gap at the University of California at Berkeley where a small minority of beatniks, radicals, and filthy speech advocates have brought such shame to and loss of confidence in a great University that applications for enrollments are down 21 percent and are expected to decline even further."[61]

That the universities would be dragged into politics became a given regardless of what was actually happening on the campuses. Political pressures tugged and pushed the universities in conflicting directions, and public policies at both the federal and state levels increasingly influenced university operations. A narrow range of hot button issues was able to ignite flashpoints of controversy after the Vietnam War era, including, prominently, such matters as divesting investments that some university constituencies found objectionable and combating "hate speech" on campus. More recently, controversies involving the Middle East, Israeli-Palestinian relations, and the war in Iraq have been the most common.

Radical critics within the universities, and many moderates, have insisted that the opening up that followed the Vietnam era protests was intellectually liberating, both to the various disciplines and to the general campus intellectual discourse. The universities generally gave poor to mixed performances in reacting to McCarthyism. This is cited by way of contrast to show signs of health in the current situation. Faculty members at leading universities in the early 1950s were dismissed from their positions for being members of the Communist Party or for failing to be "candid" with their colleagues about their past political associations.[62] The Association of American Universities, then composed of the presidents of thirty-seven leading research universities, issued a statement in 1953 declaring, "Since present membership in the Communist Party requires the acceptance of these principles [of Russian communism], such membership extinguishes the right to a university position."[63] The American Association of University Professors (AAUP) did little in that earlier period to defend professors accused of being Communist Party members or "Fifth Amendment communists" (that is, those who refused to answer questions from investigators).[64]

Other academic observers, however, have felt that a stifling orthodoxy became part of the Vietnam era legacy. Harvard's Derek Bok, for example, asserted in 1982, "For several decades [after the doctrine of academic freedom was promulgated by the AAUP in 1915], the assault came chiefly from conservative groups disturbed by theories and ideas that seemed to undermine prevailing orthodoxies. More recently, however, the greatest challenges to free expression on the campus have come from students and faculty on the left who have launched vigorous attacks on professors involved in the Vietnam War or in disputes affecting race."[65] The main evidence Bok cited was the policy of some professional associations of warning their members against allegedly "racist" research.[66] These differing interpretations of academic freedom illustrate the difficulties of separating matters of intellectual orientation from political ideology or orthodoxy. The left, at least the more militant wing, has evidently feared that criticisms of its poststructuralist epistemology and its concern with questions of identity should be equated with an assault on academic freedom itself. The right, again perhaps the most vociferous critics, has challenged postmodernism and multiculturalism as shallow intellectual fashions and potential threats to the very premises of free inquiry.

These abstruse arguments have become stylized and almost ritualistic as the combatants have grown fatigued with their own rhetoric. The center of academic debate has moved elsewhere, mostly back toward the particularities of the individual disciplines, as the identity question has run out of intellectual steam. It was always difficult, even in the heyday of the identity debates, to infer the major political themes behind the arguments, if there were any, beyond a vague utopian yearning for the perfect community in which power would be distributed evenly to all previously excluded groups. The identity debate at all events waned and never remotely provided a unifying conceptual focus for the humanities and the social sciences.

One surprising development of the 1970s and 1980s that seemed to offer promise of the kind of political argument and engagement that we are calling for in this book was the excitement generated by John Rawls in *A Theory of Justice* and the direct counterargument of his Harvard colleague and fellow philosopher Robert Nozick in *Anarchy, State, and Utopia.*[67] Rawls's call for a general theory of justice not grounded in utilitarianism attracted an astonishingly wide audience in the humanities and the social science disciplines and generated a wide-ranging debate in intellectual circles. Philosophers and political theorists at last seemed to have found a champion to justify the liberal state and defend its principles. Rawls combined elements of Kantian and Benthamite philosophy to argue for a more egalitarian distribution of society's goods and services, a theory appealing to many academics. When Nozick countered with a libertarian critique that asserted a defense of the minimum state, the basis for a genuine discussion and debate of political themes seemed to have been laid. In the end, however, neither man's work directly engaged political themes, and the grand debate never quite materialized; much less did the encounter and the hundreds of articles and commentaries generated in response to the two books deal with real-world political issues or with the practicalities of citizenship. Both men agreed that a citizen's goals in life are his or her own private affair and that scholars have no right or competence to judge.[68] There was little or nothing in Rawls's book of the give and take of real political life, the compromise, the clash of deeply held, conflicting values that make up the stuff of politics, and no engagement of actual political issues. Nozick's theory of the state was crudely libertarian, with almost no role for the state beyond maintaining public order and security. The state could hardly be distinguished from a business corporation providing a limited set of services, and the notions of citizenship and loyalty to past and future generations were wholly absent. One could in the end infer nothing of broad political significance from the Rawls-Nozick debate and detect no impact in terms of genuine political education on the campuses.

The title of Everett Ladd's and Seymour Martin Lipset's survey of faculty political attitudes, *The Divided Academy*, reflects their estimate of the post–Vietnam War mood on campus.[69] Even though college professors in general have tended to hold liberal views, they found that professors in schools of engineering, agriculture, business, and law differed significantly from their colleagues in the arts and sciences.[70] They found a fractured political awareness and differences on specific issues, along with some general predispositions. While there was the waning of political debate after the Vietnam War ended and the inward turn that we have noted, the universities have always been interested in how they should relate to the outside world and in how their own preoccupations do and should contribute to society. More recently, this debate has heated up within the universities and increasingly spilled over into the public domain. What had been an introspective debate became joined with the concerns of the broader public or of politicians and political activists. There has been a heightened public interest in how universities operate and in how they should be held accountable to society. In the remaining chapters, we turn our attention to these concerns, looking first, in the next chapter, at whether there has been a marked shift recently in faculty political attitudes.

# 5 | Political Attitudes of American Professors: Results of a 2007 National Survey

Just how dominant are liberals and Democrats on American campuses today? Does the current tilt to the left among college professors affect the classroom experience of students and the tenure chances of conservative faculty members? The assumption among many conservative pundits in America today is that college professors as a class are dangerous radicals and left-wing ideologues. Numerous books portray America's universities as havens for former hippies, who, having lost the battle for power in the America of today, have claimed the ivory tower as their exclusive fiefdom. Dinesh D'Souza, one of the cultural warriors of the 1990s, put it this way:

> Within the tall gates and old buildings, a new worldview is consolidating itself. The transformation of American campuses is so sweeping that it is no exaggeration to call it an academic revolution.[1]

Abigail Thernstrom, another conservative critic of the academy, labeled American campuses "islands of repression in a sea of freedom."[2]

One might imagine that the subsequent absence of a significant shift among college graduates to the left in American politics would give critics pause. But the indictments, if anything, have grown more sweeping. David Horowitz, perhaps the most prominent and persistent conservative critic of academia, observed, "All students are being deprived of a decent education by the leftist monopoly on campus."[3] Conservative pundit Ann Coulter had this advice for college students: "Your professors and instructors are, by and large, evil people whose main goal is to mislead you."[4] Professors are compared to tyrants, as in this attack on left-wing academics:

> I think it is a little naïve to suggest that we will fertilize academic freedom on campuses by enlightening leftists about how totalitarian they are. This is like saying that the way we could have prevented Stalin's, Mao's, and Pol Pot's killing fields is if we had just patiently informed them that their ideology and practices were not allowing dissent and intellectual diversity and then they would have understood and become more tolerant. . . . The purpose of the Left is . . . to build a new and perfect world, which means that this present existence must be destroyed, so that the slate can be wiped clean to start building the earthly paradise it dreams of. The objective for education for leftists, therefore, is indoctrination.[5]

These are just some of the attacks by conservatives on the liberal elite that they believe populates and runs America's universities and colleges.[6] Recently, Rothman, Lichter, and Nevitte have conducted a more empirical examination of alleged bias in the academy, which is impressive in the nature of their data and the bold character of their arguments.[7] Rothman and his colleagues claimed to show that faculty today are more liberal than at any time in recent history and that they likely discriminate, consciously or unconsciously, against conservatives and Christians in hiring and promotion. These claims attracted broad media attention, demonstrating a strong public interest in the question of bias in higher education.

A leftist critique of the universities also exists, of course, but it is as yet more diffuse than the conservative critique. Feminists, with University of Miami president (and President Clinton's secretary of health and human services) Donna Shalala as a prominent leader, have sought to mount an attack on the "culture" of the sciences and engineering fields for being inhospitable to women, and some have lobbied to have Title IX of the 1972 Higher Education Act Amendments reinterpreted to apply to educational programs and not merely to athletic programs.[8] Many point to the inadequate representation of blacks and Hispanics among faculty and, to a lesser extent, students. Other critics have disparaged "legacy" admission policies, and many have complained that elite universities are dominated by the privileged classes. A cacophony of voices has urged colleges and universities with large endowments to spend more on student financial aid. There are those who argue, frequently but not always from the political left, that the American university, far from being hostile to capitalism and the market, has in fact been increasingly influenced and even dominated by commercial forces and corporate values.[9] This left wing criticism, however, seldom becomes part of the broad public discourse.

The conservative critics of the academy we have just cited seem largely unaware of the historical context in which we should properly view the current clash over the political biases of the American professoriate. They posit the existence of some halcyon collegiate past before political correctness and bias took over the academy. Even a glance at the political history of American higher education reveals waves of contestation and controversy that rise and recede, usually as a by-product of broader trends in the body politic. Our preceding chapters show that American campuses are today much more open and tolerant of dissenting views than were the campuses of the eighteenth and nineteenth centuries. Professors for most of the nineteenth century were conservatives and only moved to the left with the Progressive era (the meaning of liberalism at that time is not easily classified in our contemporary terms). The relative absence of controversy in the 1950–65 golden age was somewhat misleading insofar as the universities reflected many of the conformist tendencies as well as the largely unchallenged liberal orthodoxies predominant in America in the immediate postwar era.

This chapter reports the initial findings from our own 2007 national survey of professors on matters such as basic ideology and partisanship, as well as classroom conduct and treatment of colleagues, and our snapshot is framed in the context of previous surveys conducted on the topic.

## Faculty Political Ideology

Our survey, along with every other survey that has examined the question since the 1930s, found that professors lean to the left, particularly when compared to the general population. Table 5-1 gives the raw numbers and percentages as well as the wording of the question for our main measure of professor ideology. Those who identified themselves as left liberal outnumber those on the right by approximately 3:1, and the middle is about the same size as those who lean right.

There have been numerous claims that professors today are substantially more liberal than they were in the 1960s, as the rebellious hippies who were students have become the "tenured radicals" of today. To some extent, our survey supports an increase in professors identifying with the left, at least when compared to the 1960s and 1970s. In table 5-2, we put our numbers in the context of the Carnegie studies of professorial politics, along with the study by Rothman, Lichter, and Nevitte.[10]

Table 5-1. *Faculty Ideology, 2007 National Survey*

Percent giving a specific answer to the question, How would you describe yourself ideologically?

| Answer | Frequency | Valid percent | Cumulative percent |
|---|---|---|---|
| Strongly liberal | 230 | 18.7 | 18.7 |
| Moderately liberal | 514 | 41.9 | 60.6 |
| Middle of the road | 232 | 18.9 | 79.5 |
| Moderately conservative | 213 | 17.4 | 96.9 |
| Strongly conservative | 38 | 3.1 | 100.0 |
| Total | 1,227 | 100.0 | |
| Missing | | 43 | |
| Total | 1,270 | | |

Table 5-2. *Carnegie (1969–97) and Rothman (1999) Studies of Faculty Ideology Compared to Our Study*

Percent

| Ideology | Our study, 2007 | Rothman, 1999 | Carnegie | | | | |
|---|---|---|---|---|---|---|---|
| | | | 1997 | 1989 | 1984 | 1975 | 1969 |
| Left, liberal | 61 | 62 | 62 | 62 | 39 | 41 | 45 |
| Moderate, strong conservative | 21 | 15 | 19 | 23 | 34 | 31 | 27 |

While our results show a drop of around 6–13 percent among faculty who are to the right of center since 1969–84, we find little difference compared to every subsequent Carnegie survey. Indeed, the level of stability over time is striking.

The survey that stands out among post-1984 examinations of this question is the 1999 survey by Rothman, Lichter, and Nivette, published in 2005.[11] This study originally made dramatic claims about the rise in leftism among American professors and the coinciding decline in conservatism. However, Rothman, Lichter, and Nevitte measured ideology differently than the Carnegie studies. Our survey, which used a similar style of question, found stability, not change. In 2007 Rothman and Lichter indicated that they had made a coding error in their widely reported 2005 estimate of the percentage of professors who are left liberal and revised their figure downward from 72 to 62 percent.[12]

For the sake of systematic comparison, we emulated both Rothman's and Carnegie's question styles by asking about ideology twice in the same survey at different points. Table 5-1 presents our 2007 survey results from a question

Table 5-3. *Rothman's 1999 Survey Compared to Our 2007 Survey*

Percent

| Ideology | 2007 | Rothman, 1999 |
|---|---|---|
| Left, liberal (answered 1–4) | 58 | 62 |
| Moderate, strong conservative (answered 7–10) | 18 | 15 |

Table 5-4. *Percent of Faculty Reporting Left of Center Views on Ten-Point and Five-Point Scales, by Discipline*

| Discipline | Ten-point scale | Five-point scale |
|---|---|---|
| Humanities | 71 | 75 |
| Social sciences | 58 | 59 |
| Natural sciences | 62 | 55 |

that mirrors the five points of the Carnegie question, although we updated the wording.[13] We also asked the question exactly as Rothman, Lichter, and Nivette did, using a ten-point numeric scale in which respondents were asked to place themselves on a scale from one for very liberal to ten for very conservative. When we compared our results, from exactly the same population, which showed little budging from the Carnegie results since 1989 on the five-point scale, we found substantially fewer professors to the left of center than Rothman, Lichter, and Nevitte did, but marginally more conservatives. Two explanations present themselves. Perhaps the mood of professors had shifted mildly back toward the center in the seven years between our surveys, and Rothman and his colleagues did identify a surge of leftism in their survey. But the congruence between our results and Carnegie's when the question was asked in the Carnegie style suggests that the difference is more likely a product of changes in the question in the Rothman survey, not in the professoriate (see table 5-3).[14]

Regardless of whether there was a large surge toward the left at some point in the 1980s or 1990s, our survey found that professors lean to the left to a significant degree. This finding is consistent across broad disciplinary divisions (see table 5-4). Indeed, what is new about our findings is that faculty in the hard sciences are, by one measure at least, more left or liberal than professors in the social sciences, a finding quite different from those of previous studies. Using the Rothman ten-point scale, 58 percent of social science faculty members are left of center, while 62 percent of hard science faculty members are left of center. Because our analysis of a question using the Carnegie five-point scale revealed a modest four-point split in the direction of social scientists still being more liberal than their natural science colleagues, we can safely conclude that the hard and social science faculties have become almost indistinguishable in the degree of liberalism of their views.

This finding is at odds with what Ladd and Lipset found for the late 1960s: "All the natural sciences . . . are significantly more conservative politically than the social sciences." Their study, *The Divided Academy,* was published in 1975 and offered an argument for why, in the context of the late 1960s and the early 1970s, the social sciences would attract more critical and dissenting minds: "At other times in history, and in other societies today, the natural sciences have occupied very different political positions, and in some instances have been the principal centers for social criticism and dissent. . . . A field of study becomes highly ideological when . . . it offers a fulcrum for the rejection of established social arrangements."[15] What we may be seeing is a return of the natural sciences to a contested position, in which many who study science perceive their discipline as being under assault from religious and conservative institutions.

We did find, as several surveys have found since the 1960s, that humanities faculty remain slightly more liberal than the other two divisions. But our findings about the hard sciences suggest that a change among hard scientists may be one of the most significant developments of the last decade. Indeed, since Rothman's survey in 1999 found less of a change than did our 2007 survey, the shift among the hard sciences may have occurred relatively recently.

When departments are analyzed separately, some typical patterns emerge (see table 5-5). The most liberal departments are English (85 percent), foreign language (80 percent), sociology (80 percent), history (78 percent), physics (78 percent), and religious studies (60 percent). The least liberal are economics (23 percent), agriculture (31 percent), business (34 percent), health sciences (41 percent), and engineering (46 percent). Prior studies frequently found history, sociology, and foreign languages to be on the left and economics, agriculture, business, and engineering to be on the right. Ladd and Lipset identified a gap between applied sciences and basic sciences, in which applied sciences, like agriculture and engineering, were less liberal.[16] Our survey suggests that this is probably still true today. But Ladd and Lipset did find some congruence between the ideological attitudes of the social and hard sciences, as illustrated by physics being one of the most liberal of all departments in their survey as well as in ours. In both the Rothman survey and our own, comparing such small subgroups is merely suggestive, but there is broad consistency

Table 5-5. *Partisanship and Ideology of Professors, by Select Disciplines with Ten or More Respondents*

| Discipline | Total surveyed | Party identification | | | Left, liberal (percent) |
|---|---|---|---|---|---|
| | | Democrat | Independent | Republican | |
| Agriculture | | | | | |
| Count | 13 | 5 | 4 | 4 | 4 |
| Percent | | 38.5 | 30.8 | 30.8 | 30.8 |
| Art and art history | | | | | |
| Count | 14 | 8 | 2 | 4 | 11 |
| Percent | | 56.0 | 14.0 | 28.0 | 73.3 |
| Biology | | | | | |
| Count | 78 | 50 | 19 | 7 | 60 |
| Percent | | 65.8 | 25.0 | 9.2 | 69.0 |
| Business | | | | | |
| Count | 66 | 23 | 24 | 19 | 24 |
| Percent | | 34.8 | 36.4 | 28.8 | 33.8 |
| Chemistry | | | | | |
| Count | 35 | 17 | 15 | 3 | 22 |
| Percent | | 48.6 | 42.9 | 8.6 | 51.2 |
| Communications | | | | | |
| Count | 38 | 24 | 9 | 5 | 24 |
| Percent | | 63.2 | 23.7 | 13.2 | 55.8 |
| Computer science | | | | | |
| Count | 34 | 17 | 11 | 6 | 22 |
| Percent | | 50.0 | 32.4 | 17.6 | 52.4 |
| Earth sciences | | | | | |
| Count | 15 | 9 | 5 | 1 | 11 |
| Percent | | 60.0 | 33.3 | 6.7 | 68.8 |
| Economics | | | | | |
| Count | 18 | 6 | 6 | 6 | 5 |
| Percent | | 33.3 | 33.3 | 33.3 | 22.7 |
| Education | | | | | |
| Count | 79 | 42 | 16 | 21 | 37 |
| Percent | | 53.2 | 20.3 | 26.6 | 45.1 |
| Engineering | | | | | |
| Count | 68 | 25 | 29 | 14 | 38 |
| Percent | | 36.8 | 42.6 | 20.6 | 45.8 |
| English literature | | | | | |
| Count | 53 | 39 | 11 | 3 | 53 |
| Percent | | 73.6 | 20.8 | 5.7 | 84.9 |
| Foreign language | | | | | |
| Count | 34 | 25 | 9 | 0 | 32 |
| Percent | | 73.5 | 26.5 | 0.0 | 80.0 |
| Health sciences | | | | | |
| Count | 31 | 18 | 8 | 5 | 13 |
| Percent | | 58.1 | 25.8 | 16.1 | 40.6 |
| History | | | | | |
| Count | 51 | 32 | 15 | 4 | 51 |
| Percent | | 62.7 | 29.4 | 7.8 | 77.8 |

Table 5-5 (continued). *Partisanship and Ideology of Professors, by Select Disciplines with Ten or More Respondents*

| Discipline | Total surveyed | Party identification | | | Left, liberal (percent) |
|---|---|---|---|---|---|
| | | Democrat | Independent | Republican | |
| Mathematics | | | | | |
| Count | 43 | 17 | 18 | 8 | 27 |
| Percent | | 39.5 | 41.9 | 18.6 | 50.9 |
| Music | | | | | |
| Count | 25 | 15 | 4 | 6 | 17 |
| Percent | | 60.0 | 16.0 | 24.0 | 60.7 |
| Other[a] | | | | | |
| Count | 97 | 55 | 29 | 13 | 64 |
| Percent | | 56.7 | 29.9 | 13.4 | 61.5 |
| Philosophy | | | | | |
| Count | 20 | 12 | 6 | 2 | 17 |
| Percent | | 60.0 | 30.0 | 10.0 | 70.8 |
| Physics | | | | | |
| Count | 18 | 11 | 6 | 1 | 18 |
| Percent | | 61.1 | 33.3 | 5.6 | 78.3 |
| Political science or government | | | | | |
| Count | 44 | 21 | 16 | 7 | 22 |
| Percent | | 47.7 | 36.4 | 15.9 | 46.8 |
| Psychology | | | | | |
| Count | 76 | 51 | 19 | 6 | 65 |
| Percent | | 67.1 | 25.0 | 7.9 | 80.2 |
| Religious studies | | | | | |
| Count | 24 | 11 | 13 | 0 | 15 |
| Percent | | 45.8 | 54.2 | 0.0 | 60.0 |
| Sociology | | | | | |
| Count | 39 | 28 | 10 | 1 | 32 |
| Percent | | 71.8 | 25.6 | 2.6 | 80.0 |
| Natural sciences | | | | | |
| Count | 358 | 179 | 126 | 53 | 358 |
| Percent | | 50.0 | 35.2 | 14.8 | 100.0 |
| Social sciences | | | | | |
| Count | 497 | 276 | 141 | 80 | 497 |
| Percent | | 55.5 | 28.4 | 16.1 | 100.0 |
| Arts, humanities, languages | | | | | |
| Count | 227 | 149 | 59 | 19 | 227 |
| Percent | | 65.6 | 26.0 | 8.4 | 100.0 |
| Total[b] | | | | | |
| Count | 1,097 | 614 | 330 | 153 | 1,097 |
| Percent | | 56.0 | 30.1 | 13.9 | 100.0 |

a. Respondent selected a category.

b. Totals include professors from disciplines with fewer than ten respondents, as do the larger disciplinary categories of hard sciences, social sciences, and arts, humanities, and languages. Those disciplines that could not be categorized as one of the three were included in the totals only. Totals are for those who answered the partisanship question. There were more respondents who answered just ideology, not partisanship. Most who answered only ideology were not citizens of the United States and also tended to be further to the left.

Table 5-6. *Faculty Perceptions of the Political Climate on Their Campus and Political Views of Their Departmental Colleagues*

Percent

| Political view | Campus | Department |
|---|---|---|
| Strongly liberal | 7.2 | 12.9 |
| Moderately liberal | 32.5 | 48.3 |
| Middle of the road | 26.6 | 22.7 |
| Moderately conservative | 26.8 | 13.1 |
| Strongly conservative | 6.8 | 3.0 |
| Number of respondents | 1,174 | 1,143 |

in the findings with regard to ideology and partisanship among the larger (more aggregated) disciplinary categories.

Professors are also quite Democratic in their partisan identities, as found in other recent studies. In our survey, Democrats make up 56 percent of professors, with independents taking 30 percent, and Republicans making up only 14 percent. The ratio overall of Democrats to Republicans is approximately 4:1. Rothman, Lichter, and Nevitte found 50 percent Democratic and 11 percent Republican.[17] Our study showed fewer Republicans in specific natural science disciplines, such as chemistry, biology, and mathematics, than was found either by Rothman or by Ladd and Lipset. Compared to earlier studies, the partisan orientations of the natural sciences, at least insofar as voting is concerned, seem to have undergone some change. While in the Ladd and Lipset study the gap between social and natural scientists in their partisan vote in 1968 was 19 percent (with natural scientists voting much more Republican), our survey found a gap between natural and social scientists in the 2004 presidential election of only 2 percent—in short, statistically a tie. Rothman and his colleagues found a similar rise in Democratic affiliation among natural scientists, although in their survey the social sciences were still substantially more Democratic than the natural sciences.

We also asked faculty members about their perceptions of the political balance in their department and about the general political climate on their campus (see table 5-6). Asked to describe the political views of "most members of your department," 61 percent of faculty characterized them as either strongly or moderately liberal, while only 16 percent felt that their department colleagues are moderately or strongly conservative.

However, in characterizing the general political climate of their campus, 40 percent of faculty selected liberal, while 34 percent felt that they are teaching at a conservative campus. Overall, the typical faculty member in America perceives his or her campus as roughly middle of the road (2.9 average, where 3 equals middle of the road) and his or her own department as moderately liberal (2.5).

Given that we know that faculty members tend to be liberal, perhaps any sign of self-perceived moderation should be seen as merely misperception. Thus we might expect that faculty who are very liberal or very conservative would perceive their department and their campus differently than their less ideological colleagues. Hypothetically, a very conservative professor might perceive her department as more liberal than it actually is, based on her own perception, and the same effect from the opposite end might be expected of a very liberal professor. This kind of effect is seen, for example, in some studies of voting behavior. However, we found very little evidence for this supposition of false consciousness or misperception in our survey results. Both the very and the moderately liberal faculty members tended to perceive their department as moderately liberal, while the other three groups (middle of the road, somewhat conservative, and the most conservative) saw their department as middle of the road, not what we would expect if faculty members consistently misperceive and misrepresent the real state of affairs in line with their own ideological leanings (see figure 5-1). The only evidence for this type of systematic misperception is that the two liberal categories of professors, and especially the most liberal, tended to see their campus as slightly more conservative than their colleagues who are middle of the road or conservative.[18]

Middle of the road and conservative faculty members have very little difference between their perceptions of the situation in their department or the climate on their campus. Middle of the roaders and conservatives seem to hold relatively similar views in assessing ideological tendencies, at least as judged by their answers to some of our questions. Gross and Simmons in their 2006 survey of faculty political attitudes asked about a dozen more detailed questions concerning the general climate on campus and found similar indications of moderate and conservative faculty affinities (in the most research-intensive universities at least, with more liberal attitudes among professors in liberal arts colleges and the less research-intensive universities). They also found even sharper differences in the answers to certain questions of moderates and conservatives, on the one hand, and liberals, on the other. For example, Gross and Simmons asked their respondents to indicate their level of agreement with this statement: "The adoption of attitudes often labeled 'politically correct' has made America a more civilized society than it was many years ago." Overall, 39.8 percent of respondents agreed. But while liberals expressed moderately high levels of agreement—59.8 percent—only 23.8 per-

Figure 5-1. *Perceived Campus and Departmental Ideology, by Professor's Own Ideology*

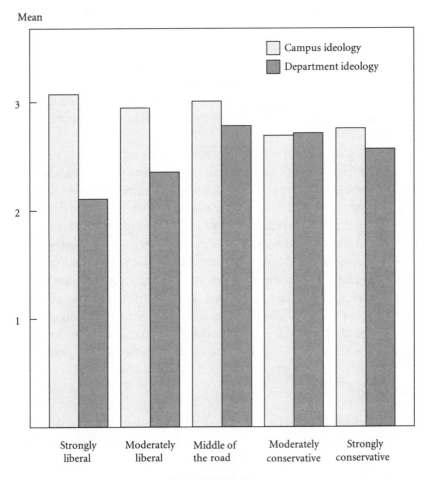

Professor's ideology

cent of moderates and 23.6 percent of conservatives agreed.[19] "Taken together," Gross and Simmons conclude, "these findings suggest that conservative professors are quite unhappy with the current campus environment, at least with regard to politics, and that some moderate professors share some of their complaints."[20] Our finding that most professors perceive the general climate on campus as moderate may be explicable in terms of the answers to two other questions posed in our survey. Respondents were asked to characterize the ideological gap between faculty and administrators and between faculty and students. Given a choice between saying that professors and administrators are ideologically similar or that faculty members are either more liberal or more conservative than administrators, 56 percent of faculty felt that professors are more liberal than administrators, while 42 percent felt that they are about the same, and only 2 percent felt that administrators are more liberal than professors. Similarly, 59 percent of faculty felt that professors are more liberal than students, 33 percent felt that they are about the same, and 8 percent felt that students are more liberal than professors. Since the "campus" includes administrators and students as well as faculty, professors may correctly perceive the climate on campus as being more moderate than the climate in their own department.

The college experience does not consist only of what happens in the classroom. The entire environment includes interactions with fellow students, administrators, and campus activities, including visiting speakers. We thus asked faculty members if their campus seeks to provide a broad range of opinions among the invited speakers, and we tried to determine whether they felt that speakers tend to be drawn mostly from one side of the political spectrum, liberal or conservative. Most of our respondents felt that speakers on their campus are ideologically diverse. Moreover, if indoctrination by left-leaning professors is a serious danger, students seem remarkably unaffected by the leftward tilt of their professors. Studies of student political views do not show a rising tide of leftism, and the mood of national politics, until the impact of the Iraq War at least, has not tilted toward liberalism over the last thirty years.[21]

## Faculty Behavior toward Students

Our expectation was that faculty would lean to the left, and, in anticipation of that, we sought to examine whether faculty ideology would result in the negative treatment of conservative students, in matters such as grading or class assignments. Such allegations are not uncommon, but little systematic evidence has supported the claim. Because few faculty would admit to grading on the basis of a student's political views, we asked faculty members to assess whether they thought such inappropriate activities are happening with other faculty on their campus. This type of "third-party" assessment is frequently used to measure prejudicial conduct when a survey cannot expect candid answers from potential offenders. This approach does come with the limitation that the professors who are answering rarely have direct knowledge of the situations they are assessing and thus presumably will be influenced to some undetermined degree by hearsay and their own predispositions.[22] Also, we admit that it is possible that faculty might be grading students unfairly and simply be cognitively unaware of it. Bias in evaluation is a subtle and difficult matter to assess, and our examination of it is suggestive only.

We asked faculty respondents, "Do you think that students unfairly receive different grades because of their political views at your university?" Only 12 percent of all faculty members felt that biased grading of this sort happens occasionally, and only 1 percent felt that it happens frequently or often. Even among conservative and Republican faculty members, few believed that biased grading is a problem.

What about bias beyond grading? Our survey asked, Do "professors at your university teach their courses in a way that unfairly favors one political view, through their selection of readings, their lectures, and their leadership of class discussion?" Faculty were much more willing to accuse their colleagues of this variety of unfairness, with 44 percent saying it happens "occasionally," 9 percent "often," but only 3 percent "very frequently."

We also felt that it was necessary to identify the direction of any putative bias. So we asked professors who felt that bias is present to assess the direction of the bias. The majority (62 percent) felt that there is no consistent pattern to the bias, while 31 percent believed that most of the time it is liberal faculty expressing bias against conservative views. Only 7 percent thought the most common bias on their campus is conservative faculty biased against liberal views. But 75 percent of all faculty believed either that there is no significant bias of either variety on their campus or that, if any bias exists, there is no consistent pattern to it.

Another frequent allegation of bias is that professors spout off about political topics that are not relevant to their subject area, subjecting conservative students to lectures about the Iraq War in chemistry courses, for example, or in other courses unrelated to foreign policy. We asked professors, How often do "professors at your university give opinions about political figures and issues that are not relevant to the course content?" Only 10 percent of faculty members said that this happens often or frequently at their institution. A majority, or 58 percent, felt that it occurs "occasionally," but 31 percent believed it occurs "seldom or never." Critics of the academy should ponder what a similar survey of professionals in a comparable workplace would find, such as at a large law firm, a hospital, or a stock brokerage.

We did try to assess how faculty members handle politics and hot button issues in their own classroom with a battery of questions about their conduct (see table 5-7). For 61 percent of professors, politics seldom comes up in their classroom because political concerns are unrelated to the topic of the course. Most professors did not, in fact, admit to informing students how they feel

Table 5-7. *Faculty Tactics for Handling Politics in the Classroom*

Percent agreeing or disagreeing with the statement

| Statement | Yes | No | Number of respondents |
|---|---|---|---|
| Politics seldom comes up in my classroom, because of the nature of the subjects I teach | 61 | 39 | 1,154 |
| I try to be an honest broker among all competing views | 95 | 5 | 1,045 |
| I let my students know how I feel about political issues, in general | 28 | 72 | 1,028 |
| I try to keep students guessing about my opinions about most issues | 43 | 57 | 814 |
| My students can probably guess who I voted for in 2004 | 45 | 55 | 868 |

about most political issues, with 72 percent saying they do not let students know their political beliefs. Keeping students guessing about their views concerning most issues is a tactic chosen by 43 percent of all faculty, but 45 percent of the professors who answered that way judged that their students could probably guess who they voted for in 2004. Overall, 95 percent of professors claimed to be making an attempt to be an "honest broker among all competing views." Some critics of higher education, both outside and inside the academy, have advocated that faculty members should simply inform students of their opinions and views, since complete objectivity is a chimerical goal. In a similar vein, some have argued that a complete value neutrality—for example, portraying all political and economic systems, or all cultures, as equally valid—represents a perverse form of cultural and moral relativism. We cannot resolve or even get at such issues in a fully satisfactory way on the basis of our survey questions, but we note that professors at least say that they reject open advocacy of their own political views in the classroom.

We do find some evidence that faculty members who lean conservative tend to be circumspect in expressing their views. Among faculty who voted for Bush in 2004, 72 percent believed that students would not be able to guess their vote accurately, while only 42 percent of faculty voting for Kerry in 2004 felt that their vote would be a mystery to students. Similarly, when asked if they let students know their political views, 46 percent of very liberal faculty members said that they do versus 28 percent of all faculty. However, the second most likely ideological group to make their political views known to students was the group self-identifying as the very conservative professors, at 33 percent. This finding suggests that those with strong ideological views on either end of the spectrum

Table 5-8. *Faculty Perceptions of Ideology in Hiring and Promotion,*
*Campuswide and Departmental, by Professor's Ideology*

Percent giving a particular answer to the question, "In hiring and promotion, do you believe
that conservative candidates and liberal candidates are treated similarly?"

| Answer | College-wide | Very conservative professors | Very liberal professors | Your department | Very conservative professors | Very liberal professors |
|---|---|---|---|---|---|---|
| No, I believe there is a strong preference for liberals | 5 | 36 | 1 | 4 | 11 | 3.5 |
| No, I believe there is a weak preference for liberals | 7 | 24 | 5 | 6 | 14 | 6.2 |
| Yes, ideology doesn't influence hiring and promotion | 81 | 36 | 85 | 85 | 69 | 84.6 |
| No, I believe there is a weak preference for conservatives | 4 | 4 | 6 | 4 | 6 | 3.5 |
| No, I believe there is a strong preference for conservatives | 4 | 4 | 5 | 2 | 0 | 2.2 |
| Number of respondents | 854 | 25 | 154 | 1,270 | 35 | 200 |

tend to make their views known. Making one's views known, however, does not
imply that professors believe in advocacy of their views in the classroom.

## Faculty Behavior toward Colleagues

According to some conservative critics of the academy, liberal professors have
created a self-perpetuating cadre of like-minded colleagues. Critics argue that
the few conservatives within the academy face difficulty in getting and keeping desirable academic posts. Smart conservatives figure this out before they
even begin or complete a graduate degree, and this bias purportedly helps to
explain the paucity of conservatives in the ivory tower. We examine this claim
further in chapter 9, directing particular attention to the claim that Christians, as well as conservatives, face discrimination in hiring and promotion.
While we leave a full examination of this question to chapter 9, our survey findings do cast some light on the issue.

In order to examine this question, we asked a series of questions about hiring and tenure. Faculty members were asked whether, first in their own
department and then across their whole campus, there is a preference for or a
bias against conservatives or Christians (see table 5-8).

College and university professors in our survey by a clear majority said that
they do not believe that ideological discrimination is a problem in their own
department. And of those few faculty members who said that they do perceive

bias, about a third thought that if there is preference, it is *for* conservatives. When subgroups are analyzed, it becomes clear that more conservatives than liberals felt that politics has entered inappropriately into hiring and promotion. Among strong conservatives, for example, 26 percent believed that there is either a strong or a weak preference for liberals in their department. However, even this group, which is the most suspicious of an ideological bias in general in academic hiring, overwhelmingly believed that ideology plays no role in hiring and tenure in their own department.

Although a higher percentage of respondents saw a preference for liberals in hiring and promotion outside their department, some saw a preference *for* conservatives in other departments. Overall, a striking 81 percent believed that ideology plays no role at all in hiring on their campuses. A majority of strong conservatives, however, alone among the ideological groups, did perceive that discrimination exists in hiring but that it occurs mostly outside of their own department.

While our survey suggests that ideological discrimination in academic hiring is a small problem, with potential victims at both ends of the political spectrum, we remain cautious about overinterpreting our data. Possibly, people of strong conservative views are seldom hired by departments that discriminate against conservatives, so conservatives do not show up at campuses and in departments that are intolerant. Perhaps we surveyed the docile survivors of widespread discrimination against conservatives, and the conservatives who were truly outspoken failed to get tenure. Thus they were not around to answer our survey. If this were the case, we would expect a significant gap in the perceptions of tenured and untenured conservatives, but we did not see such a gap.

Alternatively, those who saw bias in other departments may be reacting, or overreacting, to accounts in the college newspaper about the experiences of other departments. Perhaps the rumors of discrimination seem more plausible the less the respondent actually knows about a situation. Support for an explanation of this sort appeared when respondents were asked about their own tenure and promotion cases. Only 6 percent of the college teachers in our survey believed it likely that their own chances for tenure and promotion will be or have been affected by the reaction of their colleagues to the respondent's political views (see table 5-9). For very liberal professors, the percentage was 14 percent, and for very conservative it was 13 percent. It appears that, with faculty members who have strong political views on either end of the ideological spectrum, a very small percentage fear an adverse impact on his or her career.

Table 5-9. *Political Views as They Affect the Respondent's Own Chances for Tenure or Promotion*

Percent giving a particular answer to the question, "In your own personal case, do you believe that your chances for promotion or tenure were (or will be) affected by the reaction of your colleagues to your political views?"

| Answer | All faculty | Very liberal | Very conservative | Middle of the road |
|---|---|---|---|---|
| No, I consider it almost impossible that my political views have affected (or will affect) my chances | 75 | 69 | 54 | 81 |
| I think it is possible, but unlikely, that my political views have affected (or will affect) my chances | 19 | 22 | 32 | 17 |
| It is probable that my political views have affected (or will affect) my chances | 4 | 12 | 10 | 1 |
| Yes, I am certain that my political views have affected (or will affect) my chances | 2 | 2 | 3 | |
| Number of respondents | 1,205 | 223 | 37 | 215 |

What about that critical aspect of faculty life, collegiality? Has the paucity of conservatives in higher education restricted discussion and debate among faculty? Here we sought answers by asking faculty members about what they know best, namely, their own behavior. When asked, "Have you ever remained silent about your political or religious views because you feared the reactions of your fellow professors?" 71 percent of college professors answered never or seldom if ever, and only 6 percent felt that they censor themselves frequently. Conservatives were more likely to censor themselves occasionally than other groups, but self-censorship was almost as common among the very liberal as the very conservative professors. And for every group, strong majorities felt that self-censorship is either exceedingly rare or absent in their own discussions with colleagues.

Thus the pattern seems fairly clear: faculty members do not perceive discrimination in the situation they know best—their own—whether in conversations with colleagues or in the case of their own past or upcoming tenure. Most faculty members, even those with the strongest conservative views, do not see discrimination as a problem in their department. Only in the campus at large, when asked about the situation in other departments, do even strong conservatives believe that ideological discrimination in hiring is present. But they do not personally experience it, nor does it limit their discourse with colleagues. Ideological discrimination in hiring and promotion is a limited problem in the opinion of most professors, perhaps occurring in a

Table 5-10. *Religion in Hiring and Promotion, Campuswide,*
*by Religious Faith*

Percent giving a particular answer to the question, "In hiring and promotion, do you believe candidates with strong Christian beliefs are treated the same as candidates of other faiths and the nonreligious?"

| Answer | All faculty | Jewish | Catholic | Protestant | Other faith | Agnostic or atheist |
|---|---|---|---|---|---|---|
| No, I believe there is a strong bias against Christians | 1.8 | 0 | 0 | 3 | 2 | 1 |
| No, I believe there is a weak bias against Christians | 4.9 | 0 | 4 | 9 | 4 | 2 |
| Yes, religion doesn't influence hiring and promotion | 77.1 | 88 | 75 | 72 | 79 | 84 |
| No, I believe there is a weak preference for Christians | 7.7 | 5 | 14 | 6 | 5 | 8 |
| No, I believe there is a strong preference for Christians | 8.5 | 8 | 8 | 11 | 10 | 6 |
| Number of respondents | 854 | 64 | 164 | 348 | 136 | 183 |

few specific departments on certain campuses. Whether there are other more subtle and pervasive biases (for example, in favor of safely "tenurable" candidates), we leave for later consideration. We also note some recent evidence from the Higher Education Research Institute at the University of California, Los Angeles, suggesting that college professors *do* tend to avoid controversial subjects such as religious beliefs when "different religious perspectives in the classroom or the place of religions in the public square were at issue."[23]

The contention made by Rothman, Lichter, and Nevitte that Christians face discrimination in academic hiring, however, found little or no support in our survey.[24] While the vast majority of faculty members believed that religion plays no role in hiring and promotion in their department or on their campus, among those who did perceive religious discrimination, by almost 3:1 they believed it is a bias against non-Christians (see table 5-10). Among the minority of professors who feel that religion plays any role in hiring and promotion, Catholics were most likely to believe that Christians were favored. While 12 percent of Protestant professors believed that there is at least some bias against candidates with "strong Christian beliefs," 17 percent, on the contrary, saw at least some preference for Christians. But 72 percent of all Protestant professors believed that religion is irrelevant in hiring. Among Jewish faculty, we could not find a single one in our sample who believed that there is bias against Christians in hiring, but we did find 13 percent teaching at institutions they believed have a preference for Christians in hiring and promotion.

Table 5-11. *Faculty Perceptions of Ideological or Partisan Diversity at Their University, by Political Viewpoint*

Percent giving a particular answer to the question, Do you think a lack of ideological or partisan diversity among the faculty is a problem at your university?

| Answer | College-wide | Very conservative professors | Moderately conservative professors | Middle of the road professors | Moderately liberal professors | Very liberal professors |
|---|---|---|---|---|---|---|
| No, it is not a problem because we are diverse | 50 | 26 | 34 | 53 | 54 | 52 |
| No, it is not a problem, even though we don't have a lot of diversity | 29 | 24 | 28 | 31 | 29 | 30 |
| Yes, it is a problem, but not a major one | 17 | 37 | 28 | 13 | 14 | 14 |
| Yes, it is a serious problem | 4 | 8 | 9 | 4 | 2 | 2 |
| Yes, it is one of the most serious problems facing the university | 1 | 5 | 2 | 0 | 1 | 1 |
| Number of respondents | 1,237 | 38 | 211 | 223 | 506 | 229 |

Overall, judging by responses from faculty members at any rate, discrimination against non-Christians appears to be more widespread than discrimination against conservatives in American higher education. The main finding here is that most professors, including conservative and Christian professors, do not believe that either political ideology or religion plays a significant role in hiring and promotion.

We asked our respondents a number of specific questions about "ideological diversity," since many of the academy's critics think that such diversity is lacking on campus (see table 5-11). In our survey, 79 percent of professors answered that they do not believe that ideological diversity is a problem, with 50 percent saying that their faculty is ideologically diverse. A smaller majority of conservative professors agreed, and even among very conservative professors only 5 percent thought that ideological diversity (or the lack of it) is one of the most serious problems facing their university. Only 13 percent of the most conservative professors considered it to be a serious problem in any sense.

## Summary

Our survey of American college professors suggests a picture at odds in important respects with that painted by many of the academy's conservative critics. Faculty political attitudes have become more liberal over the entire post–World

War II period, but college faculty members have consistently been identified on the political left since the dawn of surveying. A small rise in liberalism occurred during the 1980s, but there has been little or no significant shift since 1989. The 1999 survey by Stanley Rothman and his colleagues, which received so much media attention, may have produced its most dramatic claims simply by using a different question structure and wording as well as by making an interpretative error. In any event, Rothman and his colleagues have revised their figures, so now virtually every study based on survey data is in general agreement that the percentage of self-identifying liberal-left faculty members remains approximately what it was in 1989.

There are still differences in faculty political outlook between the applied and basic sciences and among the various departments and divisions within the universities. Many of these differences reflect surprising continuities over decades of sustained study. However, one notable feature of our survey is the ostensible increase in liberalism in a number of science departments. We have suggested several reasons for this shift, including populist attacks by conservative interest groups and politicians on scientists who study evolution, stem cell research, climate research, the origins of homosexuality, and a number of other topics. In the 1940s and 1950s, many faculty members were deeply out of step with large portions of the American public on the question of racial equality. That fault line might have been most evident among humanities and social science professors. Today, many of the gaps between the views of academics and the views of the general public seem to be rooted in disputes over the validity of scientific findings. While some surveys find that a plurality of Americans do not believe in evolution and that a large majority of citizens advocate teaching both evolution and creationism in high school science courses, such views are anathema to professors in our survey, even those who consider themselves conservatives. The shifting positions of the two major political parties with regard to certain hot button science issues may help to explain why we see a modest increase in liberal and Democratic views among natural scientists.

Yet conservative critics of the academy should find much comfort in our overall findings. Far from a harsh environment for conservatives, most conservative professors in our study, if we can believe what they say, have experienced very little, if any, discrimination. They do not believe that their tenure will be or has been affected by their political views. They do not believe that their department practices ideological discrimination in hiring and tenure. Nor do they believe that conservative students are treated unfairly. As for the claim that Christians face discrimination in hiring and tenure, we found the opposite;

more faculty members perceive a preference for Christians in hiring than an antipathy toward Christians. Of course, even one professor denied employment or tenure on the basis of his political views or religious faith should be a cause for concern, but our data suggest that this is a very rare event, and the most likely victims are atheists or non-Christians.

That political bias among professors has become an issue for certain political groups seems to reflect the cultural divides in American politics more than any sweeping changes in behavior and attitudes among professors. Certainly the "culture wars" era at the American universities did feature countercultural radicals among the faculties at certain universities. Speech codes, radical multiculturalism, and curricular postmodernism were not all figments of the vivid imagination or the political tactics of conservatives. That most of the campuses and departments making headlines during the 1990s eventually moved back toward more moderate policies, however, has been underreported. The media have much preferred the narrative of the lefties in academe taking over. Academic battles, despite their occasional shrillness, do not in our opinion account for the attention given within the political arena to alleged faculty bias. The answer to why political bias has received so much attention lies rather with the interest groups, the political partisans, and the activists who have found common ground (and fundraising success) in identifying a crisis within American higher education. It is to this topic that we turn our attention in the following chapter.

# 6

## The Politics of
## Politics in the Classroom

In the preceding chapters we discuss the modest shift in faculty political attitudes that occurred in the 1980s. The traditional vocabulary of liberalism-conservatism has limitations when we seek to understand contemporary political reality.[1] So we do not rely on our survey findings alone, and in this chapter we broaden our focus to account for the political motives behind the higher education debate. Faculty political attitudes might appear more liberal because of contrasts with broader public attitudes on certain issues, such as gay rights, abortion, evolution, family values, and other matters.[2] The country has moved in what we could loosely call a center-right direction on some issues, creating more distance from college professors even if they have not changed much.[3] One of the present authors recalls his dad warning him in 1953 as he departed for college, "Well, son, there're a lot of liberals over there [at the University of Minnesota], but what are you going to do? You have to get an education, and you'll get a good education."[4] But the political issues that swirl around the universities today move in a potentially more dramatic fashion and operate according to a new and more complicated logic, which helps to explain why the idea of political bias in the classroom has surfaced as an issue in recent years.

## Classroom Bias as a Failed Issue

Demographic change of any kind is gradual; political change, though influenced by demographics, can be quite rapid. Seldom will politics merely follow a logic derived from demographics or other social trends. As with any political issue, the specific context and the behavior of political actors will determine whether, and when, an issue becomes salient. The political scientist John W. Kingdon has identified various overlapping stages in the emergence of an issue: activating elite opinion, mobilizing interest groups, attracting sustained media attention, and finding political champions to push the issue.[5]

Classroom bias, compared to issues such as global warming, workplace safety, or children's health, is a concept that is nebulous from the start. Yet the concept is amenable to the same kind of analysis: how does elite interest crystallize, how does a cause gain media attention, what triggers interest groups to organize a campaign and carry forward the fight, and when do political champions pick up the cause in legislative chambers or in the electoral arena? Under what conditions, in other words, can we expect an assault on university radicals to emerge as an issue?

In 1966 Ronald Reagan gained political momentum by attacking radicals at the University of California. He accused radicals of hurting the university, and once elected he continued to attack them for harming public higher education. Reagan's critics within the public university accused him of shortchanging the public universities (and favoring private higher education), but he never interfered with what was taught or intervened in hiring decisions or other internal decisionmaking. In the 1990s the attack on "political correctness" in the universities did not have an obvious electoral goal, but this did not dissuade a number of academic observers from detecting a far-reaching assault on higher education.[6] Elite opinion, inside and outside the academy, was activated on both sides, and a great deal of media attention focused on the "culture wars" in the universities. But Kingdon's other stages—interest group activity and political champions—did not develop in the 1990s. Thus no sustained campaign was directed toward achieving any goal, there was little focused attention, and there was even less impact on public policy at either the state or federal level. Classroom bias as a political issue has continued to run into problems. Although it has advanced to the stage of organized interest group activity, the opposing interests have largely checked and neutralized each other (not an altogether bad outcome from the point of view of many participants). But few politicians have taken up the cause, and those who have wish they had not. Thus the final and critical link—finding a political champion—has been the missing ingredient. This has been so despite the ascendance of conservative thought in national and state politics during many of these years. The overall result has been that classroom bias as a serious political issue has achieved, at best, only limited and transitory gains.

In accounting for this lack of success, a root problem has been the fundamental ambivalence about the issue within the ranks of conservatives. Conservatives do not in general favor government intervention nor do they see politicians acting as the "school boards" for the universities. The No Child Left Behind Act of 2002, pushed strongly as a signature issue during President George W. Bush's first term, scrambled some of the traditional dividing lines in national politics, drawing fire from traditional conservatives and from liberal forces associated with the teachers unions. Whatever else this controversial program achieved, it certainly did not predispose Republicans to the idea that government should regulate university curricula. Paradoxically, liberals for their own reasons have helped to fan the flames and inflate the standing of conservative activists like David Horowitz. The case of purported bias in the classroom in the end illustrates how difficult it is for any proposed reform to become a serious issue in real-world politics, to advance, in short, past the numerous obstacles that block and winnow out causes in America's pluralist politics. But issues can be kept alive, in a sort of low-boil state, because many players find a common interest in a stylized and largely symbolic form of combat.

The features that have always impeded the reformer—divided authority, judicial checks, suspicion of radicals of all sorts, America's pragmatic and cautious political culture—work against the idea that government, either federal or state, should regulate curriculum matters or other specific areas of internal university conduct. There is a high hurdle to overcome with any proposal to intervene politically into curricular matters, despite calls for greater "accountability" in higher education.[7] The pressures that surround elementary and secondary school politics have apparently moved to the arena of public higher education.

The debate has been complex, and the ideological grounds have shifted in unusual ways among the combatants. Some conservatives, in their effort to gain political traction for their critique of universities, have advanced an argument formerly made by both the old left and the new left. To wit: a powerful establishment—a power elite—controls the policy agenda and enforces a Marxian "hegemony" over the thought processes of citizens. This powerful liberal establishment is rooted in the elite universities. The mass public thus suffers from a "false consciousness": they are deluded into believing that things are all right and that the great universities are really great.[8] Conversely, liberals have happily invoked conservative themes, for example, tradition and the authority of long-standing practice argue against radical reforms that might rupture arrangements that have worked well for many years. It should be presumed that what exists probably exists for a reason. And, in general, if something ain't broke, don't fix it.

## David Horowitz as Activist

David Horowitz, gadfly critic of the universities and bête noire of the campus left, has emerged as one of the most prominent figures pushing for "intellectual diversity" on campus. This is a goal to be realized, he argues, through what he called an "academic bill of rights." Horowitz's singular influence and unique status in the pantheon of conservative critics of the universities can be attributed, as we have suggested, in part to the efforts of his enemies. A campus radical during the 1960s and now an unrelenting critic of the left, Horowitz is an ideal target for anyone hating zealotry. He has been inflated by his enemies into a serious threat to academic freedom, a position happily suited to his talent for keeping in the public eye. As one official from a higher education association in Washington remarked informally to us (not entirely in jest), "If David Horowitz didn't exist, we would have to invent him." One has to credit his hard work, his tenacity, and his ability to pick out and dramatize skillfully examples of inappropriate behavior on campus, which, indeed, are not lacking in the large and complex higher education enterprise. Horowitz's rise to national prominence began in earnest after the Ward Churchill episode had created indignation and even outrage across the nation amid continuous media coverage.

In much the way that Ward Churchill became a symbol of the leftist lunatic fringe, Horowitz became a symbol of the rightist attack on the universities. Pointing to Horowitz in order to rally one's allies, done at times as a conscious tactic and sometimes merely as an overreaction to one of his charges, made some educators uneasy. The concentration of critical fire on Horowitz could be seen as a tactical mistake and, more broadly, as the failure of a close-minded establishment to address some of Horowitz's legitimate complaints. To build Horowitz up into a David battling the higher education Goliath was not a winning strategy. Horowitz's demands were, at some level, reasonable and indeed quite in line with deeply rooted academic values. What is wrong with viewpoint diversity? Who would seriously argue against the concept that students should not be browbeaten in the classroom?

Horowitz's efforts, moreover, were notable for attempting to do what was not done by conservative critics in the 1990s: find Republican politicians or even Democratic politicians to champion his cause. He has been modestly successful in eliciting a certain amount of symbolic support for his bill of rights from state legislators in a number of Western states. Aided by the Republican control of state legislatures, Horowitz urged legislators to do *something* toward the end of requiring public colleges and universities to promote "diversity" and "balance" in hiring, advocate openness in campus forums, and ensure that conservative students are not browbeaten in class by liberal professors.

As of summer 2005, Horowitz had proposed various measures in some twenty state legislatures to implement his ideas. His proposals included calls for funding legislative "watchdog" staffs, investigating student complaints of classroom bias, and imposing annual reporting requirements on public colleges and universities.[9] Nonbinding resolutions would "urge" colleges and universities to report annually on the steps they take to ensure intellectual diversity and the free exchange of ideas. As well as encouraging positive steps, actions would also prohibit heckling speakers and holding panel discussions that are not balanced. Horowitz was subsequently joined in his advocacy vis-à-vis state legislatures by other conservative groups.[10]

In addition to viewpoint diversity, Horowitz has championed student rights. The main idea of his academic bill of rights is that students have been left out of the traditional American concept of academic freedom. This omission contravenes the original Weberian intent to include student rights under the concept of *Lehrfreiheit* and *Lernfreiheit* (the freedom to teach and to learn).[11] Students need to be protected against intimidation and proselytizing by faculty members. All too often, he claimed, liberal professors intimidate students and create an atmosphere inimical to learning. Horowitz was able to create a stir and consistently to vex the higher education establishment. Again, officials of the educational associations were alarmed not by his arguments as much as by his tactics: he was seeking to capture the attention of policymakers, not to convince his academic colleagues. And although he denied seeking government control over the universities, his influence with politicians and the media could produce such a result, even if his good intentions could be believed. He may have "talked the talk" of the academy, said his critics, but he did not play by the normal guild rules.

None of this kind of criticism bothered Horowitz, who seems to have felt validated the more he was attacked. That he, an outsider with no snug tenure berth, would be vilified because he was not a member of the club only proved that he was on to something. And this is not to speak of elementary decorum:

Horowitz was hit in the face by a pie at one campus and is routinely heckled in his campus appearances.[12] The publisher of the *Weekly Standard*, William Kristol, also was hit in the face by a pie while he was speaking at Earlham College in Indiana in 2005. Acts of incivility against conservative speakers have taken place at a number of campuses. This kind of behavior is intolerable and should be seriously addressed by university administrators. Horowitz's campus appearances have now become almost choreographed. He arrives with bodyguards and is greeted with organized protests and often with shouted insults. The story is covered in the campus and local newspapers, and Horowitz has won his point before he says a word. The hostile reception he receives enables his victimization and provides ammunition for his critique of the close-minded university.

Horowitz in the summer of 2005, however, had bigger fish to fry than visits to campuses. He had embarked on a one-man campaign to influence federal policy. In June 2005 he made numerous visits to Republican congressmen pushing the idea that the language of his academic bill of rights should be written into current legislation as a "sense of the Congress" resolution. The most promising venue seemed to be the pending reauthorization bill for higher education, the adoption of which the higher education community in 2005 had decided to push for (the higher education authorization had not been modified since 1997). Horowitz found a receptive audience with Republican congressmen, and especially staffers, who believed that the campuses *were* generally hostile to Republicans and that if the universities wanted the Higher Education Act to be reauthorized, they would have to swallow a congressional resolution demanding that they become more diverse in the viewpoints expressed on campus. Some of the Republican congressional leaders and staffers were uneasy about inserting language into the bill, remembering the uproar that had erupted over funding for language studies in 2003 (when pro-Israeli groups tried to have a board created to scrutinize funding for language programs that might be prejudiced against Israel).[13] But momentum built up behind the Horowitz campaign. "It was clear to us," said Terry W. Hartle, senior vice president of the American Council on Education (ACE), the umbrella organization representing the largest number of colleges and universities, that "David [Horowitz] had considerable traction, and while at some level we had no trouble with what he was saying, we were uncomfortable with some of the language. We worried over how you could, for example, implement a requirement for 'balance' in the classroom."[14]

Hartle sounded out colleagues in the higher education community and entered into discussions with Horowitz and Republican legislators. Horowitz was amenable to changes in his language so long as the principles he sought were retained. Most of the Washington-based educational representatives were amenable to compromising with Horowitz if doing so would modify his bill of rights language or avert restrictive legislative language that would spare their colleges and universities unworkable regulations. Some of the higher education interest groups, notably the National Education Association and the American Federation of Teachers, remained adamantly opposed to dealing with Horowitz and preferred an open fight with GOP legislators in the House of Representatives, hoping to block the bill in the Senate. John A. Boehner (R-Ohio), chair of the House Committee on Education and the Workplace, and Howard (Buck) McKeon (R-Calif.), chair of the major subcommittee, were particularly sensitive to the concerns raised by Bob Andringa, counsel to the Council of Christian Colleges and a close ally of Hartle in the June 2005 negotiations. Andringa objected that the concept of balance might interfere with his clients' freedom to hire Christian professors and to teach subjects from a Christian perspective. Would holocaust denials have to be taught in college courses on the theory that all points of view had to be represented? Boehner and McKeon had no desire to stir the ire of fundamentalist constituents and did not relish a big "culture wars" fight in the committee. But the two congressmen believed that such a fight was inevitable unless the higher education community and Horowitz could work out some sort of compromise. The congressmen suggested that the educators try to work out a joint statement that would affirm their conceptions of academic rights and responsibilities and also be acceptable to Horowitz. This was the background of the June 23, 2005, statement on academic rights and responsibilities.

## The ACE Statement of June 2005

Perhaps the peak of David Horowitz's national influence came in June 2005 when a coalition of twenty-eight mainstream national educational associations, led by the American Council on Education, approved a statement on academic rights and responsibilities that blended traditional concepts of academic freedom with an endorsement of intellectual pluralism and student rights as championed by Horowitz.[15] This whole episode was perhaps minor in the larger scheme of things, involving only the wording of a "sense of the Congress" resolution that would not have imposed any specific or binding requirement on the nation's colleges and universities. But the episode highlights nicely the conflicting forces in the politics of higher education that were contending to shape a host of other policies, and in Washington losers get rolled, so nobody wants to lose any battle. After the outcome had been worked out and the wording agreed to, Horowitz immediately hailed the statement as "a tremendous victory" for his campaign and a "huge step forward" in the cause of academic freedom. The mainstream associations also declared victory, believing that the Horowitz drive had been largely blunted and that they had gotten on the right side of a public relations campaign that they had been losing before. They were pleased that Horowitz looked on the statement as having satisfied his key demands, and congressional interest in university leftism all but evaporated. Universities could no longer be accused of being indifferent to legitimate student complaints or in any way hostile to free inquiry. As the steam rapidly went out of the drive in Congress to demand that universities stop discriminating against conservatives, the universities considered that they had at last weathered the "Ward Churchill" crisis and returned to a more hospitable climate.

The ACE statement contained a provision that, to the conservatives, implicitly acknowledged bias. To the liberals, the provision was merely an affirmation and restatement of long-standing practice: "Any member of the campus community who believes that he or she has been treated unfairly on academic matters must have access to a clear institutional process by which his or her grievance can be addressed."

Four other "principles" of a similarly anodyne character were part of the statement, the most significant of which was an endorsement of the proposition that universities should be places conducive to intellectual pluralism. The word pluralism was insisted on by those who felt that to use the word diversity would be a total capitulation to Horowitz and possibly also an affront to conservatives who disliked the term. The ACE statement represented a win for those among the educational establishment who argued that Horowitz should be co-opted, not built up by exaggerating his importance. Many thought that fighting for the sake of fighting was a losing proposition. The "pros" in the higher education lobbying community had a simple reaction: Horowitz had gotten a lot of attention and traction, and one simply had to deal with the situation by trying to come up with a compromise statement satisfying everybody. The pragmatists won out, and the Republican leaders who conceived the idea of the statement and suggested it to the educators were quietly vindicated. Only the National Education Association and the American Federation of Teachers refused to sign the statement. The remaining Horowitz foes yielded to the arguments of the majority but warned that Horowitz was a renegade whose mischief-making potential was going to be enhanced by this effort to deal with him.

The June 2005 ACE statement in the end was a political solution attractive to the main parties, even if it broke no new ground intellectually and had a certain vacuity to it. The higher education associations went on record as being receptive to legitimate concerns, and the statement reaffirmed important and long-standing principles of openness, fairness, and academic freedom. At the same time, the statement would help to ensure that Congress would not carry on the culture wars and harass colleges and universities for their alleged bias. The Republicans could strike a symbolic blow for viewpoint diversity without putting Congress in the position of becoming the school board for higher education. Horowitz and his allies could point out that they had brought the establishment to heel (or at least gotten it to see reason). Conservatives had won a victory against the academic liberals, but the liberals had won, too, since they were not injured and since Horowitz apparently had behaved himself and turned out to be more modest in his demands than they had feared. The show of unity, with almost the whole of the higher education associations signing on in support of the intellectual pluralism statement, gave a measure of protection against potential criticism from the colleges and universities.

With nearly all of the associations as signatories, the mainstream Washington associations hoped that adverse comment in the college and university constituencies would not flair up into a revolt. This turned out to be the case for the most part. The statement, in fact, passed largely unnoticed in the academic community, but the American Association of University Professors (AAUP) drew some fire from its more active members for failing to fight Horowitz to the death and for handing him a public relations victory. As it turned out, both those who said that Horowitz's influence would gradually decline and those who said that the statement would increase his visibility and his capacity for mischief proved to be correct. We pick up the story of the Pennsylvania fights over academic freedom, which were inspired in part by Horowitz after the statement, in chapter 7.

## A Retrospective Look: God and Man at Yale

How did the nation get to the stage where national associations, and major politicians, actually took part in a debate on politics in the universities? It is instructive to step back and to view how the allegations of political bias in the academy arose—to see the matter, in short, from an historical perspective. William F. Buckley's classic 1951 conservative text *God and Man at Yale* provides a useful point of departure.[16] Buckley, a pioneering figure in American journalism and in the revival of conservatism, made a case in this book against the secular and collectivist trends that he saw in the undergraduate curriculum at Yale during the time he attended Yale College (1946–50). He drew on material he wrote for the *Yale Daily* (where he served as chair and editor in his senior year). Buckley's approach was straightforward. He simply considered the main courses that most Yale undergraduates took—economics 10, sociology 10, a course in comparative economic systems, and introductory psychology and religion courses—and quoted copiously from the major textbooks used. He buttressed those quotations with references from his class notes to show the lines of argument of his professors.

Writing in a witty and provocative style, he showed that, in economics, for example, every textbook used in the introductory courses favored Keynesian "pump-priming" and government stimulus of demand and underscored the need for a government to have a strong role in the economy generally. Further, the texts endorsed highly progressive income taxes and government economic regulation and repeatedly criticized laissez-faire capitalism and individualism. The texts and the professors repeatedly stressed the need for government planning. Buckley quoted extensively from his professors' lectures to make the case that orthodoxy prevailed in favor of collectivism.

In examining sociology, psychology, and religion courses, Buckley took up his other chief preoccupation: the secular nature of Yale's curriculum and of the campus atmosphere. He quoted extensively from textbooks and class lecture notes to show that religion was not regarded as a major influence in Western civilization. Religion was scarcely referred to in some texts and then only dismissively as a relic or holdover from popular superstition. He drew on an editorial he wrote as editor of the *Yale Daily* to criticize a popular sociology professor for making a "cult of nonreligion," for making gratuitous references to Christianity, and making bad jokes, insults, and derogatory remarks about church doctrine and religious practices.[17]

We quarrel with key assumptions of Buckley's argument—in particular, the premise that the alumni are the ultimate "owners" of the university. From this, he deduces that the alumni should examine what is taught, and the university should hire only teachers that the alumni and trustees deem acceptable. Most contemporary observers (but not all) totally reject this idea. For our part, we find the notion of giving power to the trustees and alumni a holdover from an earlier era, when universities were much less hospitable to open and wide-ranging debate.

Buckley, however, did not presume to know exactly how his vision of Yale should be implemented, and he did not want to stifle debate on campus. For all of his deploring of liberal professors, he objected most to the absence of spirited debates on campus—the indifference of many of his fellow "white shoe" students to intellectual contestation—and did his best at the *Yale Daily* to enliven the intellectual atmosphere on campus. Even though he clearly wanted to reverse the trend toward secularism and return to the earlier notions of liberal individualism, he did not want to interfere with a professor's research or writing, and he did not want undergraduate teaching to be dogmatic and wedded to any ideology. But professors of religion should be able to advocate religious belief and not merely comment neutrally on the history of religious institutions.

Buckley's argument for limiting academic freedom principally to the sphere of what the professor does *outside of* the classroom found few adherents at the time. It is doubtful that he wanted classroom discussion to be bland or that professors should refrain from controversy, although he did not clearly develop his views on this score. He did not endorse the "value-free" style of inquiry that was developing in disciplines such as political science and economics at Yale and elsewhere. Buckley's focus on the university's role as transmitter of cultural and spiritual values seemed to ignore the university's research and public service functions.

Notwithstanding the book's faults, Buckley made a case that a set of rather narrow orthodoxies shaped the thinking and the teaching of his professors in a number of departments at Yale. By inference his indictment extended to other Ivy League universities. Buckley's complaints did not make much of an impact, perhaps in part because there was no wider resonance for his ideas in the nonacademic intelligentsia and in the political classes. Today's social science departments are quite different from what they were in Buckley's day. In some ways the fields are much more open and diverse than they were in the late 1940s, but in other ways they could be worse from an undergraduate's perspective. Consider, by way of contrast, today's economics departments. Using the same kind of reasoning he employed, contemporary economics departments would be considered much more market oriented than in the 1946–50 period and certainly more critical of collectivism and more open to examination of different ideologies and policy options.[18]

Economics today would probably be seen as divided on issues like the government's role in both the domestic economy and the international economic arena. In general the neoclassical synthesis has displaced Keynesianism as the leading paradigm, so the field is not without orthodoxy and methodological conformity. Indeed, though the neoclassical synthesis has been revised, recast, and also reviled, economics departments might be criticized for being too rigid methodologically and for teaching subject matter that is so highly technical and mathematized as to be of limited interest to students outside the major.[19]

Buckley's brand of conservative activism, or activism of any kind, was not the norm for student editors at Yale. A lower-profile, career-oriented posture was typical, and political passivity was a general feature of student life. Buckley's critique of his fellow students was not too different from some critiques of the career-minded students of today.

Religion has also made a comeback on many campuses today. Interest in religion has dramatically increased in various university departments. American society clearly has not followed the secular path envisaged by many of Buckley's Yale professors. Scholarship has inevitably had to respond to the revival of faith in our own society and in other parts of the world. Buckley's argument against a casual secularism in 1951 should have been taken more seriously at the time, but the idea that religion is neglected today is less plausible. Even secular scholars acknowledge religious fundamentalism as a rising force in the world. But moral and religious education overall is on something of a par with political education, needing more professional attention from educators, more serious debate on how it should be included in the curriculum, and more determined defense in the face of constant pressures to expand vocational offerings.

The natural sciences were of surprisingly little concern to Buckley. He saw no conflict between scientific inquiry and spiritual values, provided that the value neutrality of the sciences did not extend to those parts of the university— the social sciences and the humanities—that concerned him. Equally, neither communism nor anticommunism seems to have concerned him. He saw no communists on the Yale faculty; a brief allusion seems to suggest that communism as a world historical force would be a transitory phenomenon. He congratulated the Yale administration for hiring only professors committed to democracy. For Buckley, the great danger lay in hiring socialists. Socialists, he implied, were all right so long as they toed the line, *taught* capitalism in class, and limited their advocacy of socialism to their scholarly writings. In retrospect, if they were paid as research professors from sources other than tuition, then he had no objections.

## Conservatism and Sustained Media Attention

Buckley's *God and Man at Yale* made only a brief ripple in the New York publishing world. It was not picked up by the conservative news media and radio talk shows—common features today—because such media did not exist. Buckley himself, in founding the *National Review* and creating the television show *Firing Line*, played an important role in creating the conservative media and reviving conservative intellectual thought in the last quarter of the twentieth-century in America.[20] The mainstream news media, which became the frequent target of conservatives for displaying a liberal bias, have in recent years regularly run stories about political correctness and leftism on the nation's campuses. The contrast between today and the total lack of receptivity to Buckley's critique could not be more striking.

Indeed, the meta-narrative underlying many media stories about the universities has become so fixed in our cultural awareness that it requires deeper explanation. Anti-intellectual attitudes, which Hofstadter found in business, religion, and the parties, are perhaps also to be found in the media. Perhaps liberal media can deflect critical fire from themselves by targeting liberal academe. Bloggers, too, could have debased public dialogue by extremist accounts that work their way into the mainstream media outlets. But these lines of thought do not adequately account for the persistent critical themes found in the mainstream media in recent years. On the theory that literature plays some part in a society's deeper impulses, we can turn to Tom Wolfe's 2004 novel *I Am Charlotte Simmons* for clues. If literary narrative frames the attitudes of the popular (and elite) culture, the novel and its major themes merit consideration. Charlotte, the novel's heroine, is an honest, intelligent, and religious young woman from a small mountain town in North Carolina. She gets accepted at a prestigious secular university, named DuPont University in the novel. Although situated fictionally in Pennsylvania, DuPont appears to be a blend of Duke and the University of Virginia (Wolfe's own daughters attended Duke). Student life is dominated by athletics, drinking, parties, and sexual predation. The campus political atmosphere depicted in the novel is nonexistent, or, rather, there is an almost total absence of thoughtful political debate. There is, however, a certain reflexive utopianism enforced by a layer of junior bureaucrats mindlessly acting as gatekeepers of political correctness. Occasional rallies are held on campus pushing leftist causes, but these are principally countercultural happenings, and there is nothing that passes for genuine debate or discussion of any issue. The students organize such events, and virtually no faculty members attend. The administration is relentlessly fixated on enforcing speech codes and rules of conduct, while doing nothing about the excessive drinking that pervades campus life.

The faculty have no interest in politics or anything that smacks of values, being preoccupied with epistemologically mindless behavioralism and displaying a shallow and unattractive careerism. The students are equally unappealing, as they are concerned mainly with "success" and upward mobility in the consumer society. Their own shallow careerism (when they take time off from alcoholism and sexual predation) dovetails with that of the faculty so that neither finds time for education. Between the faculty's faults and the students' lack of seriousness, there is little or no room for teaching or learning, and there clearly are no time and no incentives for the liberal arts education that appeals to Wolfe. This is a caricature, of course, just as *The Bonfire of the Vanities* is not a fair portrait of New York City politics. But there is enough verisimilitude in the rich details and the engrossing narrative to capture some uncomfortable truths about the contemporary university.

In this respect, Wolfe's novel highlights those features of college life that are extensively criticized by the essayists in Robert Calvert's volume *To Restore American Democracy: Political Education and the Modern University* as discouraging any meaningful educational attention to politics.[21] Although these authors do not concentrate on campus social life—the partying, drunkenness, sexual predation, and obsession with athletics depicted by Wolfe—they do point out that students bring their "good time" culture with them to college and that the marketing activities many universities undertake are predicated on that assumption. Students, already deeply conditioned by the mass media, come to college fully expecting something like Wolfe's portrayal of campus life and, once at college, face enormous distractions that interfere with serious study.

Even the sciences do not fare well in Wolfe's allegory: scientific research at DuPont reflects a crude behavioralism. The leading light on campus is a neuroscience professor who has won the Nobel Prize for an experiment in which he removes a portion of a cat's brain, which stimulates heightened sexual activity by the animal. Other cats in a control group follow this cat's example, even though their brains are normal. They become promiscuous even though their brains have not been altered—a trope for the hypersexual ethos on campus.

The worst character in *I Am Charlotte Simmons* is an arrogant history professor who plays at the "sand box" politics on campus but has no real political principles or scruples. He is the only professor to speak at a gay rights rally on campus; he strikes the right rhetorical pose (but then, of course, the phony that he is, lets drop the admission that he himself is straight). He is on a vendetta against the athletics department, but then drops his campaign to get the coach when he discovers that the investigative reporter on the student newspaper has got damaging material on a bigwig Republican politician who has visited the campus. Like the villains of Wolfe's *The Bonfire of the Vanities,* the history professor is a man of the left and so are most of his colleagues. The villains of *The Bonfire of the Vanities* have a certain roguish élan, but the professorial figures in *I Am Charlotte Simmons* are wooden and almost formulaic figures that do not come to life. The coach, the athletes, and the students are more colorful and vivid characters, even if many are not appetizing figures.

The media portrayal of the academy often fits neatly into the Wolfian frame. So persistent is this image that some observers have sought to explain the phenomenon and have produced a spate of theories. A recent study by historian Jon Wiener of scandals in his profession finds, for example, that some instances of scholarly misconduct have been widely reported in the press, while others have been wholly or largely ignored.[22] How to explain this? Wiener asserts that the media treatment reflects a systematic pattern. On the one hand, conservative professors have been cast as innocent victims of ideologically driven university administrators, while conservative transgressions have been either ignored or downplayed in media accounts. On the other hand, liberal sinners against academic rectitude have been pilloried and generally excoriated in a kind of lynch mob media mentality. Wiener's explanation for why this is happening is that conservatives have been adroit in manipulating the media. Indeed, they have self-consciously used the media to advance their own agendas in contrast to the less media-savvy liberals who have been hapless victims.[23] Conservatives, according to Wiener, do not play fair, that is, they do not follow the accepted rules of academic discourse. Conservatives, he says, play to the wider audience through bumper-sticker slogans. This attitude may help to account for the hostile reception to David Horowitz on his numerous campus visits and why so few professors engage him directly.

In a critique of threats to academic freedom, Beshara Doumani sees a pervasive and deep-rooted danger stemming from the war on terror and from the trend toward privatization and corporate patrimony. In his view, "The unprecedented curtailment of civil liberties following the passage of the USA Patriot Act in October 2001 has affected academic freedom structurally."[24] Moreover, he adds, private advocacy groups have fueled a campaign to intrude into the classroom and thwart the free expression of ideas.[25] "Unlike in the McCarthy era, private advocacy and special interest groups are playing the lead in national campaigns to undermine freedom by replacing professional norms with arbitrary political criteria."[26] Similarly, Professor Ellen Schrecker observed in response to a question about McCarthyism versus the present era in a *Chronicle of Higher Education* colloquy, "Despite the hysteria of the times, the witch hunts [of the McCarthy era] were focused mainly on what professors—liberal and otherwise—were doing outside the classroom. That's why the attacks on the university today are *potentially* more serious. They ARE reaching into the classroom."[27] [Emphasis in the original.] Schrecker, however, said that the danger at the present moment was a potential, not an actual, threat. Harvard sociologist Neil Gross found in a paper presented at the 2007 American Sociology Association meeting that more professors currently feel threats to their academic freedom than did professors in the recent past.[28]

Thus we see why classroom bias has emerged as a political issue, even if it has not yet had an impact on policy. Political bias is seen as serious because individuals on both the left and the right see it as a matter of importance, and each side finds comfort in having an enemy to fight. The right deplores what it sees as the lack of professionalism and the misuse of a professor's class time to push political views. Those views often are extraneous to the subject matter of the course. In this line of argumentation, it is seldom explained when, and how, politics should be discussed and in what classes. The implication is that all politics and all political discussion are inappropriate (of course, patriotism, tradition, and other conservative values are presumably to be encouraged). Obviously, any serious discussion of the nation's public philosophy would have to include *both* conservative and liberal values. How can we Americans *not* seek to conserve our liberties, even while we argue over what it means to be free?

The left deplores the effort by conservative critics to manipulate the media and to inject political considerations into matters of personnel, curriculum, and teaching methods—the heart of the university. This is the inner citadel, the domain where professional standards must ensure the quality of the academic enterprise. The intensity of the debate leads to growing fervor by partisans on each side, and the debate is carried on largely by the militants on such sides. Here, therefore, we have a clear case of enemies who need each other. Conservative critics sense that they have touched a nerve when the liberals push back and hence sharpen their criticisms. Liberals, in turn, find added evidence of a right-wing assault on the academy and on academic freedom. If we may be pardoned for stepping outside our role as analysts for a moment, we say to both sides: let's not throw the baby out with the bathwater. The aim is not to banish political discussion, expunge all politics from the university, but to encourage serious discussion. If political themes and issues cannot be discussed seriously in the universities, where can they be?

The debate captures media attention precisely when the nuances are set aside and the cultural warriors clash in full panoply. As Morris Fiorina and others have argued, the most intense partners on each side of the cultural divide dominate the argument.[29] In Fiorina's strained analogy, "The bulk of the American citizenry is somewhat in the position of the unfortunate citizens of some third-world countries who try to stay out of the crossfire while Maoist guerrillas and right-wing death squads shoot at each other."[30]

To capture fully the politics behind the politics in the classroom, we must examine next the important dimension set forth earlier: the interest group networks. It is at this stage and through these channels that, in practice, the battles are largely fought. The higher education interest groups and associations provide the organizational backup, the resources, and the communications networks to put forward their ideas. The interest groups set the parameters and the overall tone of the debate and rally the foot soldiers of the campus cultural wars.

## The Role of Interest Groups

Higher education, like every other industry that depends on or is regulated by the government, has a dense, intricate, and overlapping network of associations and representatives in Washington (and in the state capitals as well). Associations represent liberal arts colleges, land grant universities, disciplinary societies, the business officers of colleges and universities, research administrators, university professors, religious colleges, presidents of major research universities, scientific societies overall and researchers in various fields, graduate deans, trustees, students, financial aid specialists, proprietary colleges, and myriad other interests affecting some or all of the more than 4,000 postsecondary institutions in the United States.

Major universities themselves, like their corporate counterparts, have opened their own Washington offices to represent their unique interests beyond the lobbying and advocacy activities they participate in through their membership associations. New entities emerge to advance specialized interests when a constituency feels itself inadequately represented by the existing organizations. Washington law firms specializing in lobbying on behalf of universities, such as Cassidy and Associates, have been an important part of the picture, perfecting the art of the "earmark" in appropriations for university clients.

The traditional higher education interest groups typically are funded by membership dues, foundations, and government grants. The interests of the numerous mainstream groups overlap, and their efforts frequently converge around matters of day-to-day concern to higher education as a whole (for example, student loans, reimbursement of indirect costs on research grants, student visas, accounting standards, and the like). There are areas of conflict, however. On matters such as earmarks or other targeted benefits to particular regions and institutions, for example, individual universities may follow a strategy of "every man for himself," relying mainly on their own Washington offices and on specialized law firms. Disputes are, however, rarely ideological among the mainstream groups. Higher education usually fails to take action on conflicted issues; it is not an industry that is unified or hierarchically organized. Unlike, say, the oil or pharmaceutical industries, higher education rarely can reach a common position when confronted with disputes among its diverse members. The intellectual pluralism statement of June 2005 is an unusual case of both discordant views and ultimate coalescing to achieve a common purpose.

The Association of American Universities (AAU) is a prominent mainstream organization made up of the presidents of the sixty-four or so of the country's most research-intensive universities. It attempted, and failed, in the 1990s to adopt a policy statement critical of earmarks. AAU president Robert Rosenzweg was a strong critic of earmarks, as were several university presidents among the AAU membership, but several other university presidents favored them (and had employed Cassidy and Associates to gain specific appropriations). The effort to take a stand against earmarks was thus stymied, inaction being the normal course in the face of disagreement. Similarly, the AAU in the 1990s also took up the issue of speech codes on campus. The effort came at the urging of Yale president Benno Schmidt, a First Amendment scholar and civil libertarian who (along with several other presidents) opposed broadly worded speech codes. Other AAU presidents defended the codes as necessary to a positive learning atmosphere and denied that there were adverse effects on campus free speech. Consequently, the AAU took no official position.

The controversies over earmarks, speech codes, and classroom bias illustrate that the traditional higher education associations will act cautiously and display great deference to members' wishes. Under normal circumstances, the associations seek to advance the common-denominator concerns of their membership. For most of the post–World War II period, the issues that mattered most to the higher education community were those of system expansion. The focus was on how to manage growth in student enrollments, faculty hiring, federal research support, and financial assistance to students. Many potential conflicts could be sidestepped in the general expansion of the whole sector. The traditional associations rarely looked for fights; they tried to avoid, if possible, the contentious issues. If driven to take strong positions, they sought safety by acting in concert with a broad coalition of colleagues.

New entrants into the overall system of higher education representation have generally not aimed to shake up the system, preferring instead to find an ecological niche among the organizational flora and fauna that mark the terrain. But higher education does not exist in a vacuum. When major issues shake the nation, the colleges and universities will be affected. Political trends inexorably have an impact on the universities and thus on their institutional representatives in the nation's capital. Ideological conflicts have now come to the interest groups that concern themselves with higher education. The most visible manifestation of this trend is the appearance of the ideologically driven associations.

## The New Ideology-Oriented Advocacy Groups

The ideological conflicts that are our concern in this chapter stemmed initially from the campus speech code controversies of the late 1980s and the 1990s. Starting in 1986, a number of widely publicized incidents of racial violence on several campuses led to the rapid adoption of codes banning discriminatory language and behavior, including, in particular, "hate speech," directed against minorities, women, ethnic groups, and gays. By some estimates, around 300 campuses had adopted such speech codes by the end of the 1980s, although the codes differed widely in breadth and specific content.[31] The overly broad wording of many such codes, and their potentially chilling effect on campus speech and even potentially on classroom instruction, precipitated the movement against political correctness (PC) on campus. In providing conservatives within the academy with a rallying cry, the anti-PC campaign resulted in a spate of books attacking campus liberalism. Counterattacks on liberals and the academic left by conservatives set the stage for the polemics of the 1990s.

A series of important federal court cases addressed the campus speech codes in the period 1992–93 and seemed to settle the issue by striking down the broadly worded codes at public colleges and universities. Surprisingly, the campus speech codes did not disappear after what seemed to be this authoritative judicial resolution of their legal standing. Rather, the number of codes *increased*. By the end of the 1990s, more than 800 colleges and universities had them.[32] Why this increase occurred is not obvious, but Jon Gould of George Mason University Law School offers a plausible explanation. He suggests that university administrators have been motivated by a combination of factors: first, they believed that eliminating speech codes would draw the ire of feminists, critical race theorists, and other campus constituencies. Administrators feared that any formal rescinding of the codes would be seen as backsliding. Second, deans and presidents judged that more narrowly formulated codes could withstand legal challenge. Legal opinions by some of their law school faculty colleagues affirmed this.[33]

Administrators believed that the failure to enforce the narrowly worded codes would remove any incentives for litigation. Thus a kind of prudential compromise was the answer: the codes would remain intact and would symbolize a university's commitment to nondiscrimination, social justice, and equality, with the trinity of class, race, and gender undisturbed. Students and faculty would live and work within a framework of shared values and behavioral norms. But civil libertarians on campus would also be mollified or at least given no specific cause for concern. The speech codes would not be enforced; their wording would be strictly limited to narrowly drawn fighting words. The codes would have limited practical effect but could help to enforce civility on campus. Gould might also have added that any community must have rules, and students should learn to observe rules of behavior.

In this general climate, a new kind of higher education interest group made its appearance. Advocacy oriented, and ideologically driven, the new entities emerged to fight the culture wars of the 1990s. David Horowitz's Students for Academic Freedom, his Center for the Study of Popular Culture, FrontPageMagazine.com, and the various other components of his project to fight campus leftism took shape over the course of the 1990s. Horowitz relied heavily on the Internet to carry on his campaign, which helped him to gain mainstream media attention.

The FIRE (Foundation for Individual Rights in Education), a small conservative foundation based in Philadelphia, grew directly out of the "water buffalo" speech code controversy at the University of Pennsylvania in the early 1990s. It was founded by University of Pennsylvania historian Alan Kors and civil liberties attorney Harvey Silverglade, whose coauthored book, *The Shadow University*, provided the intellectual foundation for the effort.[34]

The National Association of Scholars (NAS), founded in 1987 and headquartered in Princeton, New Jersey, has grown into a membership organization of some 3,500 dues-paying college and university professors who oppose what they deem to be a leftward drift in the intellectual climate at American universities. The NAS is dedicated to the notion that the principal threat to academic freedom now comes from the stifling orthodoxies within the academy itself rather than from extrinsic social and economic forces. The NAS functions as a kind of anti-AAUP, even while it in some respects imitates the AAUP's style of operations. Both are membership organizations committed to defending the professional interest of the professorate. The AAUP, however, founded in 1915 to represent the interests of the nation's college professors threatened by hostile social forces, is much larger, with some 60,000 dues-paying members. The AAU has operated to some extent with a trade union mind-set over its long history, representing individual professors in grievance proceedings against their institution, censuring colleges and universities for infractions of academic freedom and violations of tenure, and defending broadly the interests of the nation's professors. The NAS strives principally to attract publicity to its causes, chief of which is the alleged politicization of higher education by liberals. It criticizes the more traditional higher education interest groups for their timidity and failure to be critical of PC practices of faculty members.

The American Council of Trustees and Alumni (ACTA), founded in 1995, deserves special attention; it has become one of the most active, well funded, and most influential of the conservative advocacy organizations.[35] ACTA has become perhaps the leading voice of the new conservative critics of American higher education, performing the role of an umbrella organization. That is, it advises other groups on tactics, funds a host of studies and surveys by conservative scholars, and generally acts as a clearinghouse for information on behalf of its causes.

ACTA performs in some respects as an anti–Association of Governing Boards (AGB). The AGB is the long-established mainstream organization that represents college and university trustees. In contrast to the AGB, ACTA is funded by private philanthropists and foundations, often those interested in a cause. ACTA has been a bold critic of the universities from its inception and has focused on the curriculum and teaching in what it views as value-laden departments (that is, the humanities and the social sciences). ACTA has sometimes made common cause with one of the older and more traditional conservative organizations, the Intercollegiate Studies Institute (ISI) of Wilmington, Delaware. The ISI, founded in 1953, had William F. Buckley Jr. as its first president and has focused on programs to draw campus attention to the founding fathers, the American Constitution, the teaching of American history, and the importance of liberty in the American political tradition. Although ideological bedfellows, the contrast in style between the two organizations is instructive. ACTA is more attuned to the Washington political issues and the cultural ideological divide in the nation and is aggressive in its critique of the universities. ISI focuses on grassroots programs for individual students, such as funding scholarships and founding conservative magazines on campuses across the nation, and holds conferences and seminars on conservative topics. In recent years, perhaps influenced by ACTA and the national political mood, ISI has become more involved in advocacy and in broad national education issues.

ACTA's priorities have been directed toward shaking up the universities through media attention and critical outside scrutiny. The general aim has been to rescue the Western tradition from assault by the forces of postmodernism and value relativism. The trustees' role, in the ACTA worldview, should be a much more assertive one than has recently been common at the major universities. ACTA wants trustees to step in aggressively and to raise issues that have been left largely to university administrators and faculty members. Although it has never said so directly, the ACTA model seems to resemble the practices of the great Victorian reformers who founded the modern university and installed business elites on the boards.

ACTA initially pursued a contentious role against what it deemed the liberal-dominated network of higher education associations. As it has become more established, it has moderated its approach and become more of an anti-establishment arm of the establishment. At its most aggressive in November 2001 after the September 11 terrorist attacks on New York and Washington, ACTA issued a blistering report, *Defending Civilization: How Our Universities Are Failing America and What Can Be Done about It.*[36] In the report it criticized the failure to teach U.S. history in traditional terms and assailed the universities for failing to reflect basic American values. The report quoted comments made by 117 university faculty, staff members, and students in response to the September 11 attacks, comments that, in ACTA's view, showed the baleful effects of postmodernism and of anti-Western and anti-American thinking. In the wake of sharp criticism for McCarthyite tactics, ACTA removed the names from the report's appendix but retained the quotations and institutional affiliations.

ACTA has not lost its critical edge in commenting on trends in higher education, but its voice has been tempered somewhat as it has gained a wider audience. ACTA leaders have thus faced the choice confronting many interest groups: how to appeal to one's base while trying to broaden that base. The conflicting impulses within ACTA (and within the conservative movement) have become more evident over time. One ACTA thrust—its most consistent and prominent—has been the pedagogical aim of promoting the liberal arts tradition, especially the concept of the core curriculum (that is, teaching the classics of Western civilization).

Juxtaposed to the study of the classical texts of Western civilization is the diffuse enemy of postmodernism. This target includes among the villains feminism, postcolonialism, cultural studies, Marxist literary criticism, vocationalism, and all interdisciplinary studies programs that depart from the traditional disciplines and departments, including anything that can be labeled identity politics. A problem is immediately evident with this set of villains and the underlying aspirations. It might be supposed that a focus on the core curriculum is more likely to be found in the elite universities, which are less inclined to allow vocational influences to creep into the undergraduate curriculum. But ACTA's populist inclinations have made it focus on the elite universities as a major target for attack. It is obvious that the elite institutions may be the natural allies of ACTA insofar as it is committed to high culture and is the enemy of vocationalism.

The vocationalism and lack of standards that ACTA deplores are also quite different from the threat of postmodernism. Vocationalism and low academic standards are most conspicuously in evidence at the less prestigious campuses. Some faculty members in these less prestigious institutions may be largely immune from the poststructural currents coming from French intellectuals. ACTA thus suffers from a kind of organizational schizophrenia. It wants to attack the elite schools but shares with them a respect for broad humanist learning.

ACTA is also internally divided over the issues of political versus cultural conservatism. Many of its prominent backers are political liberals but cultural conservatives. Support for the Israeli state is an important benchmark; anything that smacks of an anti-Israeli bias is anathema to ACTA, even if one is otherwise a strong adherent to ACTA positions. ACTA, further, has not spoken out on the sciences and on scientific issues at all. To do so would risk raising issues that could prove embarrassing and highly divisive. Similar problems have bedeviled other conservatives. David Horowitz, for example, ran into trouble in Ohio with his political ally, state senator Larry Mumper, a cultural conservative, when he (Horowitz) said he did not think intelligent design should be taught at Ohio's universities. Conservatives were taken aback and suspected Horowitz of apostasy. ACTA has avoided evolution as an issue altogether: to speak out against intelligent design would alienate some conservatives, and nothing ACTA could say would satisfy ACTA's liberal critics anyway.

Another major ACTA thrust, which overlaps but is not entirely compatible with the cultural thrust, is the desire to achieve greater political balance at the major universities. The difficulty is that some of ACTA's donors, trustees, and backers are political liberals, such as Senator Joseph Lieberman (at the time a Democrat, now an independent, from Connecticut) and Martin Peretz, publisher of the *New Republic*. Does the goal of greater intellectual diversity include affirmative action for conservatives? ACTA, of course, favors viewpoint diversity but does not want explicit affirmative action for conservatives. Recently, ACTA has found a formula that has enabled it to act with greater decisiveness, calling on state legislatures to require universities to issue voluntary reports detailing their progress toward intellectual diversity goals.

ACTA has repudiated the Horowitz academic bill of rights as a public policy measure, but its new policy owes much to Horowitz's strategy. At a Manhattan Institute conference held at the Harvard Club in New York City in September 2005, ACTA president Anne D. Neal, in response to a question from the audience, said that she did not support Horowitz's bill of rights. Her response caused some consternation in the ranks of the conservative participants and drew pleasant surprise from her partner in debate, Dr. Roger Bowen, general secretary of the AAUP.

The third major impulse behind ACTA's activities has been internal governance reform of universities, including especially the idea that trustees should become the focal point for academic leadership. This concept has lacked clarity, however. The trustee members of ACTA can be divided, in turn, into three, not entirely compatible, groups. Some have focused on the association's pedagogical goals, urging universities to adopt more traditional courses in, for example, American history.[37] A second grouping of ACTA members who are themselves university trustees is interested in making universities into something more like private corporations. Still others have a more explicitly political agenda and are committed to the vague notion of getting rid of tenured radicals by getting rid of tenure. The focus on tenure is opposed by other ACTA members, on the pragmatic grounds that abolishing tenure would promote the unionization of university faculties. This would be anathema, for strong faculty unions would replicate at the university level the problems associated with strong teachers unions at the secondary and elementary levels. By abolishing tenure, moreover, the ACTA trustees might convert the AAUP into a stronger and more militant organization than it is today.

ACTA's internal conflicts show that it has arrived as a serious organization. Any broadly based educational interest group reflects competing interests that it strives to balance. The most serious potential fissure in ACTA is between the business leaders demanding accountability and the cultural elitists supporting the Western literary canon.

ACTA's position in the contemporary political landscape of higher education was evidenced in its tenth anniversary conference held in Washington in September 2005. Delegates from all parts of the country, including distinguished academics, university administrators, journalists, business leaders, a sprinkling of political figures from past Republican administrations, and donors, gathered in a generally upbeat and festive atmosphere to celebrate ACTA's achievements, to hear lively panel presentations, and to exchange views. The participants were not the marginalized figures practicing a politics of resentment as conservatives have sometimes been depicted.[38] The mood was cautiously optimistic. Speakers in the formal presentations and participants in conversations during the breaks were upbeat and distinctly happy cultural warriors. The message was that they have gotten the attention of the public and frightened their opponents. The liberals have been thrown onto the defensive at least temporarily. However, the forces of multiculturalism, value relativism, and postmodernism in the academy are still formidable enemies, and therefore they must keep up their efforts (and donations) as they fight the good fight.[39]

## Summary

Activating elite opinion, creating sustained media attention, and developing institutions have largely been achieved, and, along with this, key goals of the conservative movement have been attained. Conservatives constitute an active force at least in the organizational circles of the nation's capital. The impact on national policy has been weak to nonexistent, however. The states have seemed a more likely arena in which to fight some of the battles because the states have more direct involvement with higher education, at least the public colleges and universities. How has conservative advocacy made itself felt at the state level? We would now like to show how the issue of classroom bias has been employed in practice through a case study of the Pennsylvania hearings on academic freedom in 2005–06. Media attention created a climate in which the public had some awareness of "leftist faculty," an awareness that was kept alive and fanned by advocates such as Horowitz, the NAS, and ACTA. The interest groups provided the effort that raised the issue to public attention. But to have an impact on policy required a further step: a political champion. Horowitz found some potential allies with Republican congressmen, but they were unwilling to invest major political capital in a cause that was not widely endorsed by conservatives. Indeed, many conservatives were repelled by the idea of the federal government sticking its nose into curriculum matters. But Horowitz persevered and found at the state level the active political backing he needed.

# 7 | Conservative Activism in Higher Education: The Pennsylvania Hearings on Academic Freedom

Conservative activism on higher education issues has grown since the 1990s. Notable changes have occurred and some battles have been won, such as in the area of affirmative action in university admissions. California, Florida, and Texas curbed admissions policies relying on affirmative action in their public university systems. The California action came as a result of a referendum adopted by state voters, a ballot initiative backed by an African American member of the California Board of Regents, Ward Connelly. In Florida, gubernatorial and legislative action brought about significant change. The Texas developments came as a result of a federal appeals court ruling. Other states, including Michigan, have modified and limited, but not abandoned, their use of affirmative action in university admissions in the wake of two Supreme Court decisions in 2003. Christian-oriented student organizations have sought, and obtained, recognition as official student organizations with access to student activity fees on many campuses.

Opposition to embryonic stem cell research has limited federal funding to cell lines existing prior to August 9, 2001, the date on which President Bush authorized federal funds for existing cell lines. Conservatives have lobbied the federal government to sponsor research on the effects of sexual abstinence on academic performance in high school. Conservative causes in the field of education and research have made their way into the public dialogue and have achieved some degree of policy impact.

Yet the efforts to portray political bias in the classroom as a major problem have been notably less successful. Only a minority of the American public is convinced that bias in the classroom is a serious problem in American universities. The issue ranks fifth behind high tuition, binge drinking, crime on campus, and low educational standards as a concern among Americans, according to a recent survey by Neil Gross and Solon Simmons, and fewer than 10 percent of Americans think that political bias is the biggest problem facing higher education.[1] Nor did our own national survey find that college professors, even the very conservative, think that bias in the classroom is an important issue.

Why has classroom bias failed to have much of an impact? This chapter presents a case study of a situation in which the issue achieved some saliency and was the subject of an official legislative inquiry. A full-dress inquiry and a series of dramatic hearings were held across the state in 2005 and 2006. The conclusion was that bias is "rare," but that state colleges and universities should have effective grievance procedures in place so that students can complain if professors push their own political views inappropriately.

The main reason for the limited policy impact is that conservatives themselves do not agree on whether there is a problem, much less on what to do if a problem does arise in this area. The target of the inquiry—radicalism on campus—was fuzzy from the outset. Some conservative critics pointed to a reified "postmodernism" as the culprit. Postmodernism is, presumably, a blend of secularism and avant-garde pedagogy that disparages, and stands in opposition to, traditional Western values. Postmodernism, however, is a conception that grew out of the Western tradition itself and encompasses important Western values. We do not pause here to debate and define postmodernism, or modernism for that matter, nor to elaborate on our reasons for placing modernism and postmodernism securely within the Western cultural tradition. For our purposes, it suffices to note that postmodernism is not a concept readily grasped by politicians or by the general public. For that matter, academics themselves have some trouble knowing what postmodernism is and therefore knowing whether they are for or against it.

Even within the disciplines most familiar with postmodern thinking, the lines of demarcation between liberal and conservative positions are difficult to draw.[2] Are the "Old Moderns" (for example, Wolff, Stein, Eliot, Joyce, Hemingway, Pound, Faulkner, and Lawrence), who do not in general enjoy high favor and attention from today's humanities professors, different from the postmodernists? If so, how do they differ? Cultural conservatives and traditionalists in the humanities are not notably lucid on the point. The critics do not say whether the moderns are exempt from the ills of postmodernism or whether, in their view, the whole field of modern literature went to hell in a hand basket after the Victorians.

Nietzschean philosophy, which fosters value relativism, is the chief culprit according to certain cultural critics. However, if value relativism is subversive, the Western tradition has apparently undermined itself.[3] Other observers point to a kind of groupthink, which results from the absence of dissent within any social group that is too like-minded.[4] A tendency of this kind is potentially a serious problem for the academy, for on its face the argument has plausibility given the heavy preponderance of liberals over conservatives on college faculties. Elsewhere in this volume, both in chapter 5 and in chapter 8, we explore whether the evidence tends to confirm or to disconfirm the hypothesis of classroom misconduct (and we find the evidence for the hypothesis to be weak or nonexistent). It is plausible to suppose that faculty members, especially those at the elite institutions, tend to be irascible, independent-minded, and quarrelsome and rarely arrive at common opinions on any subject. They—the faculty members—may, like many of their fellow Americans, largely avoid or rarely think about politics as such, finding politics rather distasteful and focusing their energies on their own particular field. At any rate, conservatives (under one definition) are usually predisposed to be against government action as the solution to most problems. Failing a clear demonstration of the need for such, they are disinclined to rush to collective action. If government action is called for, the typical American conservative prefers to take steps at the state and local levels of government rather than at the national level (but then American conservatives are not conservative in the sense that, say, Edmund Burke was conservative, in that he presumed a strong state in his thinking).

Even if the problem of classroom bias could be demonstrated, conservatives would not first look to government for the solution. This is the root problem that has bedeviled the David Horowitz campaign from the outset. After opposing—and successfully placing some limits on—affirmative action in university admissions and hiring, conservatives have found it difficult to embrace the idea of "viewpoint diversity" if this means quotas, preferential treatment, or affirmative action for faculty conservatives.[5] Nevertheless, circumstances were such that in the summer of 2005 conservative activists in Pennsylvania saw, and seized, the opportunity to dramatize the issue of political bias on campus.

## From Federal to State Action

The state effort has to be seen against the backdrop of conservative efforts to affect federal policy. Middle East studies has been the only area that has presented a serious prospect of government intervention into curriculum matters in higher education. In the aftermath of the September 11 attacks, potential government restrictions on academic research, and thus on what is taught in the classroom, arose with respect to the renewal of federal funding for Middle East studies.[6] National politicians or federal government officials were not the initiators, but they were drawn in by one of the feuding academic factions that sought the help of politicians in battling its ideological opponents. In June 2003, Stanley Kurtz testified before the House of Representatives' Committee on Education and the Workforce that "Title VI–funded programs in Middle Eastern studies (and other area studies) tend to portray extreme and one-sided criticisms of American foreign policy."[7] As a result of this and other testimony, Representative Peter Hoekstra (R-Mich.) introduced legislation to bring Title VI funding of the Higher Education Act of 1965 for area and language programs under a new law called the International Studies and Higher Education Act (House Resolution 3077 in the 108th Congress).[8]

The troublesome part of the bill was that it proposed to create an International Higher Education Advisory Board, whose members would be appointed by congressional and executive branch officials. The board would be empowered to monitor funding for the program and to ensure that federal funds would go to programs that "reflect diverse perspectives and the full range of views." The measure passed the House but was blocked in the Senate.[9] Opponents of the measure from the Middle East studies area, from the major universities, from the Washington-based higher education associations, and from Congress immediately assailed various aspects of the proposal. In particular, they pointed to problems with the proposed board. The board's operations, even if modified to include only a limited review of a sample of academic programs across the country with the stated intent of only suggesting program "improvements," smacked of an ideological test in order for programs to qualify for funding. Senators Edward Kennedy (D-Mass.) and Tom Harkin (D-Iowa) vociferously opposed the bill, and it died in committee. The bill was reintroduced in the House of Representatives in 2005 but went nowhere.[10] National politicians were wary of injecting themselves into the middle of a highly fraught academic dispute.

On the Senate side, the most serious effort to back "intellectual diversity" on the nation's campuses probably came in April 2003 in the 108th Congress and was again sparked by controversies within the Middle East studies area. Senator Rick Santorum of Pennsylvania, the third-ranking Republican leader, announced, after he and several Republican colleagues met with a delegation of Jewish leaders from the Anti-Defamation League, the American Jewish

Organization, and other groups, that he planned to introduce legislation requiring ideological diversity on campus. He said that he would seek to cut federal funding for colleges and universities permitting professors, students, and student organizations to criticize Israel. In the face of strong opposition, Santorum backed off from his threat and did not introduce such legislation.[11] But he raised the issue, and this did not go unnoticed in his state.

## The Pennsylvania Campaign for Academic Freedom

David Horowitz, meanwhile, enthused by the success with the June 2005 statement on intellectual pluralism and aided intermittently by Anne Neal, president of the American Council of Trustees and Alumni (ACTA), refocused his efforts on the state legislatures. In particular, Horowitz had been trying to rally support for his bill of rights with state legislators in "red" states. A Republican majority usually meant that he could at least get a hearing. The June 2005 statement and the added publicity it brought him raised the stakes for Horowitz. Then in July 2005 came a breakthrough. He attracted the attention of Pennsylvania state representative Gibson C. Armstrong (R-Lancaster County), who had grown increasingly upset by what he saw as leftism on the state's campuses. Armstrong and his staff had received numerous complaints from students about professors who made sneering references to President Bush. Armstrong, a veteran and graduate of the Naval Academy, had lost friends in the U.S. peacekeeping mission in Mogadishu in the 1990s and had been enraged by the comments of a Columbia assistant professor who, on the eve of the Iraq War, had called for a "thousand Mogadishus" to teach American imperialists a lesson.

Armstrong had noticed a comment in Horowitz's blog that called attention to an incident at a Penn State branch campus. This became the precipitating event that Armstrong invoked repeatedly with his legislative colleagues to demonstrate the problem. The incident had allegedly taken place one week before the 2004 presidential election. Horowitz claimed that a biology professor had shown Michael Moore's film *Fahrenheit 9/11* in his biology class and then suggested that students vote for Senator Kerry. This was the last straw for Armstrong, who got in touch with Horowitz, and together they worked up a proposal to investigate political bias in the state's public colleges and universities. The Republicans were in the majority, so Armstrong could make it happen. In the summer and fall of 2005, Armstrong worked hard to shepherd the measure first through the Republican caucus and then, with the aid of the Republican leadership, through the legislature.

Pennsylvania, a state with a large electoral vote and competitive two-party politics, adopted House Resolution 177 in the fall of 2005, by almost a straight party-line vote of 110-90. The resolution authorized an inquiry into the commonwealth's public colleges and universities by a Select Committee on Academic Freedom in Higher Education. The resolution's language did not, in fact, draw precisely on the language of Horowitz's academic bill of rights in setting out its focus, but it was inspired and influenced by Horowitz's concerns.[12] The select committee was not authorized to draft legislation; rather, it was authorized to conduct hearings "on matters relating to the academic atmosphere and the degree to which faculty have the opportunity to instruct and students have the opportunity to learn in an environment conducive to the pursuit of knowledge and truth and the expression of independent thought at the state-related and state-owned colleges, universities, and community colleges."

The hearings should seek to determine, but not be limited to, questions such as "whether (1) faculty are hired, fired, promoted, and granted tenure on the basis of their professional competence and subject matter knowledge; . . . (2) students have an academic atmosphere, quality life on campus, reasonable access to affordable course materials that create an atmosphere conducive to learning, the development of critical thinking, and the exploration and expression of independent thought and that the students are evaluated based on their subject knowledge or ability to defend their perspective in various courses; and (3) academic freedom and the right to explore and express independent thought is [sic] available to and practiced freely by faculty and students." If a problem was found, the committee was to suggest what, if any, corrective action by the legislature might be appropriate.

Despite the clear limits, and despite the anodyne language, the measure was highly controversial from the start. The driving force behind the legislation, Representative Armstrong, was convinced that professors routinely introduced extraneous political matters into class discussions and intimidated students who tried to express opposing views in class. The biology professor who was said to have shown Michael Moore's *Fahrenheit 9/11* was, in Armstrong's view, merely the tip of a larger iceberg. The showing of the film was a clear violation of the 1940 policy statement of the American Association of University Professors (AAUP) on academic freedom and tenure, said Armstrong, for academic freedom was limited to the teaching of subject matter within one's professional competence. Armstrong reminded observers that the 1940 AAUP statement cautioned against introducing controversial material unrelated to the subject being taught.

Armstrong and his Republican colleagues were angered by their Democratic colleagues' attacks on the inquiry before it had even begun. The Democratic members of the committee, in an attempt to head off potential abuses by the committee, had devised a strategy that included the attempt to isolate the more militant Armstrong from his Republican colleagues. While the Democrats sought to depict Armstrong as an extremist, the Republicans harbored hopes of winning at least one of the Democratic members to their side.

The Republican speaker of the House chose moderate representative Thomas L. Stevenson, a senior member of the Republican team well liked by members of both parties, to chair the select committee. This was an implicit acknowledgment that Armstrong would be more effective in championing his cause if he were not running the committee. Minority leaders chose Lawrence H. Curry, a moderate Democrat with prior experience as a faculty member in Pennsylvania's higher education system, to lead the Democrats on the committee. The majority Republican Party was assigned seven members and the Democratic Party was assigned five members.

The select committee adopted a strict set of procedural rules to ensure a decorous and relatively bipartisan inquiry. The potential charges of McCarthyism were already in the air, and neither side wanted a donnybrook from the hearings. The Democrats would have been happy to break up the inquiry and embarrass the conservative Republicans if they could do so without risk of escalating the issue and giving conservatives a stronger voice within the Republican Party leadership. Indeed, they risked a more serious inquiry if they only played a spoiler role. The Republicans wanted to find evidence of liberal proselytizing but did not want to damage the commonwealth's colleges and universities. They wanted publicity for the inquiry, but not so much publicity that it would hurt the efforts of the state's colleges to recruit top students and faculty. It was a balancing act from the start: the Republicans wanted to demonstrate a problem, but not one serious enough to damage the state's colleges and universities. Democrats wanted to derail the proceedings, but not look like ideologues and partisans.

Procedural safeguards of various kinds were adopted before the hearings began. For example, no names of particular individuals or mention of specific courses that could identify individual professors at any school were to be allowed in the testimony. The hearings were to be, and were in fact, run with decorum and civility despite the intense feelings on the issue. Four hearings in different parts of the commonwealth were scheduled. A report was to be delivered to the full House on June 30, 2006, or in any case no later than the end of the legislative session at the end of November 2006.

Democrats in the legislature, who had opposed the bill from the start, made no secret of their opposition. They believed that there was no problem serious enough to merit the inquiry. They sent e-mails to their friends, allies, and constituents, warning against the dangers posed by the hearings and urging the higher education community to mobilize opposition to it. The national education associations—the AAUP and the state chapter of the AAUP—and representatives of the local teachers union needed no prompting to organize against HR 177. The select committee to them was a "truth squad" organized not to ensure the absence of politics in the classroom, but on the contrary to ensure that conservative politics were present in the classroom. Conservatives saw an opportunity to focus national attention on the issue of ideological orthodoxy in the universities. Conservatives depicted the mobilization of opposition to HR 177 before any testimony was heard as an illustration of liberal paranoia and a vindication of the inquiry. The stage was set for a showdown. Reporters, lobbyists, and observers (including ourselves) from around the nation flocked to Pennsylvania.[13]

The showdown over HR 177 proved to be something of an anticlimax. The ideological tensions between the Republicans and the Democrats, though obvious at the hearings, never erupted into an unseemly spectacle. Both sides drew back from the brink, and in this outcome the hearings probably served an important larger purpose for the nation. No one has seemed eager to repeat the experience in other states. The brawl that pundits and media observers had looked forward to, and that some partisans on each side hoped for and others feared but saw as inevitable, never quite materialized. Instead, the representatives did their work, everyone had the opportunity to speak, vigorous debate took place, but the debates did not disintegrate into an unseemly spectacle. The media soon lost interest, and coverage dwindled after the first two hearings.

The first hearing was held at the University of Pittsburgh on November 9–10, 2005, and was confined largely to preliminary sparring between the committee members and staking out the lines of questioning with university representatives. The second took place in Philadelphia at Temple University on January 9–10, 2006, which featured David Horowitz, ACTA president Anne Neal, National Association of Scholars president Steven Balch, along with Temple University president David Adamany, students, some faculty members, and others. This hearing yielded the most fireworks of any of the four hearings. In May 2006, between the third hearing in March and the projected fourth hearing, three of the Republicans on the select committee, including Representative Gibson Armstrong and Chair Tom Stevenson, were defeated in their Republican primaries. Voters were caught up in an anti-incumbent mood and were incensed by the legislature raising its own pay and then rescinding the raise, only to hand it out again in the form of expense allowances. A grassroots organization, Clean Sweep, sprang up and roiled Pennsylvania politics through the 2006 congressional elections and beyond. Incumbent politicians became something of an endangered species in the state. In this climate, the academic freedom hearings lost steam. As a result of the primary defeats of Gibson and Stevenson, much of the drama was gone. Moreover, the second hearing failed to produce significant evidence either of classroom bias or a conspiracy on the part of the Republican legislators to force conservatives on the universities.

Neither side could establish the existence of a serious threat to academic freedom in Pennsylvania's higher education system. Academic officials, usually the president or the provost, testified that there were few, if any, complaints from students about proselytizing by professors at their institutions. President David W. Adamany of Temple University stated that in his five years at Temple he had received numerous complaints from students about food, class size, dormitories, and numerous other matters but could not recall a single complaint of classroom bias from any student (and none from a faculty member about his or her colleagues). President Francine G. McNairy of Millersville University had received seven complaints in nearly six years on the job, of which only three could be construed as having to do with political pressures in the classroom (and two of those complaints were quickly resolved). Associate Provost Blannie Bowen of Penn State found records of thirteen complaints since the 2000 academic year. He had conducted an e-mail survey of all of the Penn State branch campuses and the main campus to come up with the information. Half of the thirteen complaints he uncovered had been found to be without merit after investigation. At Penn State, nonetheless, Bowen announced to the legislators in the May 2006 hearings in Harrisburg that the faculty had decided to change its grievance procedure to make the process of filing a student complaint easier and more transparent. This faculty senate action, he said, had taken place in April 2006.

A similar story came from University of Pittsburgh provost James V. Maher. There were few student complaints, and Pitt devoted strenuous efforts to ensuring that faculty members understood their professional responsibilities. Students, if aggrieved, had clear channels through which to file complaints and would receive a fair hearing if they did so. Under questioning by Armstrong, Maher appeared to concede that he would have no trouble with Horowitz's idea of an academic bill of rights if its wording corresponded to the June 2005 ACE (American Council on Education) statement. Maher said he preferred the ACE statement to Horowitz's statement, but, when pressed, he was unable to specify the language of the ACE statement he liked or the Horowitz language to which he objected. President Adamany of Temple University testified that he had not even heard of the ACE statement. The arcana of Washington's ideological battles seemed remote from the real world of Pennsylvania's universities.

Democratic members elicited denials that there were problems from the university witnesses. Under friendly questioning, the Democrats patiently drew out the university administrators on the procedural safeguards and the grievance procedures and mechanisms in place at their universities. Republicans for their part pointed to the fear of reprisals as a reason for the apparent discrepancy between the numerous informal complaints received from students by the committee and the paucity of formal complaints testified to by the university officials. Representative Armstrong pointed to "more than a dozen" complaints received from Temple University students by the select committee staff but could not reveal names and courses under the committee's strict rules of procedure outlawing the mention of individual names. His Democratic colleagues were openly skeptical. One representative summed up the Democrats' views by dubbing the proceedings "the legislative equivalent to the hunt for Bigfoot."

Armstrong got somewhat greater traction, and won some points, when he questioned witnesses on whether they regarded the hearings as a waste of time or as a threat to academic freedom. Witnesses critical of the hearings, when questioned about what in the conduct of the hearings actually constituted a threat to their academic freedom, could not specify any threat. Witnesses critical of the hearings were obliged to concede that the hearings were being conducted fairly. When questioned closely about what precise language in HR 177 was a threat to academic freedom, no one could identify any threatening language.

Temple president Adamany, a veteran of twenty-one years as a president or senior officer of state universities and skilled in dealing with legislators, effectively rebutted the idea that the universities were resisting or in any way subverting the inquiry when he testified:

> *Dr. Adamany:* Mr. Chairman, I want to extend my thanks to you and your colleagues in the select committee for holding a hearing on this very important subject of the student academic freedom rights on our campus. Some have suggested that the creation of your committee and the conduct of this hearing is [sic] a threat to academic freedom. I do not share that view. Indeed it is my belief that all subjects are appropriate for discussion by the elected representatives of the people. Moreover, since

Temple is a state-related university, the people may take a special interest in this university and its affairs.[14]

Later at the hearing at Temple, Representative Gibson Armstrong took another run at the issue with President Adamany. This time, the issue was not the classroom but faculty rallies and the general intellectual climate on campus:

*Representative Armstrong:* Recently, as part of a faculty forum, Dissent in America, there was a faculty union forum . . . to oppose House Resolution 177, which is why we're here today. Are you aware of that?

*President Adamany:* I didn't think I heard that there was a rally, but that would seem to be perfectly appropriate.

*Representative Armstrong:* Is it appropriate to rally the faculty against the government?

*President Adamany:* When you say "to rally the faculty," certainly the university did not rally the faculty. It was a meeting of people in the faculty to take a position on a matter of public concern. And it seems to me that all such rallies, conservative or liberal, are entirely appropriate ... I'm not endorsing the rally, I'm merely saying that it is appropriate for citizens to rally about matters of concern.

*Representative Armstrong:* But is it appropriate for faculty to present a one-sided forum?

*President Adamany:* I certainly can't be responsible—the university can't be responsible—for the control of meetings by individuals.

*Representative Armstrong:* This was a faculty senate–sponsored event.

*President Adamany:* Well, the faculty senate has the same right as everybody else has to hold a meeting and express their views . . . I can't control the faculty senate. And I might have disapproved of what they did if I knew more about it, but their right to do this is what I think is critical.[15]

This exchange was more pointed than most, which tended to follow closely the etiquette of the formal legislative hearing. The elaborate courtesies, "Mr. Chairman," "Thank you, sir, for your most helpful testimony," "We are grateful for your taking the time," were the governing norms. Republican members agreed with their Democratic colleagues that the legislature "did not want to be a school board for our state universities." University administrators agreed that faculty members should teach their own subject and not inject their personal political views into their classes. The university administrators were urged to incorporate the principles of the 1940 AAUP policy statement into their faculty handbooks, university policy documents, and guidelines. In most cases such guidelines were already in effect. Much time was spent on questions about the dissemination of guidelines, openness of procedures and channels of communication, and effectiveness of existing procedures. A consensus seemed to emerge among committee members over modest measures such as the need for clear guidelines for students to file complaints if their grades were affected by their political views. But even here, no one would think the legislature had any role in how such steps or measures should be implemented by the colleges and universities.

On the central issues obliquely referred to in the bland wording of HR 177—namely, whether there was "imbalance" in the classroom—the hearing had no answer. Or, more accurately, there was neither evidence that such bias existed nor a clear understanding of what question was being addressed. For if the legislature was not to "act as a school board for our universities," what was the purpose of the hearings? The basic confusion of purpose that lay at the heart of the academic bill of rights (to the extent that HR 177 meant to incorporate the Horowitz idea) became apparent. How could the state legislature take some ill-defined remedial action if, at the same time, it denied that legislatures should play a role in internal university affairs? The idea of a bill of rights appeared simultaneously to call for official action to deal with a serious problem and to deny that government intervention was appropriate. As Horowitz testified at the January 10 hearing at Temple University,

> It seems that government intervention is good when it comes to securing some rights and some freedoms, but not in intellectual rights and intellectual freedoms. The fact is that all the legislation that we, as proponents of . . . intellectual diversity, proposed has been in the form of resolutions.[16]

Government should not legislate, but it should "urge" universities to act in certain ways. Horowitz's testimony was marked by this ambivalence over the role of government. He might have helped his cause had he made a specific analogy to a "sense of the Congress" resolution of the sort that was involved in the June 2005 negotiations with the American Council on Education, but he did not clearly make this point. His testimony veered from calling for a resolution only (no law or regulatory action) to calling for no legislative action at all and then to appealing for additional government funding to establish an alternative faculty. The idea of an alternative faculty was to have a replacement for, or at least new professors to compete with, the present faculty or perhaps to have new faculty who would constitute a small department, similar to a women's studies program. This was a strange position for a defender of the traditional disciplines, but Horowitz is more of an idea man than a practical reformer. His definition of the problem was at times expansive (faculties are so hopelessly leftist that an alternate faculty should be created) and at times limited (most faculty are well intentioned, committed scholars who are intimidated by an activist leftist minority that runs things).

At one point he called for changing the student course evaluation forms to include reference to "intellectual diversity, respect for political differences, and observance of professional standards." With this alone, "I guarantee you will cure 75 percent of the problem. This doesn't require legislation; it requires doing a report and urging the university to do that."[17]

At yet another point, Horowitz seemed to dismiss the whole problem as a mere matter of public relations for the universities: "You have a public relations issue here that you need to insulate the university from. It's not that hard. Embrace intellectual diversity; make sure that the administration is seeing that its professors are professional in the classroom."[18]

To Horowitz's critics, such solicitous advice can seem disingenuous, an example of how he can wrap himself in innocuous-sounding rhetoric while waging a public demolition campaign against the universities. He remains a puzzle to observers, who testify that he can be charming and learned when he is on his good behavior but can suddenly flip a mental switch and turn into a fiery attacker. The tactic of some of the Democratic representatives, most notably co-chair Lawrence Curry, was to provoke him, and in this they succeeded.

Most serious, perhaps, for Horowitz's credibility and for the cause he had come to symbolize, was the damage he inflicted on himself when he became rattled as a witness under sharp questioning from several Democratic representatives. He was forced to admit mistakes in some of the stories he publicized on his blog, and he raised doubts about his whole approach by appearing to be indifferent to the details and the accuracy of his reports. Consider the following exchange:

*Representative Yudichak:* Because [of] everything we found in the committee, it has become hard to document the charges that are made. . . . In your testimony, you mentioned a biology class at Penn State about an anonymous student making a charge that a professor went into . . . an anti-Bush lecture. There was another charge that was reported in the Pennsylvania magazine about the Michael Moore film being shown in a biology class, which after further investigation, was incorrect. Where

Shawna Mosier, who is the leader of the Young Americans for Freedom on that university, actually did some checking, and which apparently the other organizations, including your own, did not do, and found out that it was the Michael Moore film *Bowling for Columbine*, shown in a sociology class, not in a biology class. So when these charges are refuted and can't be substantiated, that's a concern for me. . . . This is about data and higher education.

*Mr. Horowitz:* A staffer told me this, and I actually—it happens that I spoke afterwards at Columbia, and the student told me exactly the same thing about a civil engineering class. It's neither here nor there. There is no way that every student's complaint is going to be a valid one. It is very easy to get this information if the university will get it. I have a staff of two. I have two people for a national campaign.

*Representative Yudichak:* That was in—the charges that—

*Mr. Horowitz:* I am sixty-seven years old today. I would not be sitting here if I thought I could invent a problem. I am a writer. I have three *New York Times* bestsellers. I have a book coming out in three weeks. I have a million things to do, in addition to which I live in California, so I could swim every day outdoors this time of year. I wouldn't be here if I weren't persuaded from twenty years of walking around campuses and seeing this.

*Representative Yudichak:* The charge against the Penn State biology class was incorrect?

*Mr. Horowitz:* Yes. I think that was incorrect.

*Representative Yudichak:* Thank you. I'm finished.

Or consider this exchange between Horowitz and Representative Lawrence Curry, the Democratic co-chair of the select committee and subcommittee:

*Representative Curry:* How do you know that the student in Foot Hills got a D because of her point of view, as opposed to what she answered on—

*Mr. Horowitz:* It was a he. Basically, what I did for the student was I put an article up on my website called "Intimidating Liberals in Academia," or something like that, and I gave him his say. And in my view, that has an impact. If the *Philadelphia Inquirer* covers some of these problems, a lot of them would go away, but it isn't going to do it, so I do it. I don't know if a student's view was accurate. I gave him a platform.

*Representative Curry:* Why did the student get the D?

*Mr. Horowitz:* The student was a pro-choice student.

*Representative Curry:* Yes. You've said that.

*Mr. Horowitz:* And his professor was a pro-life conservative. This is the student's claim.

*Representative Curry:* The student's claim. You didn't see the exam?

*Mr. Horowitz:* No. What I did was I printed—

*Representative Curry:* So you don't know really whether it's—

*Mr. Horowitz:* No. We had another case there, which a student was involved in, which was actually an Iraqi student who was being harassed. No, but I allowed him the platform.

*Representative Curry:* But the point is, you don't know why he got that grade. But you say he got that grade because he was being—

*Mr. Horowitz:* No. He said it. I allowed him to say it, and I repeated it, and I said it.

*Representative Curry:* Earlier we talked about the question of a waste of time, which my colleague has just answered, but a concern I have is the lack of good evidence and misrepresentation and vagueness being presented both in the resolution we have to operate under and in some of the statements we hear. In one of your essays . . . you go on in this to recite about, what was raised earlier, to recite about the showing of *Fahrenheit 9/11* before the election. Now we know that that didn't happen. Now we know that it was another film in a sociology course and probably appropriately, but it wasn't *Fahrenheit 9/11*. Are you going to retract that in a public setting?

*Mr. Horowitz:* I did. I have already retracted it on my website. You don't know that the *Columbine* [film] was appropriately shown. I will tell you, I've interviewed lots of students who have *Columbine* shown. What is appropriate is, you show *Bowling for Columbine* and you—

*Representative Curry:* My question is—

*Mr. Horowitz:*—invite students on the web at "Spinsanity" and other very liberal sites. Michael Moore has been taken apart as a liar. Students need to have the critical apparatus when they deal with it.

*Representative Curry:* Listen, we better be careful about who we call liars when we have public statements asserting something that we know not to be true.

*Mr. Horowitz:* I didn't know that wasn't true until two days ago.

*Representative Curry:* But you asserted it.

*Mr. Horowitz:* So what? Everything you say is absolutely the gospel?

*Representative Curry:* I would think someone who is a writer and a scholar would be very careful to stay as close to the truth as they could.

*Mr. Horowitz:* Not only do I stay as close to the truth as I can, but I'm one of the few people that I know, in this public field, who immediately corrects whenever somebody points it out. I'm sorry that that was inaccurate. . . . I gave you an example, and I will give you the signature of a biology class where a professor went on for twenty minutes about the war in Iraq and why George Bush is a bad person and anybody who supports him is bad. That's a biology class. It's the same thing; in this case, I can give you a name.

*Representative Curry:* But the point I'm making is that on a number [of] occasions, I have been asked about *Fahrenheit 9/11* in a biology class before the election, and it was untrue.

Curry went on to attempt to pin the witness down about whether a specific episode did or did not happen. Horowitz's response suggested impatience and lack of concern with the specific veracity of his claims so long as they fit public perceptions. The two men then tried to define what government action, if any, was appropriate.

*Mr. Horowitz:* No, but a comparable thing did happen, in a biology class, a professor went off on George Bush. The point is the story would have no credibility if people thought professors were behaving professionally in the classroom, but people are well aware that they are not doing that. And they are also aware that universities aren't doing much about it. That's what we're here for. I apologize for the inaccuracy of that.

*Representative Curry:* Representatives and public commentators need to be responsible too.

*Mr. Horowitz:* Like I said, among public commentators, I don't know too many who admit mistakes as rapidly and as forthright[ly] as I do. And I don't know any who don't make mistakes.

*Representative Curry:* Let me [say] just one final thing . . . about the attention [being paid] to the gender and the race, you know, students of a gender and students of [a] race. [We] don't have much choice in that. We do have some choice in intellectual diversity. And I think there is a difference. The government has a responsibility to look out for the citizens who may be of color or who may be of a different gender. The intellectual diversity is a much more complicated issue and not so easily inserted in the regulations as you propose.

*Mr. Horowitz:* I'm not proposing any regulations. Just imagine how you would feel if the universities were entirely—like 90 percent of professors were—Republicans, and they were sending out e-mails, as you were told yesterday, on the Temple University—using the Temple University e-mail—to all students, inviting them to a rally, the theme of which is that students who protest the war are traders [traitors]. You would be—

> *Representative Curry:* Have you talked to the senders of—
>
> *Mr. Horowitz:* You would be outraged.
>
> *Representative Curry:* Have you talked to the senders of those e-mails?
>
> *Mr. Horowitz:* You know, I'm giving you a hypothetical example. I shouldn't have mentioned the testimony. I don't know that he got those e-mails, if that's what you're asking. I'm saying, how would you react if professors at your state universities, like the professors at Columbia, who were wishing for a million Mogadishians [sic], and how Representative Armstrong is at Mogadishu and he has buddies who were killed there, wishing for the massacre of American troops? He just got his tenure at Columbia, this professor. How would you like it [if] you had as many right-winged professors on a university campus, in a university setting calling Democrats traders [traitors]?
>
> *Representative Curry:* I think before we climb on a soap box, we ought to know what the real facts are, and I look forward to hearing what they are.

The Pennsylvania hearings ended with a whimper, not a bang. The defeat of Armstrong in the May 2006 Republican primary and of committee chair Tom Stevenson left the Republican side demoralized and in disarray. The press of other legislative business kept the committee from completing its report by June 30, the initial deadline. Action was deferred until the end of the session in November 2006. The final report summarized the committee's findings in these terms: "The Committee reviewed testimony from each sector of public higher education and determined that academic freedom violations are rare."[19] But it did recommend that public colleges and universities ensure that clear procedures are in place for students to express grievances if they feel that their professors are violating student rights to academic freedom. The committee could agree on nothing beyond these general statements and simply included additional comments by individual committee members interpreting the results of the inquiry as they chose. David Horowitz had his own conspiracy theory, blaming Democratic representative Lawrence Curry for subverting the hearing.[20]

Each side scored small victories. The Democrats fended off any serious attack on the public universities. The Republicans got testimony about one-sided teaching on the record and on public interest television. Universities and colleges were happy to reaffirm their commitment to high professional standards, student rights, and academic freedom. The universities did a creditable job of defending themselves, although the best tactic seemed to be to avoid provoking the representatives or engaging in arguments with unfriendly legislators. The universities could have made a stronger case for political debate and engagement in the universities, but they largely chose to avoid open engagement in favor of vigorous political debate on campus, suggesting instead or implying that professors were nonpartisan professionals not much interested in politics.

The legislators conducted the hearings for the most part with dignity and restraint. Witnesses, though occasionally idiosyncratic or opinionated, for their part avoided polemics. A host of other pressing issues emerged to dominate the Pennsylvania legislative agenda and to absorb the voters' attention. The hearings in the end did what they promised: they explored the situation. The hearings neither discovered nor created a crisis in Pennsylvania's higher education system. None of militant combatants on either side in the campus culture wars could claim victory; yet in their own eyes, both sides felt in some measure vindicated.

## Summary

The arguments over politics in the classroom have originated in society's wider political battles. Liberals, or at least the more militant of them, see conservatives as wanting to insinuate their agenda into every institutional sector and particularly into the universities as the last bastion of liberal influence. All conservatives are cast as populists eager to subvert elite institutions. This fear of a right-wing conspiracy dissipated somewhat after the Democrats regained control of Congress in 2006 and as prospects seem bright for a Democratic capture of the presidency in 2008. Conservatives, for their part, tend to view the academy as a radical stronghold, and the more militant conservatives see academics as playing politics and trying to undermine traditional American values while pretending to be nonpartisan. But conservative parents are as eager as liberal parents to get their children into the best colleges and universities.

How Americans view higher education is much more complicated than the polemics portray. The difference between sound pedagogy and advocacy in the classroom was repeatedly touched on in the Pennsylvania hearings, but never quite squarely faced nor convincingly argued. Serious observers contend that the battle over classroom bias is a spurious one, a reflection of rhetorical confusion.[21] Teachers must teach something—that is, ideas, approaches to the material, arguments—and ideas about politics or broad political themes should not be excluded. Students are capable of choosing what they want to study and with whom. Others insist that it is easy to distinguish inappropriate from appropriate political analysis in the classroom, and administrators should simply come down hard on those who violate professional norms. But one seldom encounters, and we did not see it much unfortunately in the testimony, the insistence that students should study certain obligatory course material. Among such material, knowledge of politics, rule of law, constitutional history, and democratic theory should be required in accord with the idea of a liberal arts education. What the curriculum should be in the state's colleges is certainly a pedagogical question that faculty members should debate and resolve as a professional right—and duty. But the kind of curriculum offered in the state's colleges is also a matter on which citizens in a democracy (and their elected representatives) have a right to express an opinion.

It would have been interesting if the hearings had dug deeper into this kind of question—if, for example, both the educators and the politicians had had enough confidence in each other and enough knowledge of the other's roles to have discussed the topic of curriculum openly, thoughtfully, and candidly. And it would have been illuminating if each had credited the good sense of the state's citizens to have permitted a more profound debate. But perhaps this would be asking too much from a legislative hearing and from the political process. Overall, there is little doubt that politics and the political process performed well in this case. The hearings were carried on educational television and attracted some public attention. The hearings did produce an outcome that all parties could live with, even if no one was fully satisfied. The hearings largely disposed of the issue, deciding that the problem was not serious enough to require legislation or other state action. At the same time, the universities, in making the case that they are not politicized, implicitly conceded that they could be more transparent in their procedures, and they promised to be attentive to potential student grievances in the future. They had no trouble in affirming that diversity of viewpoints was and is a vital priority for their institutions.

However, the educators perhaps overstressed the "easy" arguments, namely, that the state's colleges and universities prepare students for the economy, for competitiveness, for the professions. Stressing vocational and utilitarian objectives, some of the spokesmen from higher education implied a distaste for politics and fostered the pretense that knowledge is an objective, nonpolitical activity. Witnesses on occasion implied, or stated, that the hearings were a waste of time (when baited by Representative Armstrong, who found some traction by posing the question directly, "Do you think these hearings are a waste of time?").

The most effective witness for the universities, in our view, was President David Adamany of Temple. He struck the right note, affirming that he had no higher duty than to discuss important public policy issues with the elected representatives of the people. (Politicians recognize, and appreciate, someone skilled in their own art.) Adamany also joined the issue of debate on campus directly, arguing that the universities, including students and professors, should be debating important public issues. We agree with his argument. To shy away from debate does a disservice to the cause of liberal education and to the university's responsibilities to be centers of debate and discussion. But at the same time, it is clear that Adamany's strong advocacy for speech is not what comes naturally to the college president. College and university administrators are much more likely to be timorous and to see only the dangers and the downside of fostering genuine political debate on their campus. One small example of this point: prior to one of the Pennsylvania hearings, we attended a small luncheon with Representative Armstrong, a senior administrative official of a Pennsylvania educational institution, and several Pennsylvania professors. The conversation turned at one point to the case of a professor who had posted a campaign slogan on the door of his office. The administrator declared with some pride that he had strode to the professor's office and personally demanded the removal of the slogan, the implication being that "there's no (partisan) politics going on around here!" Representative Armstrong seemed slightly puzzled by this declaration, but before we could explore the point, the conversation veered off in another direction.[22]

Trying to determine whether a curriculum is inappropriate or slanted inevitably runs into the sometimes rarified disputes over pedagogy that are routine within the academy. It is difficult for the outsider to follow the at times arcane debates over pedagogy that roil the contemporary university. As we see in chapter 6, the politicians at the national level, even Republicans who feel that universities are one-sided, usually want to steer clear of the academy's internal ideological quarrels. State governments are more directly involved with all aspects of public higher education, including what kinds of degree programs are offered and what is taught in those programs. But state politicians, the Pennsylvania hearings suggest, are also wary of stepping too heavily into the university's core functions such as teaching, research, and hiring staff. Legislators do not want to act, in Representative Armstrong's phrase, as the "school board" for the public universities.

Colleges and universities are large and powerful institutions, they are expensive to operate, and they confer benefits for those who are fortunate enough to have earned valuable credentials. The state universities are probably more vulnerable to political pressures than are the elite private institutions. If the public universities are perceived to be elite institutions that pay high salaries to professors who disparage community values or if universities are perceived to serve only the interests of the wealthy, they will become targets for criticism. If the universities are seen as having only liberal faculty members, the problems will be exacerbated. Budgets could be cut by conservative state legislators. The state universities could be tempted to raise tuition and to become more like their private counterparts, but they do not really want to abandon their traditional base of state support.

It would be rash to conclude that political bias in the universities is finished as an issue. But there has been a lessening of intense political interest in the issue in Congress, and the Pennsylvania hearings fizzled out without demonstrating the existence of a problem. Legislators in other states are still debating the issue of political bias, but none has taken action; like their Pennsylvania colleagues, they apparently prefer to finesse the issue. But finessing issues is part of the political process and part of the invaluable service that our politicians render to society. Politicians sustain legitimacy by listening to grievances, by debating issues vigorously, and by being wise enough to take no action when doing so would be a mistake. The debate over HR 177 in Pennsylvania has raised, but not fully resolved, the fears about bias in the classroom. Now we turn to analysis of some of the questions asked, but not answered, in the Pennsylvania hearings.

# 8

## Much Ado about Little:
## Student Perspectives on Classroom Bias

In previous chapters, we discuss the political attitudes of professors and see how activists, education associations, and political figures view the issue of political bias in the universities. Now we shift the focus to what, in fact, is going on in the classrooms and on campuses across the country, looking in this chapter at how students view the issues we have been discussing.

Although professors tend to be political liberals (as has been the case for many years), do these attitudes intrude on the classroom? What do students think? This is not an issue that has been researched as thoroughly as professors' attitudes, but we rely, as best we can, on the body of work that does exist, on surveys of student attitudes, on our own student interviews and focus groups, as well as on our own direct classroom experiences extending over many years.

### Students as Educational Consumers

The commercial metaphor of students as consumers is not a favorite concept with us, but there is little doubt that it accurately describes a good deal of what goes on in colleges and universities. Students choose what they want to study, professors treat them as valued customers and cater to their preferences, and colleges and universities compete vigorously with other institutions to gain market share. Much of this is distasteful and at odds with a more elevated conception of the educational mission. What happens in a classroom should be something quite different from a routine commercial transaction. The professor has a higher obligation to define what education is than merely to cater to student "needs," as though these were readily identified by every matriculated student. Certainly, however, what students think of their professors and how they assess their educational experiences and aspirations are matters of critical importance to college teachers and administrators.

As shown in chapter 5, college professors themselves by and large do not think they are biased in class, but do students also perceive little or no political bias in the classroom? We should begin by recognizing that young people in general are not wholly candid in their dealings with older adults. Students have long been accustomed to appear to oblige their elders, while in fact getting their own way. As Louis Menand wryly notes,

> Students' heads have been designed through millions of years of evolutionary development to be impervious to hammering. . . . Concern about advocacy in the classroom seems to me to underestimate profoundly the good sense of college students. Students know perfectly well when they're being expected to toe somebody's line. They've spent their entire lives reading these kinds of signals from grown-ups, and they figure out pretty quickly Professor W insists on finding traces of patriarchal discourse in every text. . . . Students know perfectly well what their professor's take on the subject is, and if they find that take disagreeable or uninteresting, they advise their friends to register for someone else's course.[1]

Rare is the student who does not have some idea of the "hobby horses" of his or her professors. Most students quickly deduce whether Professor X believes that George III was or was not insane, what Professor Y thinks caused the French Revolution, or how Professor Z feels about the dangers or benefits of globalization. The Russian history major has heard from friends, and is ready to laugh at, professor so and so's standard quip about Catherine the Great and her horse. Students usually know or guess (correctly or incorrectly) something about the professor's views even if the professor does not directly state his or her beliefs in so many words. Most students are savvy and shrewd, even though as undergraduates they are less experienced and conversant about the topics they study than their professors. The students of today are rarely bashful, and few are easily intimidated. Students vote with their feet to avoid courses or professors they dislike. Unfavorable student evaluations create anxiety on the part of their teachers, especially those who are struggling to achieve tenure. Even among the tenured, negative evaluations are seldom ignored entirely (and deans have used course evaluations as weapons to ensure that faculty members do not get too uppity). The students of today have access to their professors via e-mail, and many students regularly pepper their teachers with e-mail queries and comments. Students are encouraged to question their professors, and they rarely have problems expressing their own views to their teachers in or out of the classroom.

Two of this volume's authors have returned to the classroom after some years in nonteaching positions, and we have been impressed by the energy and forcefulness of the present-day students. They do not fit the image of passive learners. Our younger colleague believes that his two elders are pulling his leg when he is told of the reserved, respectful students of a bygone era. No doubt he is right to reject the idea that American college students were ever quietly deferential to authority figures.

Students do not arrive at college in an unformed state. They arrive with values and conceptions of morality, religion, and the ultimate meaning of life. Students, in fact, enter college with deeply rooted belief systems that are highly resistant to change. This was indeed one of Allan Bloom's major complaints about students of the 1960s compared to earlier generations; the modern student arrived at college believing that he already had vast experiences of life and doubting that a stodgy professor had much to teach him (certainly not about the birds and the bees). Studies of pre–high school students have shown that students in their early teens already possess some political values learned largely in the family setting.[2] Basic cultural values are learned early—in the home and in childhood social relationships—and they are resistant to change.[3]

This is one source of reassurance that students will not be passive and simply allow themselves to be politically indoctrinated, even if professors try to do so. How, and when, political allegiances are formed is an interesting subject that does not have definitive answers at present. We suspect that as parents no longer eat meals regularly with their children in a formal family setting, this chance for students to form political attitudes may be affected. This may be a reason to watch carefully what happens in college, but what the loosening of social cohesion in the family probably implies is a higher degree of political apathy and antipolitical cultural attitudes on the part of young people.

Young Americans, of course, encounter numerous cultural traditions and values in the process of maturation, and each young person confronts uniquely the inevitable tensions and internal contradictions in America's cultural traditions. Still, the young adult's "default" position is to affirm her or his own family values and the dominant cultural traditions as mediated through her or his own family experience. Students, in short, refract the classroom experience through the lens of the unique blend of social, religious, political, and cultural values that each brings to it. A study by Gordon Hewett of Hamilton College and Mack Mariani of Xavier College, based on a survey of college students, found that 60 percent of students did not significantly change their political outlook during the course of college, and, with students who showed a slight leftward drift, the change mirrored exactly the shifts in the eighteen- to twenty-four-year age cohort generally.[4] This is not to suggest that colleges and universities have no influence on the values or political beliefs held by students or that they should shy away from values, politics, or beliefs about the meaning of life. Clearly, we hope that the learning experience will uplift students' visions and aspirations as well as prepare them for citizenship and for careers. We have something more to say on these points later. For the present, it suffices to state the obvious: students encounter a huge variety of choices when they decide where they will attend college and what they will study once they get there. They will have enormous freedom of choice on what courses to take in most schools, what their major field of study will be, and which professors they will select. The classroom experience is often overwhelmed by the outside influences that buffet the student during the college years, including the mass media and new peer groups that students encounter.[5] One hopes that regular classes will have some chance of competing with the enormous impact of the nonclassroom influences on students.

Students normally shrewdly evaluate, and do not just passively accept, what they hear from their professors, accepting what makes sense to them and taking the rest with a grain of salt. Witness the following exchange in an interview with a second-year law student (the law school in this case is known for being a stronghold of the "law and economics" philosophy):

Q: Do you find any particular political climate at [your] law school?
A: Oh, yes. Definitely. It's conservative, very conservative.

Q: How would this manifest itself—in class, visiting lecturers, or what?

A: Pretty much across the board. Take property, for instance. The so-called "takings" issue. Pretty much down the line, almost libertarian you might say, they'd want to limit state powers to take property. And then in contract law, for example, the sanctity of contracts should be respected—let the parties contract. Don't let the government protect one side or the other in, say, a long-term gas supply deal. Letting the market—the parties involved—work things out is better. On international law, don't rush in to protect your nationals with respect to, say, a situation where war has led a country to repudiate an obligation. The market will discipline a wayward country more effectively. Governments are too eager to rush in, and this only messes things up. Lots of stuff like that. There is a definite line in most classes. Not that it's all bad. The profs are good. It's stimulating. I enjoy it, but there's clearly a line that is there.

Q: Is that from all professors, many, a few, or what?

A: Well, maybe not all. But I would say most. We have a visiting professor this year from Michigan Law School. He gives a different view. We need that. I wish we had more visitors, more adjuncts, too.

This student has clearly grasped the essential arguments of the "law and economics" approach, even if he oversimplifies some of the arguments. The educational process has worked—that is, the student has not only learned something but also gained a critical understanding of what he has been taught. He is aware of the limits and shortcomings of the particular approach as well its strengths. This student can also place this approach within a larger intellectual framework.

Not every student, of course, achieves this level of understanding. Less able students may be more vulnerable to whatever bias there is in the classroom, just as those in the general population who have the least political sophistication may be most vulnerable to political manipulation or to media bias.[6] We have encountered instances of illogical, uninformed, and even bizarre reasoning among students. Students can have a certain groupthink of their own, and they certainly participate fully in the human capacity to err. But we are struck by the energy, vitality, and intelligence of the current generation of college students, especially those at the highly select schools. The student leaders or activists on whom we focus our attention are usually involved with various activities outside of class, such as volunteer work, debate and discussion groups, political organizations, student government, advisory services to underclassmen, theater groups, the student newspaper, and other functions. And they do this even as they diligently pursue their studies. We sometimes wonder whether students in the highly competitive atmosphere of today's elite colleges and universities are too programmed, hard-driving, and ambitious. Are they in danger of missing something that a more laid-back college experience could provide?

## Students Are Less Liberal Than Professors

Today's students tend to be somewhat more conservative than their professors. In a survey of 1,350 students in political science classes at twenty-nine universities, April Kelly-Woessner and Matthew Woessner found that 570 (43 percent) identified themselves as liberal, 383 (29 percent) labeled themselves as moderate, and 380 (29 percent) self-identified as conservative.[7] To break down the self-identifications further, 13 percent (or 175 of the total) of the students thought of themselves as "extremely liberal," and 30 percent (or 395) considered themselves as "fairly liberal." The conservative self-identifiers were divided as follows: 305 conservatives (or 23 percent of the total survey respondents) considered themselves to be "fairly conservative," while 75 (or 6 percent of the total sample) deemed themselves to be "extremely conservative."[8]

Students, as we have said, are like other Americans in that they acquire their main political attitudes before they reach college age, and they bring those attitudes to the college experience. While the available evidence does not give us a definitive answer, there does not appear to be a marked shift in most students' political preferences over the course of their college career. Students, though less liberal than their professors, tend to be somewhat more liberal than American voters in general. This may be due to a cohort effect, that is, to the influence of group involvement and life experience. The classic example of a life-cycle effect is that one's attitude on taxes may alter when one becomes a wage earner. A cohort, or generational effect, might be expected to show up when young people generally, and students in particular, are asked about their attitudes on topics such as gay rights or racial tolerance.[9] If university classrooms have become indoctrination centers, as Horowitz and some others suggest, we would expect to discern a significant degree of uniformity on many issues among students.

Student bodies, however, usually end up as quite ideologically diverse—at the large public or private universities at any rate—and thus resemble the political divisions in the general population. The student bodies are typically more ideologically diverse than are college and university faculties. One should look for other explanatory factors. Liberal families seem to prefer to send their children to the more open, diverse, and secular environment of the select four-year colleges and the research universities, while parents who place a high value on a moral and religious environment may choose to send their children to a sectarian college or university.

## Parental Expectations and College Realities

What do parents and students—and what should they—expect from the college experience? Parents and students legitimately seek an environment in which students feel comfortable, are not harassed or bullied inside or outside the classroom, and are free to develop their intellects and personalities to the fullest. However, parents and students should not expect, and are unlikely to find, an environment in which the student is never challenged, or where students only meet people who believe exactly as they do, whether those people are fellow students or faculty members. Even if parents want their children to focus on preparation for a career, they should not expect or want their children to avoid any challenge to the ideas that students bring with them to college.

The Pennsylvania hearings discussed in the previous chapter drew attention to the issue of student rights in the framework of academic freedom. The legislative task force's overall finding was that political bias in Pennsylvania's public colleges and universities is "rare." The task force did recommend, however, that colleges and universities make sure that grievance procedures are in place so that students who wish to do so can file complaints of political bias in grading or intimidation in the classroom.[10]

In testimony at the legislative hearings, witnesses engaged in thoughtful discussions of "student academic rights." David French, president of the conservative watchdog organization FIRE (Foundation for Individual Rights in Education), which tracks campus speech codes and free speech violations, stated that student rights "do not include a right to be taught what they want to hear. Their broad rights do not include a right not to be offended. Their rights do include a right to have a teacher tell all sides of the story as they see all sides of the story."[11]

Robert M. O'Neil, professor of law and former president of the University of Virginia and director of the Thomas Jefferson Center for the Protection of Free Expression, laid out a metric of student rights. He urged, "Students should not expect their values to go unchallenged as part of the university experience. Indeed, if the son or daughter of a friend had such an expectation, I would urge that he or she either not go to college or at the very least find that rare campus where nearly everyone shared the same views."[12]

It would be conceivable today, as Cass R. Sunstein notes in an analysis of the impact on higher education of modern communications and Internet access, for a student to "customize" an entire educational experience in such a way as to encounter only views that fit the student's preconceptions.[13] To do so, however, would negate the very idea of education, which requires that students, on the analogy of citizen encounters in public spaces, confront unfamiliar views and ideas in a shared experience with other students. This is an experience that could lead to modifying one's views or to deepening a prior conviction. In short, learning usually requires one to see the familiar in a new light or to gain new depth and wisdom in one's approach to life. Students do not know in advance what will move them aesthetically, enrich them intellectually, or engage them politically.

Consider this example: a student member of the Young Americans for Freedom who complained that the president of his college expressed her views in a blog that she would send to members of the college community, saying that it put pressure on students, who must be free to form their own views without faculty or administrators expressing themselves. This student's position was rejected by most of his fellow students. They, on the contrary, welcomed the president's practice of speaking out on her blog. In another incident, Mark C. Taylor, a religion and humanities professor at Williams College, stated in an op-ed piece in the *Washington Post* that he was called on the carpet by an administrator at his college and told to apologize to a student who had complained that he had attacked the student's faith.[14] Professor Taylor had urged the student "to consider whether Nietzsche's analysis of religion undermined belief in absolutes."[15] He refused the administrator's request that he apologize to the student, insisting that his obligation as a teacher required him to challenge the student's thinking. Professor Taylor rejected the notion that a test of "religious correctness" should prevail in the classroom, any more than political correctness. One could challenge some of Taylor's pedagogical theories. For example, it is not self-evident that a teacher should feel that she or he has failed if the students "are not more confused and uncertain at the end of the course than they were at the beginning" or that "the task of thinking and teaching . . . is to cultivate a faith in doubt that calls into question every certainty."

Yet it is hard to dispute Professor Taylor's central conclusion: students should confront unfamiliar and possibly challenging views as part of their education. Taylor also noted, "The twenty-first century will be dominated by religion in ways that were inconceivable a few years ago" and "unless we establish a genuine dialogue within and among all kinds of belief, ranging from religious fundamentalism to secular dogmatism, the conflicts of the future will probably be more deadly."[16] In this belief the student with deep religious beliefs would probably find support and affirmation. Good teaching requires that the teacher have the freedom to follow his or her lights in the choice of material, in how it is presented, and in how to engage the students' interest. Students will evolve in their thinking as they progress through the college experience and return to themes raised in class throughout their lives. It is also noteworthy that Professor Taylor, in this case, apparently reflects an awareness that religion is a subject that can be taught and not simply avoided as taboo. R. Eugene Rice notes, "In the 1990s, many within higher education would have agreed . . . that religion was a 'conversation stopper' and preferred to avoid the topic, especially when different perspectives in the classroom or the place of religion in the public square were at issue."[17]

## Student Views on Classroom Political Bias

The students we talked to were activists in that they participated in extracurricular campus organizations and were often volunteers with off-campus agencies; many had served as summer interns in government. Although these students would be seen as high achievers by any reasonable standard, they are indicative of the talented and energetic students who make up the student bodies of the select colleges and universities. The students accepted the notion that they were attending college to learn, to be stimulated by their professors, and to have their own views challenged by their professors and their fellow students. If anything, they wished that their professors would be more forthcoming and bolder in expressing their views in the classroom.

In our focus groups and interviews, we found no serious quarrel with David French's or Robert O'Neil's conceptions of students' academic rights. The students were in general proud of their universities. They felt that they had made the right choice in coming to the school they chose and believed that they were getting a good education. Students pointed to the occasional derogatory remark about President Bush or a partisan jab by a professor, but, like the findings of the Pennsylvania legislative hearings, these instances were rare.

The reactions of students at a focus group at a southern public university were typical. When asked if they had encountered bias in the classroom, one student observed that a chemistry professor once went off "on a tirade against Bush and the Iraq War." Another student in the group said that she had experienced grade discrimination because of her views when she attended a small private college in the West. She had transferred to her present university because of that experience. But here at the university she had never had such an experience and was extremely happy.

Another student, who described herself as a lesbian and libertarian, said that she had had trouble with a teaching assistant in one of her classes. She felt that she may have received a lower grade than she deserved because of her outspoken views. But she observed, "I guess I was being deliberately provocative sometimes, pretty far out in some of my class comments. Maybe he [the instructor] was turned off by my style." Another student, a friend of hers who had been in the class with her, drew a laugh from the group when he observed that she was "always original" in her class comments.

A few students could recall occasional jibes by a professor directed against a politician, more often against President Bush and the Republicans than against the Democrats (the Republicans were at that time in power in Congress as well as the executive branch). Most of the students, who described themselves either as centrist, center-right, or moderately liberal in their political outlook, generally viewed their classes as intellectually stimulating. There were no instances of professors tying to proselytize or to indoctrinate them.

Although we have made no effort to quantify student reactions either in focus groups or in interviews, our general findings appear broadly consistent with the studies that have sought to capture student attitudes via survey methods. Surprisingly, perhaps, a survey conducted for the American Council of Trustees and Alumni (ACTA), which was manifestly designed to provide evidence of professorial bias, showed an opposite conclusion when carefully examined. The survey, Politics in the Classroom: A Survey of Students at the Top 50 Colleges and Universities, was conducted by the Roper Center of the University of Connecticut via telephone interviews in October-November 2004, just before the 2004 elections, when one might presume that emotions and political awareness on the nation's campuses were high.[18]

ACTA sought to portray the top colleges and universities as being riddled with political bias. The questions were often poorly worded and asked for general impressions rather than tapping the students' direct experience. For example, students were asked if they strongly agreed, somewhat agreed, somewhat disagreed, or strongly disagreed with the statement, "On my campus, some professors use the classroom to present their personal political views." In a brief cover summary of the survey's findings, ACTA reported in bullet form that 46 percent of the student respondents agreed with the previous statement.[19] Besides using the indefinite term "some" professors, failing to specify whether the use was frequent, occasional, incidental to the main theme of a course, or rare, and failing to ask how firmly the student believed the report, ACTA combined the "strongly agree" category (10 percent of students) with the looser "somewhat agree" category (36 percent) to come up with the more impressive-sounding 46 percent of the students agreeing with the statement.

Similarly, students were asked to respond to the statement, "On my campus, some courses have readings which present only one side of a controversial issue." Again the "some" is indeterminate as to number, and the construction "have readings which present only one side of a controversial issue" is not free of ambiguity. One could infer that some readings were but other readings in the course were not one-sided or that different readings presented the opposing sides of a controversial issue. In any event, only 12 percent of the student respondents "strongly agreed," while another 30 percent "somewhat agreed" (thus adding up the 42 percent who ACTA said agreed with the statement). However, ACTA could have pointed to the larger number (54 percent) who disagreed with the statement (20 percent somewhat disagreeing and 28 percent strongly disagreeing).[20]

The students' responses to other questions in the survey rebut ACTA's interpretation. For example, in response to the statement, "On my campus, students don't feel free to express their honest views about affirmative action," 81 percent of the students disagreed (22 percent somewhat disagreeing and 59 percent strongly disagreeing). Only 3 percent strongly agreed with the statement.[21] Of all the respondents, 88 percent disagreed (67 percent strongly and 21 percent somewhat strongly) with this statement, "On my campus, students don't feel free to express their patriotism." Only 3 percent strongly agreed.[22]

On another question with the locution of "some professors," 77 percent of all student respondents disagreed (51 percent strongly, 26 percent somewhat strongly) with the statement, "On my campus, some professors are intolerant of certain political and social viewpoints."[23]

It is useful to break down the data by the type of institution. At large private universities (defined as having enrollments of 10,000 or more), only 3 percent of the students strongly and 5 percent somewhat agreed with the statement, "On my campus, some professors are intolerant of certain political and social viewpoints," while 88 percent of the students at those institutions disagreed.[24] Large public universities shared similar, but somewhat less pronounced, results. At the public universities, 77 percent of the respondents disagreed with the statement. The ACTA survey tends to confirm what students at the large research universities—our major interest—told us in the focus groups and interviews: classroom bias is not a major issue with them.

An interesting and somewhat strange result of the ACTA survey is that 25 percent of the student respondents at small liberal arts colleges agreed somewhat with the statement that some professors are intolerant of certain viewpoints (even though 68 percent of the student respondents at these institutions disagreed). One could speculate that the small liberal arts colleges could have smaller and more like-minded academic departments or that a less diverse and dynamic campus environment exists at these smaller institutions. Gross and Simmons found, "A slightly higher percentage of liberals is to [be] found on the faculties of liberal arts colleges than on the faculties of the elite, PhD-granting schools, while liberal arts colleges and non-elite PhD-granting schools contain the fewest conservative faculty members."[25]

One finding in the ACTA survey seems firmly grounded and relevant for our purposes. Students who identified themselves as conservative were consistently more likely, by a small percentage, to detect bias, to feel inhibited about expressing their views on controversial topics, and to worry about grade discrimination.[26] Since students' political views tend to be slightly more liberal at the most elite colleges and universities than at the other schools, conservative students at the elite schools are somewhat more likely than their fellow students to perceive political bias. In the ACTA survey, conservative students (16 percent) were twice as likely as moderate students (8 percent) or liberal students (7 percent) to feel that they are not free to express their patriotism on campus. However, large majorities of students did not believe that they are not free to express their patriotism.

The student campus activists we interviewed were ideologically diverse and were generally sophisticated in their discussions of faculty bias. An exchange in one focus group, for example, centered on the relationship between pedagogy and political ideology. A student complained that, in a legal history class, the professor insisted "on one approach. You had to do it exactly his way. There was only one valid explanation." Another student suggested that this was probably a methodological question that did not necessarily relate to the professor's politics. Before the first student could answer, a history major interjected that both of her colleagues were missing the point. Of course, she countered, "A professor will have an approach. How can you not have a perspective? You want someone to be up-front. That's what we're here for—to get the professor's view. And you can't separate out politics from what the professor thinks is important." The discussion continued, with the students examining how explicit the professor should be in stating his or her own views on controversial topics, whether teachers should always cite approaches different from their own, the responsibilities of the students to evaluate the course material, and so on.

In another session with students from an elite private university, the students discussed a visit to their campus by David Horowitz. The aim of the visit was supposedly to discuss campus bias. All members of the focus group agreed that the visit was a dismal failure. Horowitz's presentation was described as "shallow" by one student and "ridiculous" by another. The presentation was, said another student, "lacking in intellectual substance." Student protesters who attempted to shout down Horowitz, taking off their shirts and turning their backs in protest, were also roundly condemned. "The thing degenerated into a spectacle, a happening," one student summed up. "I would like to hear a serious discussion of the issue [bias on campus]. But this certainly wasn't it."

These students did not believe that their professors are biased or that their campus lacks a diversity of political views. A chapter of the Horowitz-sponsored Students for Academic Freedom existed on the campus and complained regularly and loudly about campus leftism. But the chapter was considered to be a marginal organization by most students, according to the focus group participants.

Students' own ideological preferences, of course, tend to influence their views about bias, whether it exists, and who is or is not biased. It is typical to believe that the other person is biased, not oneself. Thus one intelligent and articulate but somewhat opinionated student, when asked in an interview if he had experienced classroom bias, complained about a particular economics professor. "I could never get him to concede that globalization has increased economic inequality," he said, even though the student had argued forcefully in class and had supplied numerous references and examples to prove his point. This professor, the student decided, was hopeless, and perhaps so was the whole economics profession. They were, in his view, locked into their rigid formulations and would not listen to contrary views. Had he encountered the views of Joseph Stiglitz, the Columbia economist, on globalization or Jeffrey Sachs on world poverty? No, but he was glad to hear that someone in the field was finally beginning to see the light.

Another point—a clincher for this student—was that the professor he was complaining about was not willing to sign a petition protesting the low wages for campus hourly workers. Nor was the professor willing to support a sit-in at the university president's office on behalf of the cafeteria employees. In fact, would the member of our study team interviewing him be willing to sign the petition? Or to support the sit-in at the president's office? Our team member politely declined.

Another student, from a private university in the Northeast, described himself as an economic libertarian and complained, in contrast to the student described in the previous paragraphs, that his department had an ideological tilt to the left. "I counted twelve or thirteen courses dealing with imperialism in the catalogue. Sure, imperialism is an important subject, but thirteen courses? And then there're the courses dealing with feminism and gender." The student, a serious and knowledgeable senior, complained that there was practically nothing on military history, not enough on political history, and too little on intellectual history. Had he encountered any discrimination because of his views? Well, not really. One professor had tried to steer him away from writing a paper on two French libertarian thinkers, but this was probably because the professor didn't know much, he thought, about the French writers. The student pointed to other subtle kinds of liberal bias. A statistics professor, for example, used examples of American casualties in the Iraq War to illustrate statistical concepts. Sure, you could say that you should use current examples to illustrate a point, the student said, but he doubted that the choice was random. Despite his criticisms, he was happy with his university and felt that he had received a good education. The total environment was stimulating, and there were ample opportunities to pursue one's intellectual interests. He was considering graduate studies at the university and later did decide to pursue graduate studies at the school. "There had to be something wrong with you," he said, "if you couldn't find intellectual stimulation at the university." There was, he pointed out, an active libertarian chapter on campus, but he did not join because he disliked the people running it.

Although students may encounter what they see as bias from time to time, they are neither helpless victims nor pawns in the grip of forces beyond their control. They believe that they are, in some important sense, capable of shaping their own lives. They evaluate what they experience with the analytical tools they have learned from their professors and their peers. They are aware that they bring their own biases and perceptions to what they encounter in college and weigh these factors in making judgments. They fall short, like the rest of us, of a perfect rationality and have their share of hot buttons and idiosyncrasies. But if the corollary of conservative contentions of faculty bias is that students are credulous, this does not square with the situation we find on campus. We find little or no support either in the published literature or in our own inquiry for the thesis that students are helpless dupes.

## Course Evaluations and Grades

The Woessners' survey of 1,385 political science students showed some evidence that students' own partisan or ideological views are correlated with their ratings of the professor.[27] The Woessners found, "When students view professors as more partisan, they assign lower evaluative scores. . . . Perceptions of extreme partisanship are correlated with lower student interest, less inclination to recommend the course to others, poorer assessments of the course, and poorer assessment of the instructor."[28]

In fact, the context in which professors interact with students in America's universities today is marked by professional constraints and self-correcting mechanisms. Max Weber cautioned his colleagues in his 1918 address, "Science as a Vocation," to avoid exploiting the professor's inherent position of power vis-à-vis students, a position that seems almost quaint to anyone familiar with today's students and today's classroom context. Of course, we endorse Weber's warning that teachers should eschew political advocacy in their role as teacher. Professors should, and most do, behave with restraint and professionalism in the classroom—they "teach rather than preach." The realities of university life today are unlikely to produce, at all events, the all-powerful professors of Wilhelmine Germany.

Professors who do not pay attention to their teaching, or who are unprofessional, partisan, or dogmatic with their students, are likely to get themselves into warm, if not hot, water in a hurry. Student evaluations, now almost universal, exert influence on professorial behavior, especially among faculty members who have not yet earned tenure or are working as visitors or adjuncts. Few professors want to be regarded by their colleagues as poor teachers. And no professor wants the unpleasant scrutiny of a dean or the departmental chair that can result from poor course evaluations or from student complaints. In some schools and departments, higher teaching evaluations can lead directly to higher salaries, resulting in an increased interest in excellence. Biased professors, of the right or the left, seem to get lower evaluations.

The Woessners' overall findings in their survey of political science students are instructive: "Students prefer classes where the instructor presents himself as a political moderate. . . . As students perceive a greater partisan difference between the instructor and the student, they tend to express less satisfaction with both the course and the instructor."[29] The constraint exerted by the course evaluation is both a good and a bad thing. It is good in forcing professors to attend seriously to their teaching duties. It has less desirable consequences insofar as it may induce professors to be overly cautious and to steer clear of controversy lest they offend students. Professors with a reputation for giving higher grades also tend to be evaluated more favorably than their harder-nosed colleagues. The suggestion advanced by David Horowitz at the Pennsylvania hearings that course evaluations give students an explicit opportunity to complain about political bias in the class strikes us as exactly the wrong kind of "reform." Professors would be less apt to introduce political themes and issues into class discussions, and the task of getting the universities to take political and civic education more seriously would be made more difficult.

What about grades and the power conferred by the instructor's ability to influence the student's prospects for professional school? Does this give the instructor the whip hand because students want to obtain good grades? The desire for good grades and the wish to gain the instructor's approval are certainly important elements of the teacher-student relationship. Yet the grading process is only part of what is a complex social interaction. The problem of grade inflation—a topic beyond our scope here—suggests the ambivalence that professors may bring to the task of assigning grades. Professors want to be liked by their students, to receive favorable course evaluations, and to help students they genuinely like. Professors want to avoid inflicting pain when students perform poorly and yet to reward excellent performance. Professors vary enormously in their philosophies of grading, and administrators labor hard to get their colleagues to maintain standards and uniformity in grading policy.

Harvey C. Mansfield Jr., a professor of government at Harvard who had a reputation as a tough grader, announced at one point that he was tired of having his students suffer in comparison to the inflated grades given by other Harvard professors. Henceforth, he would assign two grades: one would be the official grade for the university's records and the student's transcript and the other would be a private grade between himself and the student. He was, he said, forced to capitulate to the grade inflation practiced at Harvard.

Professor Thorsten Veblen, something of an *enfant terrible* in his day, never gave a grade higher than a "C+." This, together with his penchant for gaining the favors of his colleagues' wives, made him an unpopular figure to his faculty colleagues and to students alike.

Could there be an unconscious bias, a subtle but pervasive tilt, in the professor's lectures that students recognize and cater to? The students we talked to had differing views on this question, and their assessments ran the gamut. The law student we quoted earlier felt that there was some tendency of the sort.

Q: Would you say that kids follow some kind of party line to get good grades or anything like that? Does it go that far?

A: Yes, I think it does somewhat. It's only human. You tend to take a cue from the professors, a little insurance maybe. Not a lot, but some. Maybe the professors don't even realize it. But it's there to some degree. I think so anyway.

This same student thought that while there was a mildly conservative climate at the undergraduate level at his university, the graduate situation was "maybe not so clear." He was a moderate liberal at a conservative school in a conservative state. This was simply a fact of life. It did not trouble him to any significant degree.

Most students we talked to doubted that their grades were significantly influenced by their expressed political views or by the instructor's politics. Some sheepishly confessed that on occasions they tried to give the professor what they thought he or she wanted, but quickly found that this tactic rarely worked. You can outsmart yourself, was the consensus, when you try to follow too closely what you think is the professor's "line." Professors have quirks and hot buttons that can be appealed to, but hard work and good preparation are the best strategies to get good grades. Even the conservative students, much like the liberal student at the conservative university, tended to take their situation in stride. They may feel that their peers are patronizing them and they may be irritated or angry from time to time, but they "accept the universe."

This is not to say that sweetness and light will invariably prevail on today's campuses. Occasionally, the dramatic happens, such as the turmoil at Duke in the 2006–07 academic year over accusations of rape against three lacrosse players.[30] A student who was a lacrosse player felt that he had been singled out for an unfavorable grade because he belonged to the lacrosse team. He sued a professor who was identified with the faculty faction that had publicly criticized the team and the campus climate and was among those who "rushed to judgment" on the players' guilt. The student won a change in the appeal procedures for students complaining about unfair grading. Professors were no longer to be the sole judge of and the only party able to change a grade. A student could now appeal to the department chair if he or she did not get a satisfactory explanation of a grade from the professor. The chairperson, if persuaded of the complaint's justice, could pass the appeal on to the dean who, in turn, could appoint a committee to investigate. This was not expected to be a routine procedure, but a new grievance procedure was established as a result of the suit. Duke thus followed a pattern that has occurred at a number of other institutions in which grievance procedures for student complaints have been clarified and formalized.

## Public Attitudes toward Higher Education

Despite methodological shortcomings, the ACTA survey discussed earlier in this chapter does indicate that some conservative students, though a minority of the conservatives, *do* detect the presence of political bias on their campus. The 2006 survey of public attitudes toward higher education by Neil Gross and Solon Simmons for the American Association of University Professors (AAUP) helps to explain the ACTA student perceptions of political bias.[31] They identify a core group in the wider public that strongly believes the campuses are biased, and it is possible (but not certain) that this group may overlap in part with, and help to explain, the student reactions (the social origins and composition of the groups in the wider society are not socially elite, so the connection could be tenuous). Gross and Simmons found that 37.5 percent of the general public considers political bias in the classroom to be a "very serious problem," even though most Americans rate other concerns as more important problems facing higher education. Asked to identify "very serious problems" facing higher education, 80.5 percent of all respondents listed the high cost of tuition, 68.2 percent listed binge drinking by college students, 48.9 percent cited low educational standards, and 45.5 percent listed crime on campus. Political bias in the classroom came in fifth, at 37.5 percent, edging out too much focus on college athletics, at 36.5 percent. Incompetent professors were next, at 34.6 percent, and lack of support for a diverse student population stood at 30.2 percent, filling out the list of eight problems.[32]

However, when asked to identify *the* most important problem, 42.8 percent pointed to the high cost of tuition, while only 8.2 percent identified political bias in the classroom as the biggest problem. Gross and Simmons identified a cluster of views shared by 56 percent of their respondents who are supportive of higher education and not concerned about alleged political bias.[33] But a sector of the public—made up largely of conservatives, Republicans, those over sixty-five, and those with low levels of educational attainment—*is* concerned about political bias in the classroom. A cluster of the respondents, about 30.3 percent of the total sample, were "critical" of higher education. The respondents in this cluster agreed, with about 91.3 percent of them sharing the view, that liberal professors have an advantage in academe, and 89.3 percent agreed that professors are too distracted by identity politics. Another 63.9 percent of these respondents viewed professors as not respectful of students who hold political views different from theirs, and 78.5 percent of respondents in this category believed that political bias in the academy is a very serious problem.

In the light of these findings, Gross and Simmons conclude that while higher education in general and professors in particular continue to enjoy considerable prestige among the population, "there is more support for critical views about bias in higher education than might otherwise be imagined and less consensus about U.S. higher education than previous research has suggested."[34]

The minority of students who perceive bias on their campus probably come from families among the small but significant minority of Americans with critical attitudes toward the higher education sector. That even a small minority of students and parents, mostly conservatives and Republicans, perceive that political bias exists in higher education should be a concern for college and university leaders.

## Student Dislike of Speech Codes

One area where we found students, whether liberal or conservative, virtually unanimous was in their dislike of speech codes and other forms of what Don-

ald A. Downs has called "therapeutic paternalism." Students referred with deri-
sion to codes of speech and conduct, dormitory regulations, and other
examples of paternalistic rules to enforce "politically correct" behavior. Thinking back to our own undergraduate days, we could each recall similar feelings
of dislike for officious deans. Nonetheless, students have to recognize that they
live within a community that will insist upon, and enforce, certain standards
of civilized conduct. Despite our own checkered past when we were undergraduate radicals, we now concur that Robert M. O'Neil, in his analysis of student
academic rights quoted earlier in this chapter, is right to insist that "students
should not expect their views and values to go unchallenged as part of their
education experience." This may mean that students occasionally will be placed
in positions where they will feel uncomfortable.

O'Neil, an ardent civil libertarian, opposes any university rule that goes
beyond regulating conduct or inhibits free expression. But he is deeply troubled
by the claim that any campus policy regulating student conduct is an infringement of speech. Regulating conduct with only a remote connection to expression
should not be regarded as a speech code subject to judicial intervention.

Students have to learn to operate within a framework of institutional rules
of civility and good conduct, O'Neil insists, and a framework of rules is not to
be automatically construed as a code inhibiting free expression. We have sym-
pathy for both the students who instinctively dislike paternalistic rules and for
the college administrators who are responsible for maintaining good order
and civil conduct on campus. The sector of the public that is critical of the
academy as being a haven for liberals is influenced in its perception by what
occurs outside of as well as inside the classroom. Many actions taken by deans
and administrators, in the name of providing a supportive environment for
learning, attract negative publicity and contribute to an impression that the
academy is politically one-sided. College administrators can be overzealous in
their interpretations of what is necessary for civility on their campus. They can
be too easily swayed by narrow campus constituencies. However that may be,
students cannot expect to be free from institutional rules when they enter college. Learning to live with rules is part of learning to live in a political
community and to practice good citizenship.

Students should be able to express grievances through recognized channels if they feel intimidated or pressured by instructors for political or other
reasons, or if they are bullied or intimidated by their fellow students. Offenders who are sanctioned must have recognized procedural rights if they face
disciplinary action from their university for violations of the rules, including
codes regulating hate speech or expressive conduct. The students' insistence on

their rights, however, has led to very formalized and legalistic disciplinary proceedings on many campuses and even to increasing instances of civil litigation.

Colleges and universities are sensitive to public perceptions and criticisms regarding classroom bias. A number of Pennsylvania institutions, including Temple, Penn State, and the University of Pittsburgh, in the wake of the 2006 legislative review of academic freedom, altered their policies to establish clearer channels for students to express grievances. The American Council on Education (ACE) statement of June 2005, presented in appendix D, states that students are entitled to have such procedural protections.[35] Several professional associations have devoted panels at their annual meetings or at special conferences to the discussion of how teachers should handle controversial issues.

Political science chairs and a number of professors we have talked to say they are keenly aware that students can be sensitive about certain issues and reluctant to state their views openly in class discussions. Colleagues thus should, and most do, take pains to reassure their students. Chairs of departments should try to sensitize new faculty colleagues to the problems of discussing controversial subject matter in class. For political scientists, knowing how to handle, and defuse, sensitive topics should be part of the normal professional armamentarium. Other colleagues scoff at the allegations of political bias. Many colleagues insist that it is part of our professional obligation to discuss sensitive and controversial issues, not to advance our own views but to advance understanding of political complexities. We strongly concur with these sentiments. Bias *is* rare, as we have tried to show in a number of ways, and professors should not be fearful of addressing political issues in their classes or of debating what constitutes good citizenship. They should not abandon the important task of political education out of fear of offending a small number of students. But as President Adamany of Temple insisted in his testimony at the Pennsylvania hearings we review in chapter 7, citizens have a right to ask whether universities live up to their ideals of fair-minded and open debate. Citizens are entitled to a serious response to the question of whether bias exists, not a contemptuous dismissal of their concerns. Some colleagues we have talked to about this project have been suspicious of our inquiry, contending that we are inventing a problem where none exists, that we are wittingly or unwittingly playing into the hands of forces hostile to higher education, or that what we are doing is "political" and not "scientific." To which we argue that not every question that is important can be answered scientifically. If people think there is a problem, there is a problem, and it is our obligation to try to provide a reasoned answer, even if some will never be wholly persuaded. A few colleagues also suggest that we are distracting attention from the real problems facing higher education: chiefly, the pernicious impact of commercialism and the capture of universities by the privileged classes. We acknowledge that these are serious issues worthy of serious discussion, but they are not the principal focus of this inquiry.

Colleagues from all points of view agree that certain hot button issues have the potential to produce tension in the classroom. Indisputably tact and sensitive awareness are among the qualities that effective teachers have to learn. This is not to say that teachers should steer clear of controversial subject matter. To shy away from controversy is to shy away from politics and the kind of civic engagement we believe is essential for the undergraduate educational experience.

## The Challenge of Civic Engagement: Can the Universities Handle Politics?

One person's political correctness is another person's deeply held belief, for professors as well as for other Americans. There are many reasons, given the sharp differences of views, why faculty members may want to avoid controversy (just as neighbors often steer clear of politics because they do not want confrontation). Consider the issue of "diversity," which has become such a bone of contention. A sizable minority of Americans (30.2 percent) apparently believes that "lack of support for a diverse student population" is a "very serious problem."[36] In this, the public apparently mirrors the divisions within the universities, or perhaps it is equally true to say that the universities reflect the attitudes of their fellow citizens. The meaning of the term diversity is not self-evident, however. To some, diversity means the recruitment of women and minorities to faculty positions and in the student body; to others, it means the recruitment of conservatives for faculty posts and among invited speakers. Diversity could mean (a view held by many educators) that more consideration should be given to economic status and social class—that is, to ensure that promising poor students regardless of race are more fully represented—in the student body. Universities are often attacked from the left for being too beholden to large donors, legacy parents, commercial interests, and the privileged classes generally. These complaints may have merit, but it is not our intention here to evaluate them. It is, of course, entirely appropriate for the universities to evaluate such issues and to debate their own roles and shortcomings (and we hope that this book will stimulate such debate).

The larger point that we focus on here is that the older role of colleges and universities—that of preparing students for life and for citizenship in our democracy—has been all but forgotten, or else has been considered too difficult a task, or the wrong task, for the modern secular university. Consider this quotation from Frederick Rudolph on the early mission of the colleges in America:

> The professors in the era of the colleges were recruited from men who believed "that in serving the cause of knowledge and truth by promoting liberal education," they were serving the cause of religion. . . . The old time college professor was often a clergyman or had at least some theological training. Of 130 members of the Union College faculty . . . 55 were clergymen. Two thirds of the professors at Dartmouth . . . had theological training.[37]

Rudolph's comments on what he deemed an anachronistic mission undertaken by the nineteenth-century colleges are instructive. Before we celebrate modernity and the march of "progress," let us challenge the quotation's subtext. Rudolph disparages the older practices and gives an unqualified endorsement of the modern university's near total disengagement from and neglect of civic and moral education. Students were taught in former days to be patriotic, to love their country, and to be aware of their moral responsibilities. This was part of the "civic republican" tradition in the nation's political ideology. The curriculum of the pre–Civil War colleges, of course, would hardly be appropriate for today's colleges and universities. It was a curriculum that was defective in many respects and would run counter to our evolving constitutional doctrines, which radically separated church from state. But the absence of the civic republican tradition in virtually any form in the modern secular university is a serious shortcoming. This deficiency has, in part, contributed to the resurgence of the religious colleges. We do not disparage the sectarian movement in higher education. On the contrary, we ask why civic engagement, once so important in the educational missions of the pre–Civil War colleges, has been so thoroughly downgraded in the research universities of today. Whether public or private, the modern research universities have great difficulty with such a mission, and so do the elite secular liberal arts colleges.

There are many reasons why the large heterogeneous modern universities can no longer follow the tradition of teaching morality and trying to follow a model of civic education.[38] University professors would revolt against the notion that their job is to inculcate cherished dogma or to indoctrinate students in any form. Currently accepted notions of professionalism for college professors predispose them to leave preaching to the preachers. Teaching civics, as the high schools have tried (unsuccessfully) to do, is a task that would be pedestrian for someone trained to search for the higher forms of truth. Communities and parents, too, would object to having students taught values unless they were majority values (and some parents would object to majority values precisely because they ignore minority values). Better to steer clear of values altogether. Our pluralistic society makes it hard for the modern university to embrace any narrow set of values that could offend one or another part of a diverse community. These factors help to explain why the modern university is so inhospitable to politics and to genuine political disputation. Volunteerism, and nonpartisan forms of community service, can be readily embraced, but the duties and obligations of national citizenship could invite disputes and disagreements. It is thus, we believe, a misconception to see the universities as having been "politicized" to an unhealthy degree. The reverse is more the case. "On the contrary," as Robert E. Calvert observes of the campus culture wars, "the combatants have in effect declared a permanent truce . . . and have thus created a political desert, a rapprochement that quietly ends the conflict over 'difference' without achieving any sense of a shared life or common good."[39] The modern university "has synthesized the radical 'progressivism' of the 'sixties' generation and the liberal (if relationally conservative) meritocratic orientation of the universities of that day into an ideologically eclectic university . . . whose purposes and authority have little to do with either liberal or political education."[40]

The truth of this observation is borne out by what we see as happening in the universities. One university president, for example, a Republican in this instance, told us he was concerned with the lack of genuine debate on his campus and with the appearance of bias resulting from the paucity of conservative voices. He told us that he has urged his deans to rise and at least to discuss the issue of real or potential political bias with the department chairpersons at the university's annual retreat for administrators. So far, he said, the deans "have been able to sidestep the issue. Their argument is that we would just create a problem when we don't have one now. They have enough problems, they say, so why raise something that is apt to rile the faculty?" The president conceded that his associates have a point. Nonetheless, he wished that more of his faculty would reflect seriously on the issue and come up with a considered approach. He doubted that there was any single correct pedagogical approach or simple model to be followed. He did not expect or want any bold or dramatic action to be taken. Some colleagues might decide to state their own views up-front in class to clear the air; some might avoid stating their own views in order to avoid pressuring students; and others might air their own position on a particular issue in class but combine this with a statement of opposing views. Some colleagues are absorbed with their specialties and have no strong political views. He certainly would not want to prescribe any particular approach or declare administrative rules for what happens in the classroom. But he felt that his faculty colleagues should reflect and decide for themselves how to handle controversial subject matter in the classroom. He would not want them to avoid discussing issues that are important to the subject of a class. The university should be a place where sensitive issues are discussed.

We were impressed by how seriously this president had thought about the issues we raise here. This president's views were similar to the concerns expressed by another Republican who had been a university president, Senator Lamar Alexander (R-Tenn.), who told Secretary of Education Margaret Spelling's Commission on Higher Education in 2005 that perceptions of political bias could hurt public higher education. Republican state legislators might weaken in their support for public higher education if they became concerned that the state university was dominated by Democrats and liberals with a political agenda. Conversely, educators might overreact and shy away from having their campus be a center for lively debate.

Americans demonstrate a strong pragmatism and a high tolerance for cognitive dissonance in their attitudes toward higher education, as they do for many other issues. While some 60 percent of Americans say that they do not believe in the truth of Darwinism, 80 percent believe that politicians should not interfere with research at colleges and universities and 79 percent disagree with the idea that government should control what is taught in the classroom.[41] College professors continue to enjoy a high degree of prestige in surveys of occupational prestige, although the gap between college professors and educators at the public school level seems to be narrowing somewhat.

Americans in general evidently do not want the college classroom to be controlled by politicians. They decisively reject the idea that government should interfere with research in the universities. In the Gross and Simmons survey, 40.4 percent of the respondents said the term "professional" describes college and university professors very well.[42] Many Americans hold conflicting ideas about higher education (as they do on other issues). Americans are supportive of the tenure system but at the same time believe that universities should be free to fire professors who join radical organizations. Civic awareness and the ability to understand complex issues are not to be taken for granted. There are a number of indicators that civic life in America is undergoing great stress. Neither the family nor the workplace seems to offer the same kind of social cohesion or stable environment for transmitting social, cultural, and civic values that they did in previous generations. The nation's educational system thus has all the more reason to confront the role it once played, and could still play, in teaching young Americans the values of citizenship.

# 9

## Do Universities Discriminate in Hiring?

This chapter addresses the persistent criticism that universities discriminate against conservatives in hiring, promotion, and tenure decisions. Universities are most often said to discriminate in the humanities and social sciences (few contend that the sciences discriminate against conservatives, but conservatives are said to be hurt by affirmative action hiring requirements). Declaring that a leftist political culture has become self-perpetuating, a 2006 profile of American college faculty by Gary A. Tobin and Aryeh K. Weinberg of the Institute for Jewish and Community Research in San Francisco concludes its fairly representative analysis in the following terms:

> Some academic disciplines, especially in the social sciences and humanities, exhibit particularly persistent political behaviors. Recruitment, hiring, and tenure review processes have either failed to adequately prevent the political imbalance within disciplines or have actively perpetuated and deepened political unity.[1]

> Science and engineering departments have been criticized from a left perspective for failing to recruit enough women and minority (other than Asian) students and for failing to hire enough women and minorities in their tenure ranks (notwithstanding the criticism from the right that they have to knuckle under to affirmative action).[2]

## Background

In order to evaluate the claims of discrimination in hiring, we need to see the broader historical context. If faculties are somewhat more liberal than they were, say, in 1984, this cannot be attributed solely or mainly to hiring practices. There are important trends in American politics generally that should be noted. The decline in the fortunes of the moderate northeastern Republican establishment is worth noting, as is the Republican Party's growing dependence on a fundamentalist Christian base and a party strategy to capitalize on wedge issues. These features have contributed to making an already liberal-leaning professoriate somewhat more liberal and less Republican. Professors, by nature suspicious of populist rhetoric and emotional appeals to the voters, had their preconceptions reinforced. Some of the rhetorical appeals, such as opposition to stem cell research and evolutionary theory, were seemingly targeted at the universities. Further, legal requirements for nondiscrimination in the treatment of women, gays, and minorities made faculty hiring more open to these groups. The addition of more women and minorities to hiring pools and eventually to faculty ranks meant that faculties began to reflect the attitudes of these more liberal groups. Just as Jews, once they joined the faculty of the elite universities after World War II, helped to produce a more secular and liberal atmosphere, the addition of women and minorities in the humanities and the social sciences nudged those departments toward new subfields of inquiry, pedagogical concerns, and social issues.

The growing importance of women in the research universities is an especially noteworthy development. The sudden departure of women from the ranks of English and other humanities fields and their entry into the social sciences and the professions of law and medicine in the 1970s caused a temporary "crisis in the humanities," and foretold how the emancipation of women could produce shifts in the academy. The return of large numbers of women over the course of the 1980s, in turn, caused this putative crisis largely to disappear.[3] Women are now 52 percent of all undergraduates, and their preponderance in certain fields is higher than that. Women make up a majority of the students at most major medical and law schools today. Women in doctoral programs in English and in languages have registered strong gains, and they are on a path toward ascendancy and even dominance in a number of departments.

The gains by women did not merely reflect the decisions made by hiring committees on campuses. Women have advanced, and continue to advance, because of broad demographic trends affecting not only the universities, but our entire society. Women are represented in large numbers in undergraduate programs, in graduate programs, in the ranks of the junior faculty, and increasingly in senior faculty positions as well as in the leadership positions of the professional associations. The presidencies of four of the eight Ivy League universities—Harvard, Princeton, Penn, and Brown—are held by women. The significance of the growing role of women is difficult to assess fully, but higher education clearly has undergone notable changes as a result. How the major universities hire and promote faculty has to be understood in the light of such major social and institutional change. But we also need to view the academic recruitment process in the light of internal shifts and some important mileposts in the post–World War II academic environment.

## The "Old-Boy" System

The career of the oldest of the present authors illustrates the differences between the current and the former appointment process in universities. In the 1950s and 1960s the major research universities, which were at that time mainly the Ivy League institutions plus a few other private and a relatively small number of good public universities, operated within a social system that can be loosely described as *benign paternalism*. The system was an old-boy network that operated hierarchically and unapologetically. Each field, each institution, and the entire community—marked by a sort of informal ranking of quality and prestige—formed an interlocking system. There was a pecking order among the various research universities. Although universities engaged in friendly (and sometimes unfriendly) competition, most of the key players knew each other, and each had a certain sense of responsibility for the entire higher education enterprise. They wanted to foster their particular field and institution, but the senior figures, nearly all of whom had served in the government in one capacity or another during the war, were generally respected leaders who in a certain sense also spoke for higher education. The leading educators were largely white Protestant males, but Jewish scientists and humanist scholars joined the faculty ranks in growing numbers after the war. Most faculty members were happy to operate within the hierarchical order and cheerfully accepted a set of paternalistic rules of the game because the rules advanced the common enterprise of learning and scientific inquiry.

There are various decisive points in the scholarly career: the choice of a major, job versus graduate study, the relationship with one's academic mentors and professors at every stage, initial placement in a research or teaching position at an appropriate institution, and the progression in various stages through the ranks to a tenured position. This is a simplified schema of a complicated phenomenon, of course, and we do not pretend that our analysis exhausts the possibilities of fruitful research on this topic.

Our colleague was first exposed to the workings of the old-boy system when he decided, as a senior at the University of Minnesota, to pursue an academic career. He discussed his interests with one of his mentors, Mulford Q. Sibley, who shortly secured for him a post as a teaching assistant at a neighboring university, with full support for four years to complete his doctoral study.

"But you must also go see Bill Anderson [Professor William Anderson]. You know he was president of the American Political Science Association. He's in American politics, and that's your main interest, right? He will undoubtedly have some thoughts for you. You know him, of course?" said Professor Sibley.

"Oh, yes. I've had a number of courses with him."

Our colleague, who was especially fond of Professor Anderson, recalls seeing the dignified figure of the professor on a winter morning soon thereafter. The professor in his black derby and overcoat paused before a stretch of ice, crouched into a runner's stance, raced to the ice patch, and made a perfect twenty-foot slide. He then resumed his customary brisk pace. Our colleague followed Professor Anderson to his office and told the professor of his interest in teaching and the offer of a teaching assistant position at the neighboring university.

"Oh, yes," said Professor Anderson. "Charlie Hyneman [of Indiana University], a good man. A very good man. But let me think here. . . . Ah, yes, hmmm. . . . No, that's not quite right for you. You should go either to Columbia and study with Dave Truman or to Harvard and study with V. O. Key. Harvard has a slight edge. V. O. is the best man in our field right now. And my classmate and good friend Johnnie Gaus [John M. Gaus] is at Harvard now. . . . Yes, you should go to Harvard. If that doesn't work out for some reason, you stay here and do your work with us."

And thus our colleague found himself at Harvard in 1959. Harvard was not a national meritocratic institution at that time (in the undergraduate programs), but it was moving in that direction, while being, to some degree, still an institution for regional elites.[4] The graduate programs were for the most part highly competitive, drawing on students and faculty from a national and international pool. The old-boy network was everywhere in evidence, but a sprinkling of very able women populated the graduate and professional programs. At least four women were in the entering class of twenty doctoral students in Harvard's Government Department in 1959.

The following scene in 1962 depicts how the old-boy network functioned for academic appointments. As a resident tutor in one of Harvard's undergraduate houses (that is, dorms), our colleague normally socialized with his fellow tutors in the Senior Common Room before dinner. Entering the Senior Common Room one evening, he saw a fellow tutor, an Anglophile who specialized in eighteenth-century English history, resting on the couch in a state of apparent shock. He was surrounded by colleagues trying to calm him.

"What's the matter with ____?"

"He's just been told by his adviser that he's going to the University of ____ [a state university in the Middle West]. Only thing available for him right now. His adviser said he'd be very happy there, but he's never been west of the Mississippi and only to Ohio once in his life. He's suffering from culture shock."

As it turned out, the adviser had been unerring in his judgment. The tutor went to the Middle West (Kansas), found the community entirely to his liking, and spent a happy and productive career there. We note in passing that there was no posted announcement for the position in question, which was not uncommon for many, especially junior, academic positions at the time.

The old-boy system was a total system. Resident tutors in the Harvard undergraduate houses were chosen by the master and fellow tutors on loose criteria of collegiality. Tutors would interview freshmen (who lived in the freshmen dorms on Harvard Yard) and decide who would be welcomed to which of the undergraduate houses.[5]

Junior faculty positions in Harvard's academic departments would be offered to certain of those finishing their doctorate on the basis of teaching need, assessments of merit within subfields that needed coverage, and decorous lobbying by other junior and senior faculty members. Junior faculty could participate in making decisions on junior appointments. However, the most senior members of the department had the final say in appointments and everything else. It was generally assumed that anyone offered an appointment at Harvard would accept, just as, in the broader scheme of things, most scholars would normally move up the pecking order to a more prestigious university if the chance arose.

The process of senior appointments was also far from transparent, even to insiders, but few doubted that a generally acceptable choice would emerge from the process. Harvard was said, but one suspected that this was folklore, to follow a simple rule of thumb: find the best person in the world in the given field. If, astonishingly, that person was not available or turned down the offer (or if, rare at the time, the colleagues could not agree on the parameters of the field), the department would proceed to the second best in the field and so on.

Even then, few at Harvard believed that this was an accurate description of how hiring was really done, but the paternalistic system did seem to serve the needs of Harvard and of higher education reasonably well. Those who were fortunate enough to be in the system benefited from it, and a fairly large pool of talent from around the country was drawn into the network to serve as the nation's future teachers, scholars, and scientific researchers. Today, however, we are far more aware of the costs of such hiring practices. Although surveys suggest that faculty members have been consistently less prejudiced against Jews, blacks, women, and other minorities than the general population, the paternalistic system was only as good as its individual practitioners. There were very few mechanisms of oversight, so systematic sexism or racism within a department, subfield, or discipline could thwart the career hopes and life goals of numerous aspirants. Paternalism was not always benign.

Still, among the myriad shortcomings of the old-boy network, partisan or ideological discrimination was rare. The first person added to Harvard's tenured ranks in the Government Department during our colleague's graduate study was Professor James Q. Wilson from the University of Chicago. Wilson became one of the nation's leading conservative intellectuals during a distinguished career at Harvard and later at University of California, Los Angeles (UCLA), his alma mater. With rare exceptions, overt politics in appointments was not an issue at Harvard in the late 1950s or at other major universities.

At the junior level, those offered appointments as instructors or assistant professors were consistently of high caliber, and many went on to become senior members of the Harvard faculty. Those who did not get an Ivy League appointment went to a major public university or to a select liberal arts college, benefiting from the rapid expansion in higher education that was beginning at the time. The freshly minted PhD from an Ivy League institution often could choose from a number of opportunities at public and private universities and liberal arts colleges. The expansion, which ultimately helped to undermine the old-boy system, helped to ensure favorable outcomes for nearly everybody who was part of the system. In a system with mostly winners, there was little incentive—from within at any rate—to challenge its fundamental premises.

The model of the sciences, which fostered the ideal of "value-free" inquiry, shaped the academic culture of that era. The McCarthy-era controversies and loyalty oath battles, which flared up on a number of campuses, including Harvard, the University of Michigan, the University of California, and elsewhere, had largely passed by the early 1960s.[6] And Vietnam was yet to come. A professor's political views were ignored, tolerated, or taken in stride in this era, which Daniel Bell characterized with the phrase "the end of ideology."[7]

When James Q. Wilson was appointed to Harvard's Government Department, he joined Edward Banfield, Henry Kissinger, William Yandell Elliott, and others with a conservative bent. But there were many liberals at Harvard in the 1950s as well, including Arthur Schlesinger Jr. (who departed for service in the Kennedy administration) and H. Stuart Hughes in history, Carl Kaysen (who joined the Kennedy administration, with former dean McGeorge Bundy, on Kennedy's National Security Council staff) and John Kenneth Galbraith in economics (who served later as ambassador to India), and Samuel H. Beer of the Government Department (who was a cofounder of the Americans for Democratic Action). These men were original, independent, and distinguished scholars who were sometimes memorably colorful figures. No one inside or outside of the university complained that any of them was inappropriately political in class or in academic forums. They all talked of broad political themes, public philosophy, political economy, constitutionalism, and public service, and all had an interest in (and participated in) the practical aspects of politics. They all relished, and the Harvard community valued, a good intellectual fight and public debate of national political issues. Conservative critic William J. Buckley Jr. became good friends with Galbraith, and the two men debated frequently on television, at campus events, and in other forums.

The nonideological calm that prevailed more or less in national politics during the Eisenhower presidency no doubt contributed to the relative calm on the nation's campuses. We do not want to overstate this point, however, for civil rights issues were certainly stirring on the campuses, as in the broad political arena. Disputes over fraternity bias clauses were a constant feature on public university campuses after the 1954 *Brown* v. *Board of Education* decision by the Supreme Court. There were also the beginnings of the cultural revolution symbolized by the beat movement, the postmodern representations in the arts, and other gathering cultural disputes. At Harvard the LSD (lysergic acid diethylamide) craze, fed by faculty members Timothy Leary and Richard Alpert, agitated the campus. Under the stimulus of the Vietnam War, these campus movements grew into the student protests and the wider culture wars that bitterly divided the universities in the late 1960s and after.

But until the tumult of the late 1960s (whose major consequences were felt after the 1960s), the universities experienced a period of calm that was unlike the 1930s or the post-1960s. The 1950–65 period was historically atypical for the universities, and the prevailing mood was anything but the natural state of affairs. Faculty hiring was assumed to be governed by objective criteria, even in the humanities and social sciences, just as the search for scientific truth guided academic research through all fields. The legitimacy of the whole system rested on the mutually reinforcing assumptions of order, hierarchy, and observance of generally accepted principles of scientific truth. To the emerging critics in the faculty, this kind of campus atmosphere was narrow, elitist, conformist, and stifling. They wanted a more spirited and freewheeling debate of large and important issues. These were not, for the most part, postmodern critics who disputed the nature of truth. The whole ethos of the 1950–65 period in the universities was unusual: the more normal state was the noisy contentions of the 1930s and the fractious and numerous divisions of the post-Vietnam era.

Our colleague chose, on completing his studies in 1964, an unconventional career path that combined a research post with a teaching position. He joined the Social Science Department of the Rand Corporation, a leading think tank, and also became a lecturer in political science at UCLA. Having two jobs and straddling two career tracks soon proved to be a mistake. He had occasion to visit his Harvard thesis adviser Don K. Price, dean of the Littauer (now the John F. Kennedy) School at Harvard, during that year. Dean Price, after listening to a saga of troubles from his former student, said, "All idols have clay feet." The gist of the counsel, offered in the most tactful and fatherly manner, was that it was too soon to make any rash decisions, so stop complaining and make the best of the situation.

After a year or so of doing just that, our colleague was surprised one morning by the visit, unannounced, of Professor Philip E. Mosely of Columbia University, a Rand trustee attending a board meeting. He had met Professor Mosely once before while visiting Columbia as a student. The two conversed amiably, but Mosely seemed to want the conversation to head somewhere. Finally, Mosely came to the point: would the younger man be interested in leaving the research organization and joining the faculty of Columbia University? As part of the ancien régime, a call could come anytime in the scholarly career, bringing an opportunity to join the faculty of a major university.

The old-boy network doubtless led to some degree of institutional discrimination in the hiring process. Top departments restricted their searches to a small number of elite universities, and colleagues consulted with a limited number of trusted friends and senior figures who brokered appointments as a matter or right and duty. Faculty members would know something in detail about a relatively small pool of individuals within their particular field, an undoubtedly rather circumscribed universe. Searches for senior positions were naturally more open and protracted. But junior faculty members who got tenure-track positions often had an advantage in the senior appointments, less so in the most prestigious research universities but clearly so in the universities that tended to recruit regionally rather than nationally. This informal, elitist, unbureaucratic, and closed system lasted well into the 1960s.

Beyond institutional discrimination—gaining an edge by doing graduate study in the more prestigious departments—this system was rife with opportunities for the display of gender, racial, and religious prejudices. Its personalized character had few safeguards against a single faculty member on a graduate admission council believing that women were not good admits because they tended to leave the academy to become mothers or another desiring not to serve as mentor to women graduate students for the same reason. Many departments were hostile environments for women because of sexual predation, a problem that the academy seldom openly addressed in this period. The sexist nature of higher education at that time is a story told well and often, and we do not retell it here. Suffice it to say, the experience of one of our George Mason University colleagues in the 1960s and 1970s was not at all uncommon. When she was contemplating entering a doctoral program, she was told by a prominent political scientist, "Women never made it in this profession except Hannah Arendt, and you're no Hannah Arendt." The same colleague was told by a senior faculty member at her first job after completing the PhD, "We've never given a woman tenure, and we never will."

The situation for blacks and other racial minorities was better in some ways but worse in others. The institutionalized discrimination began in the segregated and poorly funded primary and secondary schools in the South, where 90 percent of blacks lived prior to 1940. In the North, blacks tended to live in segregated urban areas, which frequently featured sub-par public schools. Because Harvard and other elite programs received few top-quality black applicants, few got into the old-boy network. Southern universities, with rare exceptions, did not even accept blacks during this period, which prevented them from joining white southerners who sought a graduate degree at Harvard and other programs after doing well in their undergraduate career.[8] And it would be difficult to deny that racism and prejudice were present in various forms at all levels of American education. Just because surveys showed that university professors were more tolerant than other Americans on civil rights during the 1950s and 1960s, this did not make them immune to conscious and unconscious racist attitudes. What President George W. Bush has called "the soft bigotry of low expectations" hurt blacks and others at all levels of education. One of the leading scholars of the history of American higher education accurately concluded, "Between 1950 and 1965 concerns about race were incidental at almost all prestigious colleges and universities in the United States—not just in the South. The result was that black students remained marginal and proportionally underrepresented at almost all racially desegregated campuses in the United States."[9]

Blacks were only the most prominent victims of racism and ethnic bias; Asians, Hispanics, and Native Americans were also affected. Racist and sexist attitudes were not universal, but neither were they ever wholly absent, even at the major institutions of the day. It goes almost without saying that discrimination against homosexual academics was widely tolerated. We will never know how many gifted gay, female, and nonwhite scholars were kept out of the academy prior to the 1970s, when more open, but still imperfect, systems of graduate admissions and faculty hiring were initiated. The present authors are not entirely of one mind about the merits and demerits of the old system, but we agree that despite the best efforts and intentions of its practitioners, the old-boy network undoubtedly privileged white Protestant heterosexual males throughout the academy. Among the many tensions that led to reform of this system, the lack of fairness to the groups left out was certainly prominent.

## From Paternalism to Regulated Competition

The Civil Rights Act of 1964, Title VI (1964) of the act, and Title IX (1972) of the Educational Amendments to the act, the creation of the Equal Employment Opportunities Commission, and other measures signaled that the federal government would no longer tolerate obvious discrimination against minorities and women in public and private universities receiving federal research funds and student financial aid (in practice, this meant most universities). Implementing regulations were promulgated by federal agencies and were gradually put into effect over the decade of the 1970s. The result was that universities were compelled to adopt more transparent hiring practices, to post openings, to maintain records of candidates interviewed, to conduct systematic searches, and otherwise to alter and modernize their hiring practices.

The enormous expansion of the nation's research system had, by the late 1960s, already doomed the old-boy network. It was suited to an equilibrium order where small numbers of elite schools replaced small numbers of departing faculty members in a semi–steady state universe. The elite departments could no longer hope to keep track of the talent produced within their own graduate schools, much less to monitor the expanding research and graduate departments in universities across the country. The logic of an expanding research system called for a more open, transparent, and competitive hiring process at all levels.

Democratizing tendencies in the universities had also undercut the established hierarchies and the dominant style of operations. The patrician class that once dominated the professoriate gave way to a more diverse faculty and a new egalitarian order. The rise to prominence of many Jewish scientists and humanist scholars was already under way and came to be one of the most significant developments of the post–World War II period. The student demonstrations and the crisis surrounding the campus reactions to the Vietnam War also forced universities to be more open in their hiring practices. Graduate, and to a lesser extent undergraduate, students became participants in the more formalized hiring process at many universities.

Thus a new era of *regulated competition* took shape and replaced the old order in academic recruitment. This formulation, like the idea of a paternalist order, is, of course, an ideal type, an analytic construction that oversimplifies a complex reality. Nevertheless, regulation and greater competition are the salient dimensions of the new reality. Universities became more open, cast a broader net in recruitment, and began slowly to add more women and minorities to their faculties. First at the major universities and then at the regional universities, searches became national and even international in scope. The idea of a limited elite acting as gatekeeper for entry into the faculty ranks of the research universities quickly became an anachronism. Whatever one believes about discrimination in higher education today, it is apparent that there was much more discrimination in the past than under today's rules.

The new system produced numerous benefits for faculty members and institutions, but it was not an unalloyed good. The new competitiveness meant higher salaries, greater faculty mobility, unending efforts to lure faculty away from other institutions, the "star" system of highly paid professorial chairs (often with reduced teaching levels, leading indirectly to more courses taught by graduate students and adjuncts), the practice of generating offers to get a pay raise from one's own institution, inequalities in pay within departments and resulting morale problems, and careerism replacing the near-religious concept of the call to the scholarly profession. Additionally, a considerable amount of time was diverted from more productive teaching and scholarly pursuits to seemingly endless compliance and procedural formalities. Often the latter activities degenerated into half-hearted efforts designed mainly to protect one's flank from university compliance officers and to generate paperwork when one was not quite sure what was required under the new regulations. A kind of interest group politics also became a part of search procedures at many universities, with faculty groups forming informal factions or caucuses (for example, the women's caucus, minority caucus, gay rights caucus) to bargain and "game" the system in order to gain support for various factions.

Columbia's political science chair in the 1960s, Wallace S. Sayre (author of Sayre's Law: "Question: Why are academic politics so bitter? Answer: Because the stakes are so small."), quipped to his colleagues that other universities were guilty of "piracy" in the new competitive environment. What was the definition of piracy? Any case of another university hiring a Columbia staff member was a piratical raid on Columbia, with deplorable consequences for all concerned. What was it, he was asked, when Columbia hired someone away from a sister university? It was, said the chair with a twinkle in his eye, a case of our "providing an opportunity for professional advancement."

The new rules within departments, in any event, made searches more onerous and protracted. A few senior colleagues could no longer decide matters quickly after a few informal consultations. Instead, searches became drawn out and sometimes resulted in deadlock, with a department unable to reach a decision. Such circumstances inevitably invited deans and provosts to intervene in the search process, which created additional complexities and eventually paved the way toward a greater degree of central control of the process. Faculties began to cede back to the administrators some of the authority the departments had gained in the postwar period. As the new system evolved toward more openness and transparency in the search process, universities gradually sought to hire more minorities and women. Of course, discrimination against women, gays and lesbians, and racial minorities did not magically disappear in the new system.[10]

The hiring process became so formalized that it could wear the patience of candidates and of those who had to administer the system. A job candidacy went through various expected stages, beginning with the internal debate over how to advertise the position, what areas and qualities to include, what materials to request, what rank to hire at, and even sometimes in what professional journals to advertise. Applicants sent in the requested items, typically including a résumé, letters of recommendation, examples of scholarship, evidence of teaching excellence (such as a teaching portfolio or teaching evaluations), a cover letter, and (rarely) statements of faith or teaching philosophy. A committee would then meet, in larger departments composed of scholars within a given subfield, in very small liberal arts colleges often composed of faculty across a number of disciplines. The committee would produce a long list of prospects, often after rearguing earlier battles over hiring needs. The list was pared down, and prospects were then subjected to more intense review. This could involve checking with references directly and asking more specific questions raised by comparisons of various applicants. A short list would be compiled, at which point decisions were made about which candidates to invite for a campus visit. Further recitation of procedures would be tedious and unnecessary. What we have sketched so far is the tip of a larger bureaucratic iceberg. What this laborious process means in a broad sense is assessed later, but we want to note here that if there is a bias in this system, it is in favor of the relatively safe professional, the individual with few rough edges and a strong record of scholarly publications, for departments want to hire someone who has enough of a research record to be tenurable.

Efforts are made to make the campus visits comparable for all applicants, so that even this final stage of the hiring process is systematized. In practice, the problems of achieving uniformity are formidable. Several aspects separate this modern process from its predecessor. On the negative side, it is expensive and laborious. Airfare, sometimes international airfare, along with hotel and meals, can easily total into the low five figures for a single hire. The cost in departmental time can also be extravagant. The committee meetings that precede and follow a campus visit, the need to sift through hundreds of résumés, check references, read articles, attend research presentations, and participate in departmental deliberations are onerous. It is axiomatic that more than one candidate must be interviewed, whereas in the old-boy system, a visit was more or less in the nature of a final check. The candidate, if carefully preselected, would most likely already have the job unless he or she blundered badly.

Lest one become nostalgic for the old-boy network, the modern system is not without obvious benefits. First, it is clearly more inclusive. The modern system surely does not prevent arbitrary action or undue influence by a dominant figure, but it does make the wielding of such power more difficult. Second, the more systematic nature of the process makes the criteria more transparent to all applicants and levels the playing field to some extent between graduates of less prestigious and more prestigious institutions. It also allows departments to assess teaching quality in a more rigorous fashion. Some of the ills of the old-boy system remain problems. Certainly, racism, sexism, and antipathy toward homosexuals are still present in the hiring process, but they have been substantially ameliorated.[11]

## The Effects of Affirmative Action

Some faculty members, and not merely conservatives, believe that steps to rectify prior discrimination have gone too far and have created a system in which many minorities have distinct advantages in the hiring process.[12] Two observations are pertinent here. First, despite the efforts of affirmative action programs, blacks, Hispanics, and Native Americans remain underrepresented in the professoriate. The gap may have even become larger at the elite schools if one compares the more prestigious institutions to the rest. Talented minority students, like many conservative undergraduate students, have gone to professional schools rather than into graduate programs, and this may help to explain why so few minority students have earned doctorates (notably, at the elite universities). As with some explanations of the paucity of conservatives in academia, some college administrators point to the PhD pipeline and blame career choices made at earlier stages in the process.[13]

Yet black academics and women can often be in high demand and do receive advantages in certain circumstances. "Opportunity hires" or "targets of opportunity" are the names often given to funds made available to departments that hire a qualified minority at many campuses and to searches that do not follow the formalized procedures described above.[14] In this and other ways, higher education administrators seek aggressively to "diversify" their faculties. These tactics have caused friction and controversy on numerous campuses. Whether such programs are effective ways to compensate for past discrimination is an issue that deserves much further discussion and research.

Attempting to analyze potential bias against conservatives in hiring is even more difficult than trying to assess institutional racism, for there are no clear measures of what constitutes "conservative" in a job candidate in the first place. Much less is there a valid statistical base whereby one could evaluate progress toward a goal. Using the pipeline metaphor, there are hints at potential lines of explanations. The undergraduates with conservative ideological leanings seem to choose more vocational paths and majors from the start of their college career. They may receive less mentoring than liberal students (in part because they seek less). At the conclusion of the undergraduate experience, conservative students may be more inclined to pursue professional studies or may enter the workforce immediately in greater numbers than students with a liberal predisposition. The attitude measures and the research techniques are less well developed for students than for faculty members, so conclusions are difficult to draw. Again, however, it may be a fair inference from anecdotal evidence that a student with a doctoral degree who has conservative leanings may be predisposed to seek employment other than in academe for a host of reasons. All of this adds up to a relatively small number of conservatives in the academic recruitment pipeline. Some conservative PhDs may be interested in being actively involved in the policy process, in pursuing careers directly in politics, or in being involved with nonprofit advocacy groups and may consider that the atmosphere in the universities is too theoretical and esoteric for their more activist tastes. Still others, especially those with quantitative skills, may find more lucrative employment in the private sector. In the end, however, some conservatives *do* make their way into the universities, as evidenced by our survey, which shows a not greatly dissimilar pattern from what prevailed in the earliest survey research studies of faculty political attitudes.

## The Hiring of "Safe" Professionals

The new appointment process is in theory more democratic in nature than the old. But greater democracy means more widespread consultation, more involvement of everybody in the process, and more dissatisfaction with those who have the authority to make the decisions. In the value-laden disciplines in particular, conflicts over pedagogy, disputes arising from generational change, the role and propriety of social activism, and the hardening of philosophical differences multiplied in the course of the 1970s and 1980s. The emergence of "super majorities" in appointments has become entrenched as a practical formula for ensuring a working consensus in departments, but this means that any small faction has blocking power. Any senior-level and even most junior-level appointments must be ratified by a large majority of the voting faculty members, a requirement that tends to produce common-denominator hires. The senior faculty members in the old-boy system were usually careful to avoid making an appointment that would rile up their colleagues, but in those days the respected elders could generally count on deference from their colleagues when they emerged with a candidate. The memory of the 1960s upheavals on some campuses still hangs like a vapor, making colleagues extremely cautious not to do anything that could precipitate genuine controversy. One way to reach that goal is to avoid anyone with strong political opinions or interests.

Typically even a handful of holdouts can scuttle an appointment. At times, near unanimity may be necessary, which tends to put a premium on the candidate's inoffensiveness and orthodoxy and on the informal coalition-building skills of a candidate's backers. This said, it remains extremely difficult for outsiders to get inside the decisionmaking process of even the most high-profile appointments. The case of Columbia University's effort to recruit Secretary of State Henry Kissinger at the close of the Ford administration is a case in point. Derek Bok refers to the Kissinger incident as an example of the political left's infringement of academic freedom.[15] One of us participated in this process, and as much as he would like to agree with Bok's analysis, he does not think that Bok got it quite right. Bok did not note that the proposed appointment had strong majority support within Columbia's Political Science Department throughout the incident. The department's vote was 27-8 in favor of an offer to the former secretary of state. Several of the colleagues who were against the appointment were not from the political left, and others expressed doubts that Kissinger was truly interested and, if he was interested, that he would pay attention to his university duties. The opposition leveled charges of procedural irregularities and leaked them first to the *Columbia Spectator* and then to the *New York Times.* What really caused Kissinger's backers not to fight harder to maintain the secretary's interest was the unspoken conviction among many colleagues that they did not want a political figure on the faculty. A political figure was unlikely to be interested in advancing theoretical knowledge.

A similar problem probably had caused Walt Rostow not to return to his teaching post at MIT after his service as national security adviser to President Johnson. Majority support, even a strong majority, could not overcome the blocking power of a small but determined minority. Although MIT has long been comfortable with its scientists serving in science advisory positions, the more ostensibly "political" departments such as political science seemed less comfortable in welcoming back someone with political views who was willing to discuss those views. (Rostow went to the LBJ School of Public Affairs at the University of Texas, Austin, a professional school where his government experience was welcome). In academic appointments, two intersecting principles seem to come into play. Majoritarian principles have been subordinated to minority rights, especially in the nonscientific departments. Departments frequently simmer with controversy when the boundaries of their fields are unclear or in dispute. The effect of super majoritarianism is reinforced by a tacit or overt aversion to politics—that is, to "real" politics—which by its nature seems to invite disputation. The process weeds out mavericks and those with sharp edges of any sort, ideological or personal.

Middle Eastern studies, in recent years, has become of special concern to political scientists, historians, anthropologists, area studies specialists, and liberal arts deans across the country. In 2007 the Comparative Politics Section of the American Political Science Association (APSA) organized a Symposium on Academic Freedom and the War on Terror.[16] The conference participants and organizers found, to their dismay, distressing evidence of "self-censorship" among scholars in the field, bitter ideological divisions that have led to "the degeneration of political argument into personal attack and the disregard of alternative points of view,"[17] and the abandonment of recruitment efforts by several major universities due to opposition to the candidate's political views. Polarization of the subfield into bitter pro- and anti-Israeli factions has made it difficult for universities to conduct searches for both junior and senior faculty positions. Other subfields of comparative politics and area studies have conflicts, but nothing of comparable magnitude. Latin Americanists are not attacked or scrutinized for their views of Hugo Chávez, nor are China specialists attacked for their assessments of China's human rights policies.

Since attitudes on Islamic jihad, Israeli Palestinian policy, and U.S. Middle East policy are so fraught, it has proved difficult for university search committees to secure measured and consistent appraisals of a prospective professor's credentials. Most worrisome is the effect on senior appointments. Without the leadership of a respected senior figure, universities have been unable to launch new or expanded programs of instruction and research in Middle Eastern studies, despite the vastly increased government and philanthropic interest in the field. Middle East specialists are disproportionately represented among David Horowitz's list of the "101 most dangerous professors" in America, nine from Columbia alone, largely because of the pro-Palestinian bias attributed to Edward Said, Columbia's late literary scholar, and like-minded colleagues.[18] The controversy over the failure of Norman Finkelstein to receive tenure at DePaul University in Chicago shows that a university can pay significant costs in negative publicity.[19]

The APSA symposium reported the case of a job candidate being grilled by an interviewer at a top-tier research university on Middle East policy. Dissatisfied with the candidate's answers, the interviewer exclaimed, "You don't have the right to take the Fifth Amendment on these issues! You work on the Middle East!"[20]

Defending Yale's decision to withdraw the offer of an endowed chair to Professor Juan Cole of the University of Michigan, Dr. Dan Olson, associate professor of psychiatry at Yale and author of *Joining the Club: A History of Jews at Yale*, remarked, "People whose politics are stronger than their scholarship . . . can't rely on their scholarship to find themselves a place in the academy."[21] How one should assess the "strength" of another scholar's political views vis-à-vis that of his scholarship or how to judge whether someone has a scholarly temperament are matters that resist pat solution. It is safe to assume, however, that a polarized atmosphere in a department will make the task of evaluating candidates extremely difficult. The lack of understanding of politics on the part of many faculty members further complicates the task of recruitment.

Departments do not lightly put forward someone who may be unacceptable to one or another faction within their ranks or a candidate who is not clearly tenurable. The candidate who is sought will be a safe professional, which means largely that he or she has published in scholarly journals or with major university presses. The individual is vouchsafed as no upsetter of any intellectual applecart and no inciter of fractious debate. Politics, far from being a litmus test followed by search committees, is more often ignored, avoided, or suppressed by colleagues who typically have a meritocratic and conflict-avoidance cast of mind. Utopianism and a penchant for revealed truth are more common in faculty ranks than political behavior, which necessarily involves give and take, compromise, and the ability to deal with and try to resolve disagreements.

## The Failure of Civic Engagement

These characteristics of the hiring process contribute in our view to a serious failing of the modern American university: the neglect of civic and political education in the undergraduate curriculum. Moral and political philosophy, the history of democratic institutions, the underpinnings of the rule of law, and American constitutional history—broadly, those subjects that contribute to effective citizenship—were once at the core of the traditional liberal education. Now they are conspicuous for their absence or their marginal status on most campuses. The denominational colleges of the nineteenth century, for all of their shortcomings, at least recognized that students would be leaders in society and strove to prepare them to be ethically aware and responsible citizens. There can be no return to the good old days, but universities can and should address this failing.

Today's undergraduates, especially at the elite institutions, who can be expected to occupy leadership positions in their communities, should have a liberal education that pays attention to certain core subjects. While we cannot here go too deeply into the details of a desirable curriculum, several contributors to Robert Calvert's *To Restore American Democracy: Political Education and the Modern University* lay out useful elements that we commend to the reader. Michael Walzer outlined a curriculum proposal that would include the critical issues of political philosophy, the evolution of democratic institutions, and the ethical dimensions of professional life that we commend to the reader's attention.[22] William Galston proposed a set of principles and practical suggestions, including an emphasis on the teaching of issues and disciplined discussion, as critical ingredients of a curriculum that would return citizenship to a place of central importance.[23]

The Campus Compact, an agreement among 700 or more college presidents, is a step toward recognition of the need to include citizenship in the curriculum. But it is not an adequate solution to the problem that we identify.

The Campus Compact states in part, "We share a special concern about the disengagement of college students from democratic participation. A chorus of studies reveals that students are connected to the larger purposes and aspirations of the American democracy."[24] This is a useful start, but the Campus Compact largely serves only to encourage students to participate in local community service projects. It does not envisage any larger intellectual obligation on the part of the colleges to include political philosophy, professional ethics, the rule of law, and the history of democratic institutions in the curriculum. Civic or political education deals with the rights and responsibilities of national citizenship and how students conceptualize their role in American democracy.

Political science departments are not exclusively responsible for political education, but they are important in how universities teach politics in general and how they promote civic engagement. Political science departments can contribute to a favorable atmosphere for the debate of issues on campus. The public for the most part believes that those who hold professorships have important responsibilities to the public. It should not be surprising that many Americans are interested in how faculty appointments are made and whether the academy is a closed elite or is receptive to broad social issues and influences. A colleague from a state university commented to us, "I don't think it's great for our image when we have rational choice colleagues declaring that it's pointless for the individual citizen to vote."

Citizens sometimes worry that what goes on in the universities is so rarefied that it has nothing to do with life or reality as they know it. When we in the academy argue that universities can be most useful, and serve the country or the state most effectively, by not trying to be too immediately useful, this is an argument that they will accept to a degree. People instinctively understand that the world is growing increasingly complex and that esoteric knowledge will be vital to achieve a number of practical purposes. However, citizens also wonder whether faculty members are really part of the wider political battle and are only pretending to be above the fray, while pushing a one-sided agenda. We have argued in this book that the universities do not have a political bias and that professors do not see themselves in a political role (on the contrary, we think they, if anything, have an antipolitical mind-set). But it is not credible to insist that political considerations have *never* affected and can never affect university decisions in any way and, in particular, have never played a role in faculty appointments whatsoever. This is simply not credible, and it is not true. Equally, we should not expect that questions about the nature of what is taught are reserved only for the faculty and are beyond the public's ken or its sphere of rightful concern. State legislators and concerned citizens have a right to express their views about what in broad terms should be taught. Many states used to require that the history of the state be a required subject and that students should study state politics. Nor are faculty appointments entirely off limits or inappropriate as subjects for public debate. The public has some right to have, and to express, views on whether and how universities should help to prepare their graduates for effective citizenship. Citizens also have the right to have views about what kinds of individuals make the best teachers, and whether research credentials should be the only or the major criteria for appointments. We are not proposing that there should be voting on individual professorial appointments, but we think that universities should invite comments and reflections in various forums on what constitutes an education for citizenship and the qualities of professors to teach citizenship. The Pennsylvania hearings, discussed in chapter 7, demonstrate that it can be a healthy exercise for state universities to have to respond to legitimate concerns of elected representatives. There are constraints that will guard against demagogy. Legislators do not want to injure their public universities in which they take understandable and deeply felt pride.

The legal hurdles and the procedures in the academic hiring process, as we have outlined, have helped to guard against racial and gender bias. Ideological bias is a more difficult matter to contend with through law or regulations. We do not know for sure how, or whether, ideological beliefs influence how a faculty colleague might evaluate or prefer one candidate over another. Nor are we entirely of one mind in deciding how one *should* evaluate candidates or assess such intangibles as a "scholarly temperament," which most academics in the abstract would deem a desirable quality in a future colleague. But we agree that it is not desirable for universities to root out all politics, political views, and individuals with a strong interest in political issues and in actual politics from their faculties. This would be, we think, to throw the baby out with the bathwater. We do not want to banish political debate from the campuses; rather, we want more, and a higher level, of political debate on the campuses. The conservatives bent on driving politics out of the classroom seem at times to be unwittingly in league with the utopian radicals who believe in revealed (and objective) truth and abhor politics. Political scientists, of all of the scholarly disciplines, would seem to have a responsibility for making the case that "disciplined disputation" (this phrase is William Galston's) should be part of a liberal education. Universities from time to time should actively recruit qualified individuals who have had practical experience in politics and who would be good teachers even if they do not have a string of scholarly publications.

The discussion of politics is necessarily part of a lively intellectual atmosphere on campus. Yet, inexplicably, political scientists do not often see it as their role to promote citizenship in the curriculum and, by and large, pay little attention to such matters on the theory that they are too "applied" for their tastes. Debate of political topics is all too often derided as mere journalism and unworthy of serious scholarly attention. There is also a fear that civility will be lost, that serious academics cannot discuss issues without polemics, and that anyone who raises controversial issues is a provocateur who will contaminate the environment.

The case of Middle Eastern studies suggests the seriousness of the problem. We should hope the universities would be a source of thoughtful discussion of issues of great importance to the country. The experience at many campuses belies that supposition. Schools have been burned by the ideological currents swirling about Middle Eastern studies. Middle Eastern studies departments, which are made up largely of colleagues who study language and culture, often teach the politics of the Middle East in a highly polemical way. Since the field is deeply divided on ideological grounds, mainstream departments frequently steer clear of Middle Eastern policy disputes and may give up on making appointments altogether in this area. And if invited speakers incite public outrage or campus disturbances by militant student groups, what university will have incentives to feature speakers on Middle East issues? On the one hand, American universities are better positioned to have reasonable debates than some European and Middle Eastern institutions, where Israeli scholars are overtly or tacitly banned or forced to keep a low profile. On the other hand, interest groups and newspapers sympathetic to Israel are sometimes obstreperous players who disrupt debates and even classes on American campuses. Internal debates can become so intense that student groups sometimes disrupt the meetings and discussions of their opponents on campus. On these occasions, university administrators have to act decisively to uphold free expression, to punish those who disrupt the meetings of others, and yet to provide the conditions for robust campus debates.

The notion that professors have no political views, and as professionals should have no political views, is deeply rooted in the contemporary academic culture, including even in the political science profession. The social sciences generally were born in the Progressive era's celebration of neutral expertise. A political scientist, or any other professor, is entitled to, and should be expected to have, political viewpoints, but professors are also expected to—and the vast majority do—behave professionally in the classroom. Faculty members can, should, and, according to our data, largely do avoid advocating their political views in the classroom. But they should be free to talk, think, write, and debate politics outside the classroom and to teach *about* politics appropriately in the classroom. Indeed, we believe that most departments, and particularly political science departments, will benefit from having vigorous and frequent exchanges of political views among faculty members and between faculty members and their students. Striving to avoid, or pretending to avoid, all politics is not a practicable or desirable goal for the academy.

Academic colleagues seldom know much in detail about candidates for junior positions, including their political views. This is not a bad thing, but in part it is because candidates do not want to risk their chances by making a false step and because they have been trained to value research as their primary professional goal. The professional norms at present overwhelmingly predispose the individual toward a commitment to research and scholarly publication. The game is somewhat different with senior appointments. Anyone up for a senior appointment is bound to be closely scrutinized, and the "due diligence" will turn up knowledge of the candidate's family situation, finances, background, aesthetic views, political views, collegial tendencies (or lack thereof), temperament, marital status (often a divorce creates the incentive for a change of venue), research interests, teaching ability, and many other details. Any of these factors may affect the hiring decision. Greater candor about the hiring process would be in everybody's interest. Other things being equal, a candidate's conservative views might be deemed an asset (given the paucity of conservatives on the campus), but at any rate should not be held against the candidate. If someone objected or considered a candidate's view to be a reason to oppose the appointment, she or he could stand up and say why. Conflict can be handled civilly and need not degenerate into the kind of rancor that has developed in the Middle Eastern studies subfield. Deans can be helpful by not stepping in to take over a process, but holding the department's feet to the fire and compelling it to reach a decision.

The discipline of political science in the United States has never been radicalized at any time despite the efforts toward that end by a handful of radical colleagues. The major effort to achieve a more explicitly "political" approach to the study of politics came in the Vietnam era. A group of scholars formed the Caucus for a New Political Science, which sought a new and critical paradigm for the discipline.[25] But the caucus recruited relatively few political scientists to its ranks and in the end achieved only a modest influence within the profession. The caucus remains in existence, but it is a waning, rather than an ascending, force. Its limited influence has stemmed principally from the widespread opposition to its leftist premises.[26] Had it tried to broaden its appeal by moderating its message, and not simply remained implacably anti-capitalist and hostile to the existing order, it might have had more of an impact within the profession. Most members of the profession continue to believe that the teaching of political science and the research efforts should not be partisan or devoted to advancing an explicitly political agenda, particularly one that is contemptuous of American institutions. There have been relatively few genuine radicals in political science at any time and only a handful of these have been Marxist. Nor has political science been greatly affected by the postmodern trends that have influenced, for example, English, history, anthropology, and some other fields. Identity politics has left traces, but it fair to say that Foucault's "power/knowledge" concepts have had only a few strong adherents in political theory and virtually none in empirical political science, in philosophy, or in economics.[27]

## Are Conservatives Forced to Take Jobs at Lower-Ranked Schools?

Certainly, our own and other surveys have shown that professors in political science, and the social sciences generally, have tended to be liberal, as measured by their answers to standard survey questions. Have faculties reinforced these liberal tendencies by systematic exclusion of conservatives, as critics have charged? Academics, who generally dislike populist tendencies, whether in the body politic or in their collegial ranks, could be suspicious of an assertive conservative. Such a potential colleague might be seen as a radical in a staid department. Conservatives, being in the minority on college campuses, may feel like victims and, as such, might overcompensate and needle their liberal colleagues. According to this theory, conservatives would be considered poor colleagues and thus be denied the most desirable appointments.

We have seldom encountered conservative faculty members who fit the victim or the passive-aggressive model. Almost no one with this sort of mentality is to be found in the ranks of conservative faculty members at the major research universities. Conservatives at the major universities, while small in numbers, are frequently among the most outspoken and influential voices on campus. They are, in our experience, usually self-confident, assertive individuals quite at home in argument and gifted with the verbal agility that is respected in the professoriate. Moreover, our survey shows that most faculty members, including most conservatives, consider it highly unlikely that politics has affected their chances for tenure or promotion. As discussed in an earlier chapter, 91 percent of all faculty and 75 percent of even the very conservative faculty believe either that ideology plays no role in hiring and tenure in their department or that conservatives are actually preferred.

Nevertheless, it is widely believed that conservatives are at a disadvantage, and some conservative critics—notably Stanley Rothman and his colleagues—have not been content simply to make the assertion. They have done a careful study and advanced an empirical argument purporting to prove that productive conservative scholars have been compelled to accept lesser academic posts than their achievements merit.[28] Specifically, Rothman and his colleagues claim in their widely read article that conservatives, Republicans, and Christians face systematic discrimination in hiring at the most prestigious universities and that this discrimination has caused them to accept lesser posts. They examined this question using an innovative self-assessment measure of academic quality, including time spent on research, the number of articles, books, and book chapters written, the number of conferences attended, and service on editorial boards of disciplinary journals. They also combined into a complex model the Carnegie classification system of universities and colleges with the *U.S. News and World Report* rankings of institutional quality and linked those indexes with measures of ideology, partisanship, and religion, along with race, gender, marital status, and sexual orientation.[29] Using the model, they then examined which factors predict the quality of the institution at which the professor teaches.

While the authors do not claim to have conclusively proven that conservatives, Republicans, and Christians are treated unfairly, they do claim the following:

> In effect, the ideological orientations of professors are about one-fifth as important as their professional achievements in determining the quality of the school that hires and retains or promotes them . . . [and] Republicans, women, and practicing Christians fare significantly worse than their colleagues at similar levels of achievement. . . . The results do not definitely prove that ideology accounts for differences in professional standing. It is entirely possible that other unmeasured factors may account for those variations. That said, the results are consistent with the hypothesis that political conservatism confers a disadvantage in the competition for professional advancement. These results suggest that conservative complaints of the presence and effects of liberal homogeneity in academia deserve to be taken seriously. . . . In conjunction with other recent studies, our findings suggest strongly that a leftward shift has occurred on college campuses in recent years, to the extent that political conservatives have become an endangered species in some departments.[30]

In commentary on the article, Rothman observed that "the most likely conclusion" is that "being conservative counts against you. . . . It does not surprise me, because I've observed it happening."[31]

Why have liberals discriminated against conservatives, in Rothman's opinion? In an interview, Rothman stated that liberal academics are more prone to actions that violate the norms of civility, whereas conservatives seek to preserve civility and only engage in politics reluctantly:

> Part of the answer to that, it seems to me, lies in the nature of radicalism. The left is persuaded that collective political action can remake the world, and political action gives meaning to their lives. . . . Conservatives, on the other hand, tend to believe that love, work, family, and culture are the stuff of which life is made. They turn to politics reluctantly and, only as a last resort, to defend themselves. They are also persuaded that civility plays an important role in the preservation of a decent community and are reluctant to violate the rules of civility. While radicals also believe that they can achieve immortality by remaking the world, conservatives do not believe that immortality is possible except through religion and/or their children.[32]

How convincing is this argument? There are, first, some initial technical problems with the data analysis. Rothman and his colleagues say that they could not examine the combined effect of party and ideology so as "to provide a comparison of the statistical power of the various measures." But this claim does not stand up to close scrutiny. We apologize to the reader here for using technical concepts, but it is necessary to be precise. The correlation coefficient between partisan identity and the ten-part ideology scale in the data set that comprises most of Rothman's cases is barely 0.10, which is below acceptable levels (most statisticians want the multivariate regression coefficient to be up to 0.70).

Including both party and ideology in the same model may cause the small effects of one or both variables simply to disappear. This is only one of several problems. For inexplicable reasons, the authors leave out historically black colleges. Perhaps most important, their measure of ideology is unique, and the interpretation of it is uniquely flawed. Suffice it to say, their methodological shortcomings lead us to have doubts about the whole approach.

The assertion that conservatives, Republicans, and Christians teach at schools significantly beneath what they should merit as scholars is a new variant on the more familiar observations about the large numbers of liberals and Democratic Party identifiers in academe. Ladd and Lipset, for example, cite an earlier study (done in the 1950s) in support of their own conclusion (in 1975) that "professors in large, public schools are the most predisposed toward the Democratic Party and professors in small denominational schools are the most Republican."[33] Even if we were to assume that there has been, in fact, a rise in the percentage of faculty members who call themselves liberal since 1984, could there be other explanations than increasing liberal discrimination against conservative job applicants? One explanation might be not that academic hiring has changed so much as that the nation's political parties have changed on a number of issues that matter to professors.

Consider the partisan shift in attitudes toward spending on higher education. Political scientists are not surprised when corporate executives vote Republican in large numbers or when public schoolteachers vote Democratic. According to James Madison, among other students of public opinion, self-interest is a primary motive in human behavior. The Republican Party once contained many legislators and leaders who favored high levels of national and state spending on education. Eisenhower after the Soviet sputnik successes favored greatly increased spending on science education and urged passage of the National Defense Education Act, which benefited the universities. Nelson Rockefeller and other liberal Republicans at both the state and national levels were among the best allies that higher education ever had in their generous support of public university systems. As the national parties have evolved into more consistent ideological archetypes, these moderate Republicans are less evident within the party. The party has come to oppose, at least rhetorically, many discretionary government domestic spending programs and, almost without exception, opposes efforts to increase taxes.

To the extent that academics behave like an interest group, the less sympathetic attitudes toward expansion of public support for education have an obvious impact on professors' pocketbooks. Many professors are dependent on government spending for research support or, in the case of state universities, for their basic salary. Faculty at public universities can experience a direct loss in potential income growth with the election of a tax-cutting Republican governor. It may be presumed that faculty at both private and public universities who depend on federal research grants to provide partial salary support (the federal research may allow a professor to receive an increment of up to two-ninths of salary during the summer months) and to gain prominence in their field have tended to vote Democratic. A professor may reasonably doubt that his or her interests will be served by anyone "slashing" expenditures. Thus to the extent that we have seen a shift in partisan and ideological loyalty among professors, economic interests, probably refracted through professional socialization, may provide an explanation.

The evolution of the modern Republican Party has other aspects with symbolic significance for academics. Most faculty members are attached to the scientific method as a way of thinking and a worldview, notwithstanding the internal debates about whether science is a "constructed" human activity. The Republican Party of 1969 or even 1984 was not notably less wedded to science as a worldview than were the Democrats. Indeed, when certain antiscientific leftist views were current in some Democratic circles, academic proponents of the scientific method could have reasonably felt more at home in the Republican Party than in the Democratic Party. While some of the recent claims of a Republican "war on science" are a caricature and a political tactic employed by the left, some elements in the Republican Party have radically shifted their attitudes toward scientific reasoning and have advocated the teaching of intelligent design either alongside or as an alternative to evolutionary biology.

A consistent finding in our national survey is that professors, particularly those in the hard and social sciences, are almost uniformly opposed to creationism and its teaching. The Republican rhetorical flirtation with creationism runs counter to those basic convictions. Party leaders at the state and national level have rallied with evangelicals to embrace the teaching of creationism, catering to an activist base that includes many religious fundamentalists. In some surveys, a plurality of Americans are in favor of creationism, while academics as a social group are almost insignificant in elections. Thus Republicans are making a conscious political choice, but one with negative consequences for their support among college professors.

Moreover, creationism is only one of the hot button issues on which Republicans have taken a stance guaranteed to offend many in the academy. Whether the question is stem cell research, the Terry Schiavo case, the reining in of federal scientists who want to talk about global climate change, or delay in the approval of the morning-after (or Plan B) birth control pill, Republicans have said and done things that have cost them support within the academy.

Perhaps most offensive to the beliefs of the vast majority of professors is the attack by some Republicans on homosexuality and homosexual rights. American educators of differing political persuasions are, on the question of homosexuality, firmly committed to tolerance. Our national survey, as well as every other recent study of academic attitudes of which we are aware, confirms that faculty are far to the left of the general population on the question of gay rights. Even conservative academics tend to favor homosexual rights much more than conservatives in the general population. In 1969 there was no partisan distinctiveness on the rights of homosexuals. Today, same-sex marriage is among the most contested social issues in politics, and the Republican Party has repeatedly taken stances on family values that attract those who oppose same-sex marriage and offend those who approve of or at least tolerate gays and lesbians. Some Republicans have also opposed gay adoptions. Republican willingness to push for a constitutional amendment to limit marriage to a man and a woman has run against the much more liberal attitudes toward gay rights among college faculty.

The Republicans have become a successful ideological party that opposes (rhetorically) many domestic spending proposals and takes positions on evolution, gay rights, birth control, euthanasia, and other sensitive issues likely to be opposed by most academics. This is part of a broader trend within American politics. Academics, while they were mostly Republican after the Civil War, began to be torn between the two parties at the turn of the century. While many were opposed to the unregulated capitalism of the Gilded Age, which they identified with the Republicans, they were also turned off by the populist forces of William Jennings Bryan within the Democratic coalition. In particular, the anti-intellectualism of Bryan's opposition to science and evolution repulsed Progressives in the academy. And again in 1968, faculty support for George Wallace was so low as to be almost ummeasurable. In the broad century-long sweep of American politics, Bryan and Wallace were popular among some of the same social groups. Bryan, who swept the white South in all three of his failed attempts for the presidency, used rhetoric on some issues that anticipated the fiery Alabama governor of sixty years later. Although Bryan was not as much of an outlier on racial issues as was George Wallace, his populist anti-intellectualism and social conservatism were preached from the same political bible. The arrival of the Wallace vote in the Republican coalition, a shift that began in 1972 and was completed in the 1980s, is one of the key moments in modern American politics, a tsunami that washed away the New Deal coalition.[34] Professors demonstrated a remarkable antipathy for Wallace, just as they did two generations before for his ideological precursor, Bryan.

The modern inheritors of the Wallace vote, from Richard Nixon to Ronald Reagan to Trent Lott to George W. Bush, have been Republicans. Indeed, the populist white southern conservatism that Wallace typified now forms a central bloc within the modern Republican Party. Until the Democrats swept back into power in 2006 with control of both houses of Congress, a white southern conservative Texan sat in the White House, white southern conservatives presided over the Senate Republicans, and white southern conservatives were the dominant figures in the House of Representatives. A political party led by modern-day inheritors of the anti-intellectualism of George Wallace and William Jennings Bryan would predictably move generally Democratic faculty to a still more Democratic voting profile. Republicans, meanwhile, could point to the shifts in the Democratic Party after the Chicago convention of 1968 as evidence that intellectuals, and Democrats generally, were secular elitists who did not share mainstream American values. If this explanation is even partially accurate, the drift in faculty sentiments toward a more liberal posture is more plausibly explained by these macro political trends than by discrimination in faculty hiring. A final retrospective note: professors in the 1968 intraparty contests tended to favor, in numbers far higher than the general population, Nelson Rockefeller among Republicans. Rockefeller, the last icon of Republican domestic liberalism, has few modern heirs in his party. Liberal Republicans in Congress are as scarce as social conservatives on the faculty at Berkeley.

With the vanishing of Rockefeller Republicans, Republican professors may have found less reason to remain Republican, although some Democrats, appalled by McGovernism, switched their allegiances in an opposite direction and eventually became part of the neoconservative movement. Recent research on faculty partisanship suggests that conservative faculty members are almost as likely to be libertarian as to be Republican. The libertarian wing of the Republican Party, as represented by figures as diverse as Barry Goldwater, William Weld, and Ron Paul, has been repeatedly at odds with the social conservatives in the party. Barry Goldwater, an iconic figure of the Republican conservative movement, ended up deeply at odds with modern social conservatives on issues like abortion and gay rights. Nelson Rockefeller and Barry Goldwater represented the major Republican divide in the 1960s. Today both men would have found themselves without many friends in their party. Thus Rothman and his colleagues may be correct in observing that faculty members have become more liberal since 1984, but the reasons for this may have less to do with developments within the university than with wider trends and partisan shifts in the broad political arena during this period.

The large number of liberals at the higher-quality institutions, moreover, is unlikely to be simply the result of decisions made at those schools. The institutions that systematically discriminate on the basis of religion in hiring are primarily the religious institutions, and they are legally protected in doing so (Congress exempted religious colleges from the application of federal nondiscrimination statutes). These schools tend to have the most conservative faculties, a feature that can be attractive to some colleagues. One of the authors of this study had to write various "statement of faith" essays as part of the application process at denominational schools when he was job hunting. It is illegal for Smith Barney or WalMart to discriminate in hiring on the basis of religion or for secular universities to do so. However, a denominational college or university may refuse to hire atheists and Wiccans and may legally hire only Christian or Jewish faculty. Or a denominational college may hire only members of a specific denomination. The denominational schools that exercise this right tend to have lower ratings in the Carnegie and *U.S. News and World Report* rankings. They are also overwhelmingly Christian and often conservative in their theology and, presumably, their politics.

Moreover, data going back to 1913 show that high faculty achievement has often been accompanied by a more secular and less religious outlook. At the beginning of the twentieth century, the more secular the professor, the higher in general was the quality of the professor's institution. This connection became pronounced by 1933 and still more so in more recent surveys on the subject. Because denominational colleges are permitted to select believers over nonbelievers as faculty members, it is not surprising that they have more Christians on their faculties. Because these institutions tend to be lower ranking, it is also not surprising that Christians tend to be located at less prestigious institutions.

Another lacuna in the Rothman analysis is that he and his colleagues do not explore the relationship between religious faith and conservatism among faculty. According to Ladd and Lipset, liberalism among faculty members is highly correlated with a secular outlook. In 1969 strongly religious faculty were only 33 percent liberal, those who were largely indifferent to religion were 56 percent liberal, and those "basically opposed to religion" were 75 percent liberal.[35] It is reasonable to expect that this relationship may well be stronger today among faculty than it was in 1969. If practicing Christians tend to be Republicans or conservatives, schools that seek to hire only practicing Christians seem highly likely to have more Republicans and conservatives. It is this link among religious orientation, political outlook, and hiring practices at the denominational colleges, rather than discrimination by the major universities, that more plausibly explains Rothman's finding that Christians and Republicans are disproportionately located at less prestigious colleges and universities.

A much smaller number of schools, such as Hillsdale College in Michigan, seek to hire professors who are explicitly conservative but not necessarily religious. As with the more religious schools, they are not generally highly ranked institutions. In the 1950s Paul Lazarsfeld and Walter Thielens found that conservative social scientists were more likely to be at local or regional colleges that were less prestigious than the national universities.[36] Ladd and Lipset found the same result for the 1970s. A relationship between success in the academy and liberal political views is a subject that has been noted, and discussed, for a number of years.

Self-selection may also play a role in why faculty who are Christian, Republican, and conservative end up teaching at lower-ranked schools. Among those small denominational schools that do employ Jews, Wiccans, and atheists, it is likely that scholars of these persuasions would, if they had a choice, prefer to teach elsewhere. It is the rare person who can contemplate a career at an institution whose values are totally antithetical to his or her own. Many talented academics with deeply held religious views may turn down offers from highly ranked schools in order to teach at less prestigious institutions because they wish to work at a college that supports their religious faith.[37] Thus conservatives, for personal, family, or other reasons, may end up on the faculty of a lower-ranked institution. Scholars of an ideological feather may flock together. A campus with a conservative identity, such as Pepperdine College, may well have an easier time attracting and keeping conservative scholars, and Pepperdine also encourages its faculty to be active in public debate and citizenship activities. It seems plausible that some conservative faculty will simply choose to remain in a more comfortable setting at a lower-ranked institution. A certain school of thought in a given department or close friendships among one's colleagues can decisively influence one's choice of career. Being a big fish in a small pond is appealing to some people.

A certain "ecology" is at work here as well. Universities are not disconnected from their surroundings or from broader societal trends. Colleges and universities with more conservative campus environments are often located in more conservative states. Less competitive institutions may hire from a local rather than the national pool of applicants.

Many of the country's leading universities are located in blue states such as California, New England, New Jersey, and New York. Now that New Hampshire has turned "purple" in national elections, there are no Ivy League institutions in the red states. In the red states that have leading public universities, these campuses are often located in—and help to form—liberal oases in more conservative surroundings. One thinks of the universities located in Iowa City, Atlanta, Athens (Georgia), Austin, Fargo, College Station (Pennsylvania), and Bloomington (Indiana). The growing ideological divisions in the U.S. population have affected people's choice of life style and where to live, and we can expect that this development could also affect faculty members. A brilliant conservative biologist on the faculty of a mid-range state university might reject an East Coast offer so that her children can grow up with what she believes are wholesome southern community values. All of these self-selection factors are more likely to account for the effects found by Rothman and his colleagues than a deliberate effort to bar conservatives from academic posts.

## Academic Hiring Is Too Timid

Our analysis suggests that the conventional wisdom has misperceived the nature of the hiring problem at universities. The notion that universities systematically favor liberals and exclude conservatives is wrong and misses the mark in our view. Faculty search committees largely pursue neutral expertise and specialized knowledge, and these qualities are usually defined in conventional academic terms, that is, faculties excessively stress research and publication in the hiring process. This kind of default position means that they usually emerge with colleagues averse to, uninterested in, and incompetent to discuss political issues in any serious sense. A reflexive leftism, or utopianism, may be a by-product of this intellectual orientation. Overt partisanship clearly is not desirable in the hiring of college teachers, and paying attention to scholarly merits is a worthy ideal. Politics can inappropriately enter into the academic hiring process in many forms, however, as evident in the identity politics of the 1960s and 1970s, when an implicit social justice mission unconsciously or consciously influenced the thinking on many campuses. More often, however, in an effort to avoid political bias of any kind, searches avoid anything political and regard all such awareness as unprofessional. A good scholar with a slight penchant for polemics has to be a great scholar with only a very slight tendency toward polemics to be appointed to a prestigious post. Universities typically stick closely to the conventional profile of the productive scholar. This means someone who has published in scholarly journals, as opposed to writing op-ed pieces or contributing to non-peer-reviewed opinion journals.

The many hurdles through which a nomination typically proceeds tend to weed out idiosyncratic views and to prevent the appointment of "friends and neighbors." But a more subtle bias may creep in on behalf of conventional candidates who look like, and behave like, "safe" professionals. This sort of bias has become deeply rooted and contrasts unfavorably with at least some aspects of the old-boy network. The old boys were self-confident enough and had enough autonomy to hire persons with rough edges and unconventional views, and they did not have to justify their choices by pointing to scholarly publications. They could put forward someone they felt was well rounded and promising, and they were not troubled by excessive "democracy" in their departments. They were also shrewd enough to make sure, if they were located in a state university with a conservative population, to have at least some faculty members with whom their fellow citizens could identify. To the old boys, it was unproblematic to serve in government advisory posts and to take leave for public service. They were rooted in their institutions, were often unashamed patriots, and did not aspire to be some kind of rootless intellectual citizen of the world.

We cannot escape the conclusion that the sort of narrow professionalism that prevails in hiring has worked against the presence of conservative intellectuals on campus. Citizenship as we use the term in this book does not have partisan overtones, but the relative scarcity of conservative views on many campuses assuredly complicates the idea of citizenship. Citizenship means encountering divergent views in the public square and having to work out compromises that enable people with different views to live together. For a state university in a conservative state, it is a matter of simple prudence to avoid the impression that faculties are overwhelmingly made up of liberals. It is also unwise to embrace the rhetoric, common among some university administrators, that the globalizing university should educate students to be citizens of the world instead of preparing them to be American citizens who live in an increasingly interdependent world.

University officials sometimes say that the reason they do not hire conservatives is that they cannot find any emerging from the ranks of graduate students at the best universities. One can only recruit from the existing pool of candidates, a parody of the old arguments about the impossibility of finding women or minority candidates. A variant on this is that they cannot find any conservatives who are "real" scholars as opposed to militants, publicists, activists, bloggers, or Trojan horse conspirators put forward to subvert the universities from within. That someone goes to a think tank rather than a university after graduate studies is sometimes taken as proof that the individual lacks scholarly inclinations. In fact, some prospects may steer away from the academic job market because they suspect that the system is rigged against them or because they want to engage more actively in public life than the universities seem inclined to do.

The whole hiring process may, indeed, be less transparent in some ways than it was even under the old boys. The legally protected minorities under affirmative action or "diversity" guidelines are often adroit at advancing their own position and can count on effective advocacy from their friends. Conservatives are rarely skilled at this kind of maneuver because diversity has been an idea of the left, and they may have few friends or advocates within faculty ranks to look out for them. We do not advocate affirmative action for conservatives, if by this is meant quotas, but we have some advice for both conservatives and liberals to enhance the conservative presence on campus. We urge our conservative colleagues to reconsider their aversion to diversity in principle and to rethink any disinclination on their part to seek academic posts. To put the point provocatively, we urge conservatives to stop being cry babies and to jump into the competition for these sought-after teaching posts instead of complaining from the outside. And liberal colleagues, for their part, might ponder whether it is logical to defend recruitment on the basis of race, gender, or sexual preference criteria but to be untroubled by the absence of conservative viewpoints in their departments. Diversity of ideas is the most important diversity of all for the university's intellectual vitality. Liberals in departments such as political science, history, sociology, anthropology, and English and in some of the professional schools, who have been committed to the idea that diversity enhances the learning environment, should accept the logic of their own position. They might well consider innovative solutions to the comparative paucity of conservatives among the professoriate.[38]

Diversity has come under attack from many sides lately, including those like Walter Benn Michaels who see it a subterfuge for universities to fight symbolic evils of the past while ignoring the class divide in America's elite universities.[39] Diversity is defended by others, including ourselves, who see the task of racial and gender equality as an unfinished challenge. This is not inconsistent with the need to open up the elite universities to more poor and working-class students.[40]

Promoting democratic citizenship is a concept that, properly understood, should include conservatives and liberals, radicals and libertarians, debating the meaning of concepts such as civic republicanism, new and old liberalism, rule of law, public philosophy, and democratic majoritarianism. Government should not attempt to impose any hiring strategy on the academic community, and no serious politician advocates such a course. This idea is repugnant and is rejected by most Americans. But if universities are to embrace more fully the idea of teaching about civic republicanism and the history of democratic institutions, for example, or to promote the discussion of national policy issues, it is important that students be exposed to both the liberal and conservative traditions of the American past.

Deans, provosts, and in smaller institutions even presidents now appear to be players in the appointment process to a degree that has not been seen since the days of the powerful late Victorian educational leaders who founded the modern university. Some of the same pressures are buffeting the universities. Powerful donors threaten to withdraw financial support if they dislike what particular faculty members say. University presidents in principle want faculty to participate in public debate but in practice fear reprisals against their institution by government leaders and wealthy private donors.

A third phase in academic appointments, what we could call something of a *democratic centralism,* may be emerging. In this system overall institutional priorities are being displaced, or at least modified, and departmental autonomy in the hiring of faculty and in the direction of new research programs is no longer the dominant or sacrosanct practice. This new process could have negative effects since deans, provosts, and presidents worry excessively about the reactions of alumni, powerful donors, the muckraking press, and state legislators in deciding what areas to expand and which programs to promote. Universities, however, can serve their students, their communities, and the nation better by fostering *more,* not *less,* political debate on campus and by not being afraid to join in the wider public dialogue on critical national issues.

We come then to a paradoxical conclusion. While we find little support for the idea that conservatives or Christians are subjected to systemic discrimination in faculty hiring, we believe that colleges and universities should be more concerned than they currently are about the low number of conservatives in their faculty ranks. We believe that committed conservatives, radicals of the left, and politically active professors of any persuasion have been negatively affected by the overly cautious hiring practices of modern academia. We are concerned that the highly publicized controversies of the recent past will only encourage these cautious tendencies. Universities should draw the opposite lesson from the high-profile controversies and contemplate how to foster more politics and robust political debate on campus. No one can pretend that this will be easy; the incentives work in the opposite direction. The cat, once burned, does not relish a new jump onto the hot stove. Presidents and deans do not want to offend any constituency or to stir up the potentially explosive divisions within the faculty ranks. Professors want to do research and, for the most part, do not want to engage each other in an extended conversation about the curriculum or about public issues. Students want to advance their career and to have the widest flexibility in choosing what to study; they dislike being told what to do or what to study. These are the realities that confront any attempt to pursue changes. Given the formidable obstacles, how might desirable change be accomplished? We offer some reflections of a general nature in the next chapter.

# 10

## Conclusions

This book has set out to explore political bias in the nation's universities. We have reached conclusions that are in some ways reassuringly familiar and in other ways quite surprising to us. To use social science terms, we have confirmed some hypotheses but disconfirmed others, including some of the ideas that started us on the inquiry in the first place.

### The Myth of the Politicized Universities

The idea that the elite universities are rife with leftist politics, or any politics for that matter, is at odds with the evidence. Students, for the most part, do not feel that their professors have engaged in efforts to proselytize them or to use the classroom for partisan purposes. Professors, of course, do not believe, as our survey showed, that they act unprofessionally. More to the point, they do not believe that they suffer from discrimination. Even professors who identified themselves as conservatives apparently do not believe that they have been discriminated against in their career, nor do they in general feel forced to self-censor in conversations with colleagues on political matters.

In the most far-reaching examination of classroom bias at the state level, Pennsylvania legislators found that political bias in the state's public college and university classrooms is "rare." The dire fears of both the political left and the right, we think, have proved to be groundless. Conservative interest groups at the national level and conservative activists like the indefatigable David Horowitz helped to stir up the issue of classroom bias and to launch the Pennsylvania inquiry. But the hearings showed that the issue is, in fact, largely a nonissue. The countermobilization of the American Association of University Professors (AAUP) against what some members saw as a growing right-wing conspiracy also proved to be much ado about little, for no potent right-wing conspiracy against academic freedom could be discovered. The peak of interest in classroom bias has apparently passed as the culture wars have diminished.

On the issue of discrimination in academic hiring, we found little evidence to support the idea of any kind of political test in hiring at the nation's major colleges and universities. Discrimination was more common in the old days when a benign paternalism operated in higher education, at least in the sense that white males from the elite universities had a distinct advantage in getting the best jobs. A hierarchical system prevailed in higher education for a long time: an old-boy network dominated decisionmaking in the major universities on a whole range of issues. With the rise of antidiscrimination statutes and regulations, and with the general expansion of the higher education system, the hiring process was forced to change and to become more open. Women and minorities gained entry into higher education in increasing numbers. Women, especially, made gains in a number of disciplines, both in the ranks of students and in the ranks of college teachers. The ranks of students and teachers are obviously interdependent: as women increasingly went into graduate studies, they filled the employment pools from which colleges and universities recruited their new teachers. Boards of trustees and the administrative hierarchies also came to resemble more closely the diverse population of students they served.

## Our National Survey of Faculty Political Attitudes

Colleges and universities thus came to hire from a broader pool of applicants, adding more women and minorities to faculty ranks. This tended to reinforce the modestly left political orientations of an already moderately liberal professoriate. Our national survey of faculty political attitudes in 2007, like most earlier surveys, showed that faculty members were generally left-liberal in their political orientations. We also found that some fields, notably some of the sciences and engineering fields that previously were more conservative, have become more liberal—in short, more like the social sciences and humanities. But we did not find any sharp increase in the degree of liberalism overall during the past decade. Viewing our findings in the context of surveys conducted since the late 1960s, we were struck by the continuity of faculty political attitudes. A shift toward more liberal attitudes did occur in the 1980s: professors shifted from the 40 percent range in identifying themselves as either left or liberal to the low 60 percent range. But part of this shift can be attributed to three factors: the significant increase in women and the small rise of racial minorities, the dropping of two-year colleges from the surveys, and a small change in the wording of the survey questions. It is thus probable that there was some shift in the 1980s, but the shift was not as sudden or as dramatic as the figures would suggest.

Viewed in a broad historical perspective, faculties in the nineteenth century were generally Republican and conservative, but they began to display mugwump tendencies (still Republican, but distressed about some aspect of their party and wavering in their political loyalties) toward the end of the century. The professoriate did not coalesce around any clear partisan identification until the New Deal. College professors at that time began to identify with the Democratic Party and to become liberal in their outlook. The shift was reinforced in the aftermath of World War II with the addition of large numbers of liberal Jewish scholars, and a somewhat loose identification with the Democratic Party became more pronounced when the Democrats embraced the cause of civil rights.

But the campuses over the 1950–65 period were less politically engaged than they had been in the depression era. The Vietnam War student upheavals changed the climate on campuses across the country, igniting political activism around the antiwar movement on numerous campuses. With the end of the Vietnam War and the draft, the energy behind political activism dissipated. Once the cluster of issues connected with the war period was resolved, including classified research on campus, the status of the Reserve Officers' Training Corps, government restrictions on grants, and student deferments, the campuses disengaged from politics, with some intense debates taking place over divestiture of investments in South Africa. The campuses turned inward and away from wider political engagement. The "identity debates" of the 1970s and 1980s came to substitute a concern with the issues of race, gender, and sexual orientation, as they applied to the campus itself, for a wider engagement with national politics. The pattern of self-identified liberalism in surveys, along with a generally aloof attitude toward political activism in the real world, persisted over the remaining half of the twentieth century and into the twenty-first century until the terrorist attacks of 9/11 brought a new mood.

## *The Displacement of Politics and Values*

The universities after the Vietnam War period of activism have been anything but hotbeds of political discussion and activism. On the contrary, we believe that there has not been enough politics or enough serious political debate on campus for many years. In the broad nonpartisan terms in which the concepts should be properly understood, the universities have neglected political issues and seem to have taken little or no interest in what used to be called civics and civic education. The terrorist attacks of September 11, 2001, ignited new political interest on the nation's campuses, but of an unsatisfactory sort, mostly a rancorous and short-sighted clash over the nature of Islamic radicalism and the appropriate U.S. policy toward the Middle East. The least well-informed voices have often been heard, and the level and tone of these debates have left much to be desired.

Many American universities, at their birth in the last decades of the nineteenth century, were strongly influenced by Progressive ideas. Progressive ideas were not unified, and it is not surprising that their impact on the universities would be contradictory. The universities were understood to serve society (one part of the Progressive legacy) but to eschew partisanship and to distrust politics and politicians (another part of the Progressive legacy). The urban political machine was the Progressives' archetypical enemy. The Victorian reformers who ran the universities did so in what we would consider today a rather high-handed fashion and in what they said was law. The presidents shifted their views rather quickly (too quickly, in our view) away from the idea that faculty members should participate in public service and public debates and toward the idea that they should steer clear of controversy; instead, universities came to serve the individualistic ethic that went along with commercial success. Presidents and trustees became concerned, in short, that professors who spoke out on controversial issues were troublemakers who could damage their institution. We do not have to note the obvious similarities in this respect between the Progressive era and today.

The notions of academic freedom put forth by the founding fathers of the AAUP in 1914–15 incorporated the ideal of subject matter expertise as the centerpiece. The sanctity of the classroom was privileged over the involvement of faculty in public debate outside of class and off the campus. Professors were to teach their field of expertise and to conduct research in their specific discipline, and they could contribute to society so long as they did so by means of their objective expertise, not through participation in the political process. Academic freedom was not understood to mean vigorous participation in controversial public debates. For this reason, college presidents could fire faculty whom they regarded as troublemakers and still believe that they were subscribing to the tenets of academic freedom.

Almost by definition, any faculty member who became controversial was deemed to have forfeited academic freedom protections (if one acted scientifically, there would be no controversy). Although schools of public administration, business, law, medicine, social work, and other professions were established, the tradition of preparation for citizenship and civic engagement did not generally include direct participation in politics (only technical boards and civil service departments). Thus law, medicine, and business schools were increasingly vehicles for the new middle classes to enter into private sector careers, not public service and not elective politics. Some schools, such as Syracuse University's Maxwell School of Citizenship and Public Affairs, were devoted to citizenship training and required all undergraduates to study civics. But the undergraduate civics requirement was later weakened at Syracuse and only survives today as an elective. The Maxwell School's best-known programs became the more specialized professional offerings for master's-level students. As elsewhere, the faculty increasingly focused on individual research specialties and taught at the undergraduate level what they researched.

In the humanities there was a related shift as courses devoted to large philosophical issues and to broadly humanistic concerns were displaced by the formalistic scrutiny of texts and later by gender, race, and sexual orientation themes. Alexander Meiklejohn, a professor of government and constitutional law and president of Amherst College from 1912 to 1924, preached a vision of undergraduate education that included many of the dimensions we find appealing. His vision inspired many other colleges and universities in the first half of the twentieth century. By mid-century, however, such ideas were no longer influential. Undergraduate humanities at many elite colleges and universities became heavily influenced by the ideals of specialized research that marked graduate studies, and the broad Meikeljohn pedagogy was downgraded or abandoned.[1]

In its neglect of citizenship, values, and broadly humanistic learning, the modern research university has departed from what was a major mission of the pre–Civil War denominational colleges. The old colleges felt a responsibility for the moral and political education of their students. The colonial colleges—that is, those twenty-five institutions founded before 1800—were explicit in their mission statements. Higher education was to prepare students to live and think so as to contribute to the new American democracy. Benjamin Rush, who was instrumental in forming two of them (Dickinson College, Franklin and Marshall College) proclaimed, "[These institutions were] to teach our citizens to think for themselves, and thereby to deliver them from the influence and dictates of a few designing men."[2] The offerings were mainly classical learning, and of course we are not recommending any simple return to the past. We do not endorse an exercise in nostalgia, but we do consider the nearly total abdication of responsibility for moral and political education to be a serious shortcoming of the contemporary university. This is why for some parents the Christian-oriented or -affiliated colleges are appealing, and the pluralism of our system is certainly an asset. But most students will continue to attend secular public and private institutions, and we want these schools to address at least the citizenship requirement, even if they cannot or should not transform themselves into denominational institutions.

The public face of the universities from 1950 to 1965 rested on the ethic of scientific research and objective truth-seeking. The ideological debates of the 1930s were set aside; such disputes were seen as relics from the past. The questioning of first principles was replaced in the broad scheme of things; the democratic unity of the Free World in its opposition to communist totalitarianism was a broad enough umbrella to give unity of purpose.

The purposes of the "multi-versity" during this period could incorporate the idea of public service in an unproblematic fashion. The universities could participate in economic modernization in the Third World, in military research, and in language study in the immediate aftermath of World War II to "know the enemy," for example, without precipitating fractious internal disputes, until the Vietnam War shredded the consensus. The mission of the university seemed misleadingly clear for a time: to expand in faculty size and student numbers, to serve the ends of America's new role as world leader, and to advance scientific understanding across the broad frontiers of research. The university entered into a kind of informal compact with American society. Society would get economic growth, improved health, and military strength from this tacit bargain, and the universities would be awarded generous research support and student financial assistance to fuel the postwar expansion, on terms that largely protected the autonomy of the universities.[3] This 1950–65 period, as we argue in earlier chapters, was the unusual rather than the normal state of affairs. The 1950–65 period was historically less typical than either the strife-ridden 1930s or the contentious future ushered in by the Vietnam War era and its aftermath. The postwar consensus that had prevailed in American politics and shaped the relationship between the universities and the federal government seemed to offer the prospect of an untroubled future. Such was not to be, and those who have in mind the 1950–65 university as an implicit or explicit model are bound to suffer disappointment. The universities were (and are) forced to confront the more profound questions relating to mission and purpose that they faced at their founding.

## The Eclectic University and an Uncertain Future

The more eclectic university that emerged in the last decades of the twentieth century does not lend itself to easy characterization. The universities have continued to view themselves as in some sense providing "service" to society, if by no other means than by responding to the needs of the new student body. The multi-versity concept advanced by Clark Kerr before the height of the Vietnam crises is not totally dead, but it is much more problematic as a statement of a unifying mission for the modern university. The resurgence of tradition and of more traditional ideas has also been evident, marking a reaction to the new curriculum ideas and the new service role in general. Witness the words of Dr. Jacques Barzun, provost of Columbia: "I have nothing against the university studying social problems or commenting on what is going on out of its fund of knowledge. But the university is getting to resemble the Red Cross more than a university, with direct help to whoever is suffering."[4] Traditional conceptions of the university's role notwithstanding, the universities in the post-Vietnam era felt committed to promoting social justice, somehow defined, and most often in terms of admitting disadvantaged minority students and offering programs that appealed to them. The scientific ideal that had dominated so many fields of study, even in the humanities and social sciences, no longer holds quite the same sway, and knowledge has been deemed a product of social construction and held up to new critical scrutiny. In some measure, for a number of fields that have escaped from a narrow "scientism," the changes affecting the universities have been a healthy corrective. The boundaries of subjects have become broader and the topics studied more inclusive and more open to the debate of core values.

The natural sciences still are vital and central to the university and, in many ways, continue to set the overall tone and direction for the modern research university. The sciences have escaped most of the controversies swirling around the humanities and the social sciences, but they also have to some degree been drawn into the cultural arguments that have afflicted (but also energized) the "softer" disciplines. The scholars who study the sociology of science, science affairs, and technological change have grown more critical of science's internal folkways and its wider social impact and less inclined to be mere celebratory chroniclers of science's achievements. The scientists, who always enjoyed friendly relations with the humanities (and somewhat less so with the social sciences), have struck back at the excesses of some of the newer types of scholarship.[5] That there is no longer a unifying mission or a dominant intellectual conception for the universities is not necessarily bad. The heterogeneous modern university can perhaps have no single or simply defined mission and no prospect of escaping public scrutiny by presenting a unified front to the external world. The stage is set for revisiting the kind of fundamental issues that were presented to the Victorian reformer architects of the modern university. Thomas Haskell put the point in its most basic terms: "What are universities *for*?"[6]

Are universities to be primarily devoted to research? Mainly transmitters of cultural values and arenas for the debate of large value-laden issues? Plural communities of scholars pursuing truth in their separate ways or mobilized entities promoting social justice, assisting the federal government, or pursuing some other collective ends? These are only a few of the numerous questions that come to mind. Not least in such a list of major issues is what role is to be played by higher education, and what special role, if any, is to be played by the elite research universities in achieving national purposes. Do these elite institutions have a special obligation, either to set goals for the entire higher education system or to stand apart from the rest and to serve a unique purpose of their own?

We are not comfortable with the idea that the major universities should be engines for general social change; they are neither organized for nor suited to such a role. We do believe that the major universities and the selective liberal arts colleges have a general obligation to provide moral and political education for their students in the framework of a liberal education, a responsibility many of them neglect at present. It appears that going to college produces a change in attitudes among students on specific issues such as gender equality and gay rights, just as higher education in the past produced more tolerance and support among whites for African Americans' civil rights. This may be part of citizenship, but we are talking about a broader goal and one that may be possible mainly in the elite schools. Reviving the concept of citizenship, restoring the idea that colleges and universities can grapple with the big issues of life, and empowering humanists and social scientists to be more than specialists in narrow fields of learning will come more readily from the major schools. A mass higher education system can never be patterned wholly on an Ivy League model. Today, however, there is a tendency for many institutions to imitate the undesirable features of the research model and thus to serve their students and communities poorly.

The elite universities and colleges cannot serve all of the nation's educational needs nor can they or should they conform to any uniform mold. The variety of our system caters to different educational needs. Parents who seek values and a religious orientation can send their children to the denominational colleges or to the more recently established schools with a distinctive social philosophy. We have no quarrel with the system's pluralism, and we agree that the nation draws strength from the different traditions and opportunities that are offered to students. We welcome the appearance of new institutions that challenge the perceived secular and liberal bias of higher education, such as Patrick Henry University, which has as it mission the education of future conservative leaders of America. Patrick Henry is already experiencing predictable problems in serving a student body made up of less academically advanced home schoolers and more intellectually assertive, skeptical students who resist the school's orthodoxies.[7] Any college explicitly devoted to a particular ideology, conservative or liberal, faces similar challenges. Such institutions enrich American higher education even as they attack it. Market forces will operate here, as students, parents, donors, graduate schools, and employers choose among the graduates of the different schools.

It is improbable that any fixed curriculum could be widely adopted. But students today both want and would benefit from the opportunity to study, among other aspects of a liberal education, the great Western classics, the major religious traditions, constitutional history, and the ethical challenges involved with their future professions. Institutions with a strong core curriculum, such as Columbia College (of Columbia University), find continued strong student interest in the required courses of literature and the humanities (two semesters), contemporary civilization (two semesters, with strong doses of political philosophy), music humanities (one semester), and art humanities (one semester). Yale's Directed Studies Program, offering courses similar to Columbia's core curriculum, has been increasingly popular with undergraduates and now attracts 10 percent of the freshman class (with a long waiting list). Princeton's Madison Center offers lectures and highly popular programs in constitutionalism that are very much what we have in mind when we ask for courses to strengthen citizenship. Tufts University similarly is among the select universities that emphasize citizenship in the undergraduate curriculum. Duke's Focus Program attracts one-third of entering freshmen and women to an interdisciplinary, team-taught, year-long seminar on integrated themes that has been highly successful, and the concept will likely be extended to a similar course for sophomores. The Gerst Program at Duke is devoted specifically to citizenship issues.[8] The University of Maryland, College Park, offers a highly popular and selective honors program, which features a structured curriculum, separate residential living facilities, and close tutorial contact with a designated core of faculty members.

The freedom of choice for students and their exposure to numerous influences are hardly under threat. Most students, even at the selective institutions, are besieged with blogs, omnipresent media, and the dominant popular culture in all of its manifestations—the "invisible tutors," in Benjamin R. Barber's phrase—that shape their environment. Their exposure to the formal classroom requirements under even ideal circumstances can be nearly overwhelmed by outside pressures. The opportunities to indulge their special tastes and interests are almost limitless. What is missing is the exposure to shared values, common tastes, and a communal experience that gives shape to the educational experience. Unlimited freedom of choice, as Cass R. Sunstein argues in an analysis of the impact of new communication technologies, enables students to learn rapidly outside the formal classroom but erodes the shared cultural experiences and exposure to common values that make for effective citizenship.[9] Faculties must assert their responsibility to ensure a liberal education for their students and not merely encourage eclecticism and dispersion of the student's intellectual energies. Premature specialization and vocationalism are pervasive in the universities today, while faculties are often disengaged from the task of framing common educational standards.

## The Weakening of America's Civic Traditions

We have suggested that politics and the serious discussion of political issues—the critical ingredients of a civic education—are conspicuously missing in today's university curricula. William A. Galston notes that, in contrast to the nineteenth-century colleges' definitions of their educational mission, "one can number on the fingers of two hands the contemporary American colleges and universities that devote even one-tenth of their efforts and resources to civic education."[10] The reasons for this neglect go back to the Progressive tradition. The Progressive legacy privileged the expert over the politician, and the university notions of public service pointed toward service on technical boards, regulatory bodies, and civil service systems at a remove from the political parties and electoral competition. The individualist ethos also channeled students into a career in the burgeoning commercial sector. The universities served as vehicles for upward mobility for the new middle classes.

Civic education inevitably is closely linked to the discipline of political science, although other disciplines such as history, law, economics, sociology, philosophy, literature, and others are relevant. Behavioralism and the rational choice paradigm in political science have put a premium on theoretical formulation and empirical research and have relegated civics to a marginal status in the profession. The issues that have engaged political scientists for decades have not included much concern with the institutions, procedures, and responsibilities of citizenship. While there have been notable exceptions, such as Robert Putnam's work on social capital and its role in citizenship, he and others remain more of the exceptions than the mainstream of political science. Normative political theory enjoyed a brief revival in the 1980s but has more recently lapsed back into a niche status in the profession.

Americans are normally averse to politics and reveal deep-seated antistatist attitudes. University professors are not immune from those popular sentiments.[11] Americans dislike conflict and controversy and see politics as inevitably involving unpleasant discord and contention. American civic life seemingly has eroded in recent years, and the universities, far from trying to combat the trend, have acquiesced to the erosive forces.

The way in which many of the post–Vietnam War era controversies have been handled by faculties and administrators has damaged the concepts of civility. Democratic citizenship, if it is to be taught, must also be practiced on campus. The fractious disputes that divided many faculties and departments offer a poor illustration of democratic citizenship in action. And administrators, sometimes overly frightened by the prospects of discord, have stepped in and short-circuited disputes that should have been allowed to run their course in the departments.

Departments such as economics and philosophy that potentially should contribute to political debate have at times devoted themselves to the narrow, highly technical areas of their fields, which are inaccessible to undergraduates and even to colleagues in other disciplines. It seems as if professors in those fields have either avoided politics or dissolved politics into conceptual technicalities. Perhaps this helps to explain why political themes emerged in English and modern languages, which became the home for many orphan subjects such as the politics of sexuality and ethnicity. Political matters have consequently been debated by colleagues without the benefit of a clear intellectual paradigm or historical depth. We do not mean to criticize any discipline in particular or to suggest that disciplinary lines should be policed by specified departments or university administrators. Many of the major works of scholarship, of course, stimulate cross-pollination over disciplinary and departmental lines. And political views, like ethical views, are not and should not be the province of professional specialists alone. We merely suggest that citizenship and practical politics should be studied within all departments of political science, while other departments may also include political themes in their offerings.

How should the universities engage students intellectually to equip them to be effective citizens? What kind of courses in moral and political philosophy are suitable for this purpose, and how should students be taught to be ethically sensitive members of their future profession? Should the universities teach the great religious traditions as part of the liberal arts education, and can they do this without denigrating any particular religious tradition? If the high schools do not teach civics, should the universities do so?

## The Universities after 9/11

The post–September 11 environment facing the universities has made our concerns both more urgent and more difficult to achieve. Suspicion of government interference has heightened in the academic community. Conservatives have questioned the patriotism of professors, especially the scholars who study the Islamic world and, in particular, those who belong to postcolonial scholarly traditions. Just when the nation needs the enlightened debate of complex issues, especially those concerning the Middle East and Islam, the tensions produced by the Iraq War and by long-standing disputes within the academy have led to hesitancy in speaking out on sensitive issues. Those who do speak are often the ones who are least knowledgeable on the specific issues and who are shrill and undisciplined. It is an indictment of the modern university, the mass media, or both that the most prominent professor in the aftermath of 9/11 was Ward Churchill, a professor of ethnic studies at the University of Colorado whose extreme and eccentric views were taken up by blogs and then by the mainstream media. Churchill's views were debated for weeks and even months as if his formulation represented the real dialogue on campuses and the reflections of knowledgeable experts. Serious scholars have fled from what to them seems pointless and unproductive confrontation. Etiquette, civility, restraint—the elements of a fruitful dialogue—have to be cultivated and, when lost, are not easily restored. Where there is no tradition of serious debate, those traditions cannot be created instantly. Free speech can sometimes be rough and tumble and raw, but if more professors would seriously take up the challenge and engage their students in the debate of national issues, the campuses would not seem so ill-prepared and irrelevant in times of national crisis. As one student, who had been an engineering major as an undergraduate, told us, "It was weird, like living in a bubble cut off from the world. Everybody was caught up with their own little concerns, but then I got to know several of my professors well and I started talking to them outside of class. They sort of opened up, and I got really interested in politics."

Democratic citizenship is not less but more urgent after 9/11, and the nation's major universities should face the task of educating future citizens, both leaders and followers, with genuine commitment. This responsibility means the willingness to hire faculty members who can commit themselves to educational tasks beyond traditional research and publication interests. These tasks would include a serious commitment to undergraduate teaching, to public service, to interests in and engagement with political issues, and to "campus citizenship," even though some colleagues would scoff at such a notion. Tenure can be a serious impediment if universities cling to a very restrictive definition of the criteria for appointments. There is little danger that quality of the faculty will be compromised if one makes some appointments with less exclusive reliance on evidence of scholarly publication and specialized research interests.

We urge our faculty colleagues to be bolder in appointments and to be less wedded to the sure-bet tenurable candidate. We believe that universities would also benefit from having more ideologically diverse faculties to engage in these common educational tasks, including some genuine radicals as well as conservatives. Lest this seem like an appalling suggestion, we urge the reader to remember that even though many professors show up as liberal and left on our survey, most of these are American-style liberals who are neither the radicals nor the genuine conservatives of the sort one would more regularly encounter in European universities. Professors who have spent their career in a small department among like-minded colleagues and who have rarely confronted a genuinely dissenting view are not ideally suited to teach or even to practice good citizenship.

Citizenship refers to what we have in common, the shared experiences and values that unite otherwise very diverse groups of citizens. The educational experience can either facilitate or put obstacles on the path to fostering the ideal of citizenship. The formal classroom has to contend with the outside forces that compete for the student's attention. The faculty can help or hinder the goals we seek by how they interpret their roles. The university does more for its students if the faculty define some core courses and requirements so that the diverse student body confronts, and shares, their reactions to the unifying course materials. Faculty members should engage, and even confront, each other until they can define core subjects and materials to be taught. The core subjects should include moral and political philosophy, the history of democratic political institutions, the principles and practices of the rule of law, and the ethical obligations of human and professional life. At some campuses, this need might be served by the addition of a course or two. In others, the existing distribution requirements may well have to be revised in order to expose students more effectively to the idea of citizenship. We do not believe that the variety of American colleges and universities will permit, nor does it require, a one-size-fits-all solution. But greater attention to citizenship education would be highly desirable for virtually every college and university.

Professors pride themselves on their openness to fresh ideas and their willingness to engage in free-wheeling debate. This may be why allegations of faculty bias have been so infuriating for so many in the academy. Professors are not immune, however, from the normal human tendency to be influenced by their immediate environment. Research has shown that like-minded groups reinforce fixed views and even predispose individuals to hold more extreme views after discussions within their own circle.[12]

Our 2007 national survey showed that faculties clearly tend toward liberal views: 19 percent identified themselves as strongly liberal as opposed to 3 percent as strongly conservative, 42 percent as moderately liberal, and 17 percent as moderately conservative.[13] Similarly, on partisan identifications, 53 percent identified themselves as Democrats, a large group of nearly one-third said they are independents, and only 13 percent said they are Republicans or Libertarians. These figures do not mean that faculty debates will always lack different viewpoints; our own experiences as faculty members teach us that simple labels or broad categories can mask significant differences. The figures do suggest that many faculty members will routinely encounter echoes of their own political views in interactions with their immediate colleagues. What is indisputable is that many departments, and even some entire campuses, may have so few conservatives and Republicans that those particular viewpoints are almost absent among the faculty. Despite conservative gains in expressing their views in the media, talk shows, and the publishing industry, the reality is that on campus "conservative intellectuals remain stymied. Their relationship in the universities in which they found their calling and to the curriculum and the scholarship they studied . . . remains tenuous."[14]

The underrepresentation of conservatives in the academy, as we have discussed in chapter 9, needs much further study, but several factors seem to operate here. Conservatives may be deterred from seeking academic posts at key points in their career trajectory. Conservatives may shun graduate education in favor of other professional paths. They may choose to enter the workplace immediately, or they may seek further education in a professional school. If they have completed graduate study and earned a doctorate, they may shun trying for a teaching position in favor of a career in a think tank, in journalism, in business, or as a political activist. We therefore call on our faculty colleagues to take pains to hire people with distinct views, including conservative thinkers, and to find innovative ways to address the relative absence of conservative viewpoints on campus. For example, we find intriguing the work by Kelly-Woessner and Woessner, which uses survey data of undergraduates to suggest that one way of encouraging more conservatives to pursue a graduate degree is to make graduate campuses more family friendly. Conservatives, for their part, should not self-exile themselves from an academic career, which many want and are afraid to pursue.

Changing the climate in colleges and universities to make genuine political debate more common and more valued and embracing the cause of education for citizenship in the curriculum will not be easy tasks. Nor will bringing more conservative thinkers into faculty ranks or into the college curricula. Like any real change in academic life, these goals can only be achieved over time as new generations of scholars, students, and administrators move through the system. New practices will gradually take root only if they accord with the principles and the practicalities of civility and decentralized self-governance that prevail in the universities. Most Americans and most political leaders do not want government to take on the task of changing the curriculum or the academy's hiring practices. As laid down by Justice Felix Frankfurter in the 1957 Supreme Court case of *Sweezy* v. *New Hampshire*, "who shall teach" and "what shall be taught" are constitutionally protected principles of academic freedom that shield universities against government intervention in those areas.

If government is not the vehicle for effecting change in the universities, should trustees seek a greater role? Trustees are not well suited to micromanage university life; it is probably unwise, too, for university administrators to try to become latter-day versions of the great Victorian figures who ran universities like the captains of industry ran their companies in the Gilded Age. If colleges and universities were run like business corporations, the commercial values and the vocational pressures that are already so powerful in our society would make it even more difficult to nurture the goals of liberal education that we advocate in this book. The universities have to justify themselves to society at large, and, of course, they should enter into dialogue with all of their complex constituencies in order to define their missions in changing circumstances. Colleges and universities are a part of American life and of civil society, and they have to grapple with the implications that follow from those realities. But they serve society best over the long run when they are free to pursue their goals somewhat insulated from the short-run pressures to which government and commercial enterprises are immediately responsive.

# Appendix A
## The Survey Instrument

This appendix presents the survey instrument that provided the data for several of our chapters. It was written by our team and distributed via the web to a random sample of college and university professors in the United States.

## Faculty Survey

This is a survey about three aspects of university life: the classroom, general campus climate, and hiring and promotion of faculty.

The survey is short and entirely anonymous. There will never be any link between the answers that you give and your own identity. We will never report results in such small subgroups that you could be personally identified. We have given you an individual password for two reasons: first, so we can prevent multiple responses by the same respondent to the survey or responses from nonfaculty and, second, as a way of knowing which faculty have not yet responded to our e-mail. Once you respond, the link between that password and your e-mail is destroyed.

First, a quick assessment of your political ideology:

1. How would you place your views on this scale, generally speaking, where 1 means "very left" and 10 means "very right"?

(1) Very left
(2)
(3)
(4)
(5)
(6)
(7)
(8)
(9)
(10) Very right

DK Don't know or not sure.

## Classroom Questions

2. Do you think that undergraduates sometimes unfairly receive different grades because of their political views at your university?

a. This never or seldom happens at my university

b. I believe this happens at my university, but never or seldom in my department

c. I have heard credible accounts of ideology affecting grading in my department

d. I have witnessed or seen firsthand evidence of student ideology affecting grading in my department

e. Don't know.

3. Beyond grading, do you think that professors at your university teach their undergraduate courses in a way that unfairly favors one political view, through their selection of readings, their lectures, and their leadership of class discussions?

a. This never or seldom happens at my university

b. I believe this happens at my university, but never or seldom in my department

c. I have heard credible accounts of biased teaching in my department

d. I have witnessed or seen firsthand evidence of biased teaching in my department

e. Don't know.

4. How often do you think professors at your university give opinions about political figures and issues that are not relevant to the course content?

a. This never or seldom happens at my university

b. I believe this happens at my university, but never or seldom in my department

c. I have heard credible accounts of biased teaching in my department

d. I have witnessed or seen firsthand evidence of biased teaching in my department

e. Don't know.

5. If you believe that at least some professors at your university express their political views unfairly in either grading, teaching, or both, which of the following descriptions best fits what you believe happens?

a. Most of the time it is conservative professors biased against liberal views

b. Most of the time it is liberal professors biased against conservative views

c. There is no fixed pattern; a few professors of all ideologies are biased against opposing views

d. Faculty bias is absent or extremely rare at my campus

e. Don't know.

6. Has a student ever complained that your grading or teaching had been influenced by your political views?

a. No

b. Yes, once

c. Yes, a few times

d. Yes, several times

e. Don't know.

Below you are given some descriptions about how to handle political issues in the classroom. Which of these strategies do you employ at least occasionally in your classroom?

7. I make no effort to appear neutral on political issues that I have a strong opinion about; students know my opinions most of the time.

Yes / No / Not sure

8. I attempt to be an honest broker for all possible viewpoints in my classroom.

Yes / No / Not sure

9. I strongly voice multiple views on political questions, and I make an effort to ensure that students never know my views on such questions.
Yes / No / Not sure

10. It isn't necessary in my field for a professor to have a policy one way or the other since controversial political issues seldom come up in class discussions.
Yes / No / Not sure

## Campus Climate

These questions examine ideological bias beyond the classroom itself.

11. Which of these best describes your campus's general political climate?
a. Strongly liberal
b. Moderately liberal
c. Middle of the road
d. Moderately conservative
e. Strongly conservative
f. Don't know.

12. In general, which of these descriptions best describes the contrast between faculty ideology and student ideology on your campus?
a. Students are more liberal than professors
b. Professors are more liberal than students
c. Students and professors are about the same ideologically
d. Don't know or not sure.

13. In general, which of these descriptions best describes the contrast between faculty ideology and administrator ideology?
a. Administrators are more liberal than professors
b. Professors are more liberal than administrators
c. Professors and administers are about the same ideologically
d. Don't know or not sure.

14. Do you think that, in general, your campus invites a diverse group of guest speakers?
a. No, our campus tends to have mostly speakers from the liberal or left viewpoint

b. No, our campus tends to have mostly speakers from the conservative viewpoint

c. Yes, in a given academic year, there will be speakers from many ideological views present on campus

d. Don't know or not sure.

15. Has your campus, in the last five years, had a campus incident that made you worry about the university's commitment to free speech and ideological diversity?

a. Yes, several such incidents

b. Yes, at least one such incident

c. None that I can recall

d. Don't know or not sure.

Would you like to briefly describe one or more of these incidents?

16. Does your campus have a speech code that bans offensive or insulting speech?

a. Yes

b. No

c. Don't know.

## Hiring and Promotion

17. Which would best characterize the political views of members of your department?

a. Strongly liberal

b. Moderately liberal

c. Middle of the road

d. Moderately conservative

e. Strongly conservative

f. Don't know or not applicable.

18. In hiring and promotion in your department, do you believe that conservative candidates are treated the same as liberal candidates?

a. No, there is a strong preference for liberals

b. No, there is a weak preference for liberals

c. No, there is a weak preference for conservatives

d. No, there is a strong preference for conservatives

e. Yes, they are treated approximately the same, without bias.

19. Based on credible accounts you have heard on your campus, do you believe that conservative candidates are treated the same as liberal candidates in hiring and promotion in other parts of your university?

a. No, I believe that there is a strong preference for liberals

b. No, I believe that there is a weak preference for liberals

c. No, I believe that there is a weak preference for conservatives

d. No, I believe that there is a strong preference for conservatives

e. Yes, I believe that they are treated approximately the same, without bias

f. Don't know.

20. In hiring and promotion in your department, do you believe candidates with strong Christian beliefs are treated the same as other candidates?

a. No, there is a strong preference for Christian candidates

b. No, there is a weak preference for Christian candidates

c. No, there is a weak bias against Christian candidates

d. No, there is a strong bias against Christian candidates

e. Yes, they are treated approximately the same, without bias

f. Don't know.

21. Based on credible accounts you have heard on campus, do you believe candidates with strong Christian beliefs are treated the same as other candidates in hiring and promotion in other parts of your university?

a. No, I believe that there is a strong preference for Christian candidates

b. No, I believe that there is a weak preference for Christian candidates

c. No, I believe that there is a weak bias against Christian candidates

d. No, I believe that there is a strong bias against Christian candidates

e. Yes, I believe that they are treated approximately the same, without bias

f. Don't know.

22. In your own personal case, do you believe that your chances for promotion or tenure were (or will be) affected by the reaction of your colleagues to your political views?

a. Yes, it is certain that my political views affected (or will affect) my chances

b. I think it probable that my political views affected (or will affect) my chances

c. I think it possible, but unlikely, that my political views affected (or will affect) my chances

d. I consider it almost impossible that my political views affected (or will affect) my chances

e. Don't know or not sure.

23. Have you ever remained silent about your political or religious views because you feared the reactions of your fellow professors?
    a. Yes, frequently
    b. Yes, on occasion
    c. Seldom, if ever
    d. Never
    e. Don't know, not sure.

## Demographic Section

This section contains questions about your individual political and religious views and practices as well as some demographic information.

24. What university currently employs you? (We'll have boxes for all the ones where we are working.)

25. What is your academic status?
    a. Full professor
    b. Associate professor
    c. Assistant professor
    d. Visitor adjunct
    e. Other.

25.5 (Asked only of associates and visitors, as their tenure status is not inherent in their position.) What is your tenure status? (Visitors will be asked, What is your tenure status at your home institution?)
    a. Tenured
    b. Tenure track
    c. Nontenure track
    d. Other, don't know.

26. What is your discipline? (LIST)

27. How long have you worked at this university? Please enter the number of years.

28. In what year did you finish your PhD?

29. What is your age?

30. What is your sex?
M / F

31. What is your race?
a. Black
b. White
c. Asian
d. Hispanic
e. Multiracial
f. Other.

32. Do you identify with a specific ethnicity? Type in: _____.

33. What is your nationality?
a. United States
b. Dual with U.S. and other
c. Other.

34. Generally speaking, do you think of yourself as a Republican, a Democrat, an independent, or do you have some other political affiliation?
a. Republican
b. Democrat
c. Independent
d. Other.

34.5. (IF REPUBLICAN or DEMOCRAT) How strong of a (Republican/Democrat) do you feel?
a. Very strong
b. Fairly strong
c. Not very strong
d. Don't know.

35. (VERSION 1). How would you describe yourself ideologically?
a. Left
b. Liberal
c. Middle of the road
d. Moderately conservative
e. Strongly conservative

f. Other

g. Don't know.

35. (VERSION 2) How would you describe yourself ideologically?

a. Very liberal

b. Moderately liberal

c. Middle of the road

d. Moderately conservative

e. Strongly conservative

f. Other

g. Don't know.

36. Here is a series of different statements about some broad issues. For each one, please select whether you strongly agree, somewhat agree, somewhat disagree, or strongly disagree.

a. The government should work to ensure that everyone has a job

b. The government should work to reduce the income gap between rich and poor

c. The less government regulation of business the better

d. With hard work and perseverance, anyone can succeed in this country

e. Competition is harmful. It brings out the worst in people

f. The minimum wage should be significantly increased

g. Homosexuality is as acceptable a lifestyle as heterosexuality

h. It is a woman's right to decide whether or not to have an abortion

i. It is all right for a couple to live together without intending to get married

j. God created human beings pretty much in their present form at one time within the last 10,000 years or so

k. Human beings have developed over millions of years from less advanced forms of life, but God had no part in this process

l. The public schools should teach the theory of intelligent design as well as the theory of evolution as equal explanations for the emergence of life

m. More environmental protection is needed, even if it raises prices or costs jobs.

Responses to each of these statements:

(1) Strongly agree

(2) Somewhat agree

(3) Somewhat disagree

(4) Strongly disagree

(9) Don't know or not sure.

## Religion

And finally we would like to ask just a few questions about religion.

37. How important is religion in your life?
a. Very important
b. Somewhat important
c. Not at all important
d. Don't know or not sure.

38. How often do you attend religious services?
a. More than once a week
b. Once a week
c. Almost weekly
d. Once or twice a month
e. A few times a year
f. Seldom or never
g. Don't know or not sure.

39. What is your religious preference? Is it Protestant, Catholic, Jewish, some other religion, or no religion?
a. Protestant
b. Catholic
c. Jewish
d. Muslim
e. Hindu
f. Other (specify):
g. No religion
h. Don't know or not sure.

39.5. (If Christian) What specific church denomination is that?

| | |
|---|---|
| (1) Adventist | (17) Jehovah's Witnesses |
| (2) Alliance | (18) Lutheran |
| (3) Anglican | (19) Mennonite |
| (4) Baptist | (20) Methodist |
| (5) Brethren | (21) Mormon |
| (6) Catholic | (22) Nondenominational |
| (7) Charismatic | (23) Orthodox |
| (8) Christian Science | (24) Pentecostal |

(9) Church of Christ
(10) Church of God
(11) Congregational
(12) Episcopalian
(13) Evangelical
(14) Quakers, Friends
(15) Fundamentalist
(16) Holiness

(25) Presbyterian
(26) Protestant
(27) Reformed
(28) Unitarian or Universalist
(29) United Church (Canada)
(30) United Church of Christ (United States)
(31) Other (specify):
(99) Don't know or not sure.

# Appendix B
## Sampling Methodology

The population of interest was U.S. college and university faculty, defined as the primary faculty who come into contact with undergraduates in the course of teaching academic subjects. Unfortunately, there is no available sampling frame that we could simply adapt to our purposes. Commercially available lists are inadequate in their coverage. Further, universities often protect their lists of faculty (for example, many universities will not distribute copies of their phone book to outsiders), or, when available, such a list normally would not distinguish between names of those who are eligible within our criteria and those who are not. Most universities, however, do publicize details about their faculty, both as a source of prestige and to inform current and prospective students. Nearly all universities identify their faculty on various pages of the school's website. The University of Virginia's Center for Survey Research was asked to develop a sampling plan and to execute the scientific sampling methods required for the study. We gratefully acknowledge the assistance of its staff in implementing the survey.

### Sample Size

In order to obtain 1,000 complete questionnaires at a conservatively projected 33 percent completion rate, a sample of at least 3,000 professors was needed.

Although it would maximize random selection to select participants across every school, this would have been prohibitive in both time and money inasmuch as each school selected would have to be inventoried to select a participant. Thus we used a multistage sampling design with probability proportional to size sampling at the first stage and equal counts of professors selected from each school at the second stage. This design yielded an equal probability of selection for each member of the population. We decided that eighteen professors could be selected at each school. Thus, in order to yield at least 3,000 professors, 169 schools would be ideal.

In summary, we chose 169 schools and selected eighteen professors from each school to yield 3,060 names for the study sample. Sampling was done in two or three stages, depending on the available information, with the first stage selecting institutions and the remaining stage(s) selecting individual professors.

## Selecting the Sample of Institutions

A complete list of U.S. colleges and universities from which to sample was obtained from the American Association of University Professors Research Office, at no cost. The list included all four-year institutions as well as universities in the United States and reported the total number of full-time faculty split by function (instruction, research, and public service). The list also included each school's class, as defined by the Carnegie Classification of Institutions of Higher Education. The original data were produced by the U.S. Department of Education's Integrated Postsecondary Education Data System in the fall of 2004. This could potentially introduce a small bias into our sampling to the extent that our master list omits any colleges created since 2004. However, this number is likely to be small and could well be zero.

## Selecting the Schools

To ensure that the sample was appropriately representative of different types of colleges and universities, the sample of schools was stratified. A separate sample was selected for doctoral, master's, and baccalaureate institutions based on the Carnegie Classification. The number of schools drawn from each stratum was proportionate to its size. This would ensure that the number of institutions would generate that stratum's share of faculty members.

| Carnegie type | Population | | | Selected sample | | |
|---|---|---|---|---|---|---|
| | Schools | Instructors | Percent | Schools | Instructors | Percent |
| Doctoral | 259 | 204,213 | 52.9 | 89 | 1,602 | 52.4 |
| Master's | 604 | 127,758 | 33.1 | 56 | 1,008 | 32.9 |
| Baccalaureate | 592 | 53,796 | 13.9 | 24 | 432 | 14.1 |
| Total | 1,455 | 385,767 | 100.0 | 169 | 3,060 | 100 |

The list of institutions included the number of faculty devoted to instruction, which was used as the measure of the school's size. A specially written program of commands in Statistical Package for the Social Sciences was used to select institutions proportional to this indicator of size, labeled FT_Instr (full-time instructor) in the data file. The sampling procedure was run separately for each list, representing the institutions from each of the three Carnegie types of institutions.

## Selecting the Sample of Professors

As criteria for eligibility, participants had to be an instructor of an academic subject. Eligible participants included professors of any rank, including instructors and lecturers. Those not eligible included administrators (unless also faculty), program coordinators, librarians, research staff, lab instructors, technical instructors or lesson givers (that is, instructors of a musical instrument), or athletic coaches. Faculty members at schools of theology or design affiliated with a school were excluded because the instructors do not meet these criteria. Military instructors (that is, Reserve Officers' Training Corps) were included (only at their primary institution).

Participants also had to teach undergraduates. Faculty at schools of law and medicine were assumed not to teach undergraduates. However, business and nursing schools were often found to include undergraduate students. Therefore, eligibility was determined on a case-by-case basis according to information readily available on the institution's website.

Participants had to be full-time teachers. Faculty members were assumed to be full time unless listed otherwise or titled "adjunct." Those with titles of lecturers or instructors were considered eligible, but those labeled as retired or emeritus faculty were assumed not to be teaching full time unless otherwise specified.

Participants were counted at their primary institution. Faculty listed as visiting a selected school were not considered eligible, but those who were listed as on sabbatical at another institution were eligible.

## Full List Sample

We eventually determined that the university directory could sometimes be accessed in full and that the university catalogs sometimes contained a full list of faculty. This was not part of the initial attempts because it was thought that the department pages would be the most up-to-date (which remains a valid assumption). There were thirty-five cases for which the initial attempts were insufficient to sample, and it was possible to find a full list of faculty. Sometimes there was a full list on a single web page; other times the list was printed in a university's handbook or in a phonebook. For thirty schools, there was a machine readable list that could be copied or imported into Microsoft Excel and easily numbered. An Excel macro that generated random numbers without replacement was used in those cases to select the eighteen persons.

For five schools in which the names were located in a printed directory, eighteen page numbers were randomly selected using the Excel RAND function, then a random number between one and thirty was generated for each chosen page, representing the selected person's position on the page (again using the Excel RAND function).

As with all the sampling, if the initially chosen person was obviously ineligible (for example, listed as an administrator or adjunct professor), the next eligible person on the list was selected.

## Random Selection of Groups

The majority of schools (134) were sampled by groups in a two-stage sampling procedure (following the selection of the school at the first stage). First, the searcher separated the potential participants into groups, defined in a variety of ways depending on the appearance of the data. In many cases, groups represented departmental affiliation, but groups could also be created by the searcher according to any visual differences in the information display. Files generated from the initial attempts were used where practical, but in some cases groupings were created directly from the layout of the university's website. For instance, searchers were given the option of finding the university's master list of departments and assuming that each link would yield a list of faculty in that departmental "group." In cases where a university directory was searchable and large numbers, though not the whole list, of faculty were available, grouping by letter of the alphabet (that is, twenty-six groups) was employed.

When defining groups by department, searchers tried to avoid including any given faculty member more than once by excluding interdisciplinary departments or programs (in most of these cases, it was clear that all affiliated faculty had dual appointments).

After defining and determining the total number of groups, the searcher pushed an action button in Excel, which triggered a macro that selected twelve numbers without replacement between one and that total number, representing the twelve selected groups. The searcher then identified the selected groups and determined how many potential participants were included in each group. A second action button triggered a different macro, which aggregated the populations of these selected groups and then randomly selected eighteen numbers within that limit. The macro also determined the group and sequential individual within that group that had been selected. These Excel procedures were programmed at the Center for Survey Research by Debby Kermer, with the assistance of Tom Guterbock.

## Gathering Professor Contact Information

After each participant was identified, it was then necessary to determine the contact information for that person. Searchers were given the name of the person selected, the source of the information (usually a web address), as well as any additional information that was present in the sampling file. In many cases, the additional information included the person's department or terms relating to his or her topic of study and occasionally a link to the individual's webpage. Because of the wide variety of information initially available as well as the variety of website layouts encountered, searchers were encouraged to employ whatever strategy they found most useful. Searchers used a variety of methods, employing a variety of search engines (including the university's internal search engine, the university's directory search, and global Internet engines such as Google) and a variety of search terms (such as the person's name, e-mail address, and topic of study). Information was found from a variety of sources: the university directory, the department directory or standardized webpage, the person's personal webpage, or the contact or reprint information from a recently published article.

## Validation Calling

To assess the validity of the data set as well as to obtain some information that may not have been available on the Internet, attempts were made to verify the information on a total of 475 individuals through the telephone: 300 were selected randomly in order to get reliable error rates, and an additional 175 were chosen because of concerns about the available contact information or eligibility of those cases.

It was predicted that the major cost of calling would be the time necessary to find an available, knowledgeable person at a school and that less time would be needed to verify each additional participant at a single school. Therefore, to balance the benefits of having fewer schools with appropriate coverage and random selection, it was decided to select the random 300 individuals in two stages. First, seventy-five schools were randomly selected using random number generation. Then four people from each of those schools were randomly chosen. Including all 475 cases that were part of the verification process, 107 schools were called.

Callers were given the main university number or directory assistance, where available. They were instructed to attempt to verify all contact information as well as whether the person was a full-time instructor of undergraduates. Subsequent calls were made until the address was verified, up to five calling attempts. Corrected information was noted and entered into the database.

The results of the validation calling for the 300 randomly selected participants are reported here because they provide insight into the characteristics of the selected sample.

## Eligibility

Of the 300 randomly chosen, 205 were confirmed as eligible, and 44 were confirmed as ineligible. The status of the remaining 59 could not be confirmed. The 44 who were ineligible were as follows:

—Twelve were part time or adjunct,

—Nine were in graduate programs or only taught graduate students,

—Eight were confirmed as having been teaching faculty, but were now deans or other administrators,

—Four were retiring (switched to part time) or had retired,

—Four were mostly administrative or directors of institutes,

—Four were research professors or technical instructors,

—One was visiting,

—One was confirmed as having been full time, but as having switched to part time,

—One was a graduate student, and

—One had left for another university.

With an additional 76 of the suspect cases confirmed as ineligible, 120 of the sampled participants were deemed ineligible during this phase. These records were eliminated from the data set and not replaced, leaving 2,940 professors, representing 169 U.S. colleges and universities, as the target sample to be recruited as survey participants if eligible.

## Correctness of the Information

Attempts were made to verify the information of the 264 (of the random 300) who were eligible or of uncertain eligibility. Of those, 91 were confirmed with no changes at all. An additional 133 had some type of information changed.

Of addresses, 141 were confirmed as correct with no changes, with an additional 62 needing only one change. Most of the changes were minor, such as misspellings, or represented the removal of excess information. Ten addresses could not be verified, and an additional 7 addresses were only partially verified. All changes were updated in the database.

## Data Cleaning

A final check of the mailing and e-mailing data was conducted to find missing or seemingly incomplete data. The addresses for the group of participants from each school were compared to one another to look for patterns. Empty data fields were typically filled with information that was present in the majority of the other records for that school, unless there was reason to suggest that the information was not relevant. Further, addresses that had been verified were compared with others from the same school that had not been verified to determine whether information was missing. In the event that an e-mail address was unknown but the school had an easily distinguishable pattern (that is, the first letter of the first name followed by the last name), missing e-mails were imputed using that pattern. An additional forty-two e-mails were determined using this method. The team at George Mason University attempted to verify a few remaining e-mail addresses by calling the departments.

In all cases, both the name and the university were known. Thus if no additional mailing information could be found, the mailing address consisted simply of the person's name, then the university name, and finally the appropriate city, state, and zip code.

## Mailing

Invitations to complete the survey were mailed on February 20, 2007, by the Center for Survey Research. The envelopes were emblazoned with the George Mason University logo, and a mailing label with the participant's name and address was attached. The letter was printed on George Mason University stationery and contained the signatures of the investigators at the bottom. A second page, printed on pale yellow paper, specified the e-mail address (if known) to which a direct link to the survey would be sent and detailed the other methods through which the survey could be accessed. Finally, a crisp new dollar bill was inserted as an incentive. Research has found that offering such an incentive up-front creates a sense of social obligation, which improves response rates more than offering payment for completing the survey. All subsequent steps in communicating with the target sample cases were carried out by the George Mason University research team.

## E-mail Contacts

We hired Websurveyor.com to contact the professors who had been identified by the University of Virginia and had received the initial letter and dollar via the mail. The Websurveyor interface allowed us to see who had received the e-mail, who had gone to the website, and who had completed the survey. Each recipient was given an individual link to the survey site, so that he or she could only fill out one survey.

A week after our first contact, we sent a reminder. A third reminder was sent, and then we decided not to contact again, as our response was quite high, and we did not wish to be seen as annoying spam.

## Follow-up Calling

Approximately ninety e-mails were "bounced back" when Websurveyor sent out the initial e-mail from the list provided. Several of the e-mails were found to have clerical errors, and these were corrected. The remaining numbers were contacted by phone. In approximately half the cases, the e-mail address was ascertained, and a survey was sent. In the remainder, various reasons were discovered for failure of the e-mail, such as retirement, a failed tenure case, serious illness, and death.

Three recipients of the e-mail about the survey preferred to do the survey over the phone, and they called in and were interviewed.

The efficacy of the dollar method was duly noted, not only in our response rate, but also in the number of professors who felt duty bound to return the dollar if they did not complete the survey. More than forty envelopes were mailed back to the principal investigator, often with an apology or complaint along with the crisp dollar.

## Response Rate

Of 2,940 professors who were contacted via e-mail, mail, and, in some cases, phone, 1,270 ultimately took the survey, for a response rate of 43 percent. This rate compares very favorably with similar studies of faculty ideology.

We did not have the budget to engage in a formal examination of nonresponders to discover why they chose not to take our survey. It is possible that some recipients had very effective "spam guards," although our contractor assured us that their e-mails tended to get through such screening software. No school in our study had a response rate of 0 percent, leading us to assume that any spam guards that worked were not institutional. Based on e-mails and notes on returned mailings, time was probably the most common cause of refusal, cited by a majority of those who gave a reason for not completing the survey.

However, many recipients of the e-mail requesting participation in the survey took the time to complain about the survey or indeed the very idea of surveying faculty about ideology. The most common suspicion was that the survey was part of a right-wing attack on the academy. Our team wondered if this was in part because of George Mason University's reputation as a relatively conservative institution within higher education. More than a dozen professors wanted to know the source of our funds for the study. If the refusal rate was higher for left-leaning professors because of this suspicion, it is possible that a bias could have been introduced into our findings. For example, one respondent wrote,

> I am very concerned about filling out this survey because of the presence at George Mason University of a very far right-wing Center for Media and Public Affairs headed by S. Robert Lichter. Is there any way to be assured that this survey has no connections whatsoever to the virulent CMPA and/or to academic groups such as those sponsored by David Horowitz et al.? These groups claim to be nonpartisan and non-ideological, which is of course false. What are the safeguards your researchers have put in place, if any?

A prominent historian wrote,

> I feel that the survey seems to accept the basic premise that there is a substantial issue in universities about political bias in hiring, promotion, etc., which I deny. Why not investigate whether people being left handed or right handed correlates with promotion, or the state in which they were born, or a million other variables?

Another well-known scholar wrote,

> Just listing the questions at a time when there seems to be a national move-
> ment brewing to persuade students to tape their professors in an effort to
> spot inappropriate left-wing indoctrination attempts in America's class-
> rooms pretty much erases my uncertainty. Unless you can give me some
> clarity about what you're investigating, I don't think I'm interested.

A number of respondents complained about various questions that measured
ideology on the grounds that the measure was incomplete or imperfect. One scientist wrote eruditely about how our evolution question (based on the one in
Rothman and others) misstated how humans emerged, complained that the
whole thing was a conservative conspiracy, and concluded with the following:

> If I have misjudged your intent you may be interested to know that even
> though many of my colleagues hold strong beliefs I have never witnessed
> an academic bias against a student based on constitutionally protected
> speech. However, I have been witness to many instances of bias in the
> classroom; bias against ignorance—more commonly referred to as
> "grades."

Other respondents took the time to e-mail us that they did not have the
time to do the survey. A final communication in response to our final plea to
take the survey seems a particularly appropriate anonymous last word, since
it mirrors some of our findings:

> I didn't [complete the survey originally] because life is short, and I had
> work to do . . . Having now taken it, all I can really say is that I very
> much doubt you'll find out much of value this way. Universities are
> places with complicated intellectual cultures and, whether "right" or
> "left," are full of smart people who care mostly about rather narrow top-
> ics of research. If the topic is adjacent to contemporary political issues,
> politics might come up; otherwise it doesn't.

# Appendix C
## Focus Group Questions

Thanks for taking the time to join our discussion about campus political climate here at _____. My name is _____, and I will serve as the moderator for today's focus group. Assisting me is _____. Our purpose today is to get information from you about what students think about this campus's political climate. A focus group is a popular method for finding out how a group of people really feel about an issue or topic. We are not trying to reach a consensus here in which you all end up agreeing; we are just trying to assess what the range of student views is. So feel free to disagree with each other. One quick caution: some of these issues are controversial and can be very personal or emotional, such as abortion, gay rights, or the war in Iraq. Don't be afraid to say what you really feel, but also treat each other with respect during this discussion.

I am here to ask questions, listen, and make sure everyone has a chance to share. If a good conversation gets going among all of you, I might not ask a question for a while. If I see that one person isn't saying much, I may ask that person a question, and if you're talking a lot, I may ask you to give others a chance. A focus group works best when everyone participates.

We are tape recording the session because we don't want to miss any of your comments. However, you will never be identified by name for anything you say today, so you may speak freely.

1. Okay, let's begin by having each person give their name and their major here at the university.

2. Thanks. Now, just to get the ball rolling, how would you describe this campus's political climate? Do most students and most faculty share similar views? Do people here talk a lot about politics? What do you think?

3. One way to divide the question of campus political climate is into what happens in the classroom, such as lectures, discussion, and grading, and what happens outside it, such as in the dorms, guest speakers, that kind of thing. Can we talk first about the political climate in the classroom? In general, what's your impression of the professors here? Do you think they are mostly liberal, mostly conservative, somewhere in the middle, or do they keep quiet about it? (Probe Democrats/Republicans; probe religious/secular.

Did you know how most of your professors voted in the 2004 election, from what they said in class? How about how they feel about Iraq? Evolution?

What about in classes like math, science, archeology—classes where politics doesn't normally come up—do professors ever talk about politics in those classes in your experience?

4. Have any of you experienced situations where you felt one of your professors was being one-sided in presenting an issue?

5. Have any of you ever felt afraid to disagree with a professor on a political issue in class or in an assignment? Could you describe that time?

6. Have any of you ever believed that your grade in a course was negatively affected because the professor was punishing you for your political views?

7. Okay, thanks so much for your comments so far. Let's talk about the other aspect of political climate: what happens outside the classroom. Do you think, overall, this is a liberal or conservative campus? Do you think there is peer pressure on students to take a particular view on politics?

8. Do you think this is a campus where the right to disagree with the majority on a political question is valued?

9. What about guest speakers? Do you think the speakers that appear on campus represent a diversity of viewpoints, or do they tend to be from one side of the political world or the other?

10. Have there been any high-profile incidents involving campus political climate that we haven't talked about already that you think are important?

Thanks so much for your time today.

## Appendix D
## American Council on Education
## Statement on Academic Rights and
## Responsibilities

Intellectual pluralism and academic freedom are central principles of American higher education. Recently, these issues have captured the attention of the media, political leaders, and those in the academy. This is not the first time in the nation's history that these issues have become public controversies, but the current interest in intellectual discourse on campus suggests that the meaning of these terms, and the rights and responsibilities of individual members of the campus community, should be reiterated.

Without question, academic freedom and intellectual pluralism are complex topics with multiple dimensions that affect both students and faculty. Moreover, America's colleges and universities vary enormously, making it impossible to create a single definition or set of standards that will work equally well for all fields of academic study and all institutions in all circumstances. Individual campuses must give meaning and definition to these concepts within the context of disciplinary standards and institutional mission.

Despite the difficulty of prescribing a universal definition, we believe that there are some central, overarching principles that are widely shared within the academic community and deserve to be stated affirmatively as a basis for discussion of these issues on campuses and elsewhere.

American higher education is characterized by a great diversity of institutions, each with its own mission and purpose. This diversity is a central feature and strength of our colleges and universities and must be valued and protected. The particular purpose of each school, as defined by the institution itself, should set the tone for the academic activities undertaken on campus.

Colleges and universities should welcome intellectual pluralism and the free exchange of ideas. Such a commitment will inevitably encourage debate over complex and difficult issues about which individuals will disagree. Such discussions should be held in an environment characterized by openness, tolerance, and civility.

Academic decisions including grades should be based solely on considerations that are intellectually relevant to the subject matter under consideration. Neither students nor faculty should be disadvantaged or evaluated on the basis of their political opinions. Any member of the campus community who believes he or she has been treated unfairly on academic matters must have access to a clear institutional process by which his or her grievance can be addressed.

The validity of academic ideas, theories, arguments, and views should be measured against the intellectual standards of relevant academic and professional disciplines. Application of these intellectual standards does not mean that all ideas have equal merit. The responsibility to judge the merits of competing academic ideas rests with colleges and universities and is determined by reference to the standards of the academic profession as established by the community of scholars at each institution.

Government's recognition and respect for the independence of colleges and universities is essential for academic and intellectual excellence. Because colleges and universities have great discretion and autonomy over academic affairs, they have a particular obligation to ensure that academic freedom is protected for all members of the campus community and that academic decisions are based on intellectual standards consistent with the mission of each institution.

*June 23, 2005*

*The following organizations have endorsed this statement:*
American Association of Community Colleges
American Association of State Colleges and Universities
American Association of University Professors
American Council on Education
American Dental Education Association
American Political Science Association
Association of American Colleges and Universities

Association of American Law Schools
Association of American Universities
Association of Catholic Colleges and Universities
Association of Governing Boards of Universities and Colleges
Association of Higher Education Facilities Officers
Association of Jesuit Colleges and Universities
The College Board
College Student Educators International
College and University Professional Association for Human Resources
Council for Advancement and Support of Education
Council for Christian Colleges and Universities
Council for Higher Education Accreditation
Council for Opportunity in Education
Council of Graduate Schools
Council of Independent Colleges
EDUCAUSE
National Association of Independent Colleges and Universities
National Association of State Universities and Land-Grant Colleges
National Association of Student Personnel Administrators
University Continuing Education Association

# Appendix E
## House Resolution 177

PRIOR PRINTER'S NOS. 1280, 2451
PRINTER'S NO. 2553
THE GENERAL ASSEMBLY OF PENNSYLVANIA
HOUSE RESOLUTION
**No. 177**
Session of 2005

INTRODUCED BY ARMSTRONG, BARRAR, BENNINGHOFF, BIRMELIN, BOYD, CALTAGIRONE, CLYMER, CRAHALLA, CREIGHTON, FAIRCHILD, FICHTER, FORCIER, GABIG, GILLESPIE, GINGRICH, HERSHEY, JAMES, W. KELLER, KILLION, LEH, METCALFE, R. MILLER, MUSTIO, PHILLIPS, READSHAW, ROBERTS, ROHRER, SCHRODER, STERN, R. STEVENSON, E. Z. TAYLOR, TRUE, WILT, YOUNGBLOOD, DENLINGER, CIVERA, RAPP, FLEAGLE, FLICK, BASTIAN, BROWNE, HARPER AND PAYNE, MARCH 29, 2005

AS AMENDED, HOUSE OF REPRESENTATIVES, JULY 5, 2005

A RESOLUTION
Establishing a select committee to examine the academic atmosphere and the degree to which faculty have the opportunity to instruct and students have the

opportunity to learn in an environment conducive to the pursuit of knowledge and truth at State-related and State-owned colleges and universities and community colleges in this Commonwealth.

WHEREAS, Academic freedom and intellectual diversity are values indispensable to the American colleges and universities; and

WHEREAS, From its first formulation in the General Report of the Committee on Academic Freedom and Tenure of the American Association of University Professors, the concept of academic freedom has been premised on the idea that human knowledge is a never-ending pursuit of the truth, that there is no humanly accessible truth that is not, in principle, open to challenge, and that no party or intellectual faction has a monopoly on wisdom; and

WHEREAS, Academic freedom is likely to thrive in an environment of intellectual diversity that protects and fosters independence of thought and speech; and

WHEREAS, Students and faculty should be protected from the imposition of ideological orthodoxy, and faculty members have the responsibility to not take advantage of their authority position to introduce inappropriate or irrelevant subject matter outside their field of study; therefore be it

RESOLVED, That a select committee composed of the Subcommittee on Higher Education of the Education Committee, plus one member appointed by the Speaker of the House of Representatives and one member appointed by the Minority Leader of the House of Representatives, examine, study and inform the House of Representatives on matters relating to the academic atmosphere and the degree to which faculty have the opportunity to instruct and students have the opportunity to learn in an environment conducive to the pursuit of knowledge and truth and the expression of independent thought at State-related and State-owned colleges, universities and community colleges, including, but not limited to, whether:

(1) faculty are hired, fired, promoted and granted tenure based on their professional competence and subject matter knowledge and with a view of helping students explore and understand various methodologies and perspectives;

(2) students have an academic environment, quality life on campus and reasonable access to course materials that create an environment conducive to learning, the development of critical thinking and the exploration and expression of independent thought and that the students are evaluated based on their subject knowledge; and

(3) that students are graded based on academic merit, without regard for ideological views, and that academic freedom and the right to explore and express independent thought is available to and practiced freely by faculty and students; and be it further

RESOLVED, That the chairman of the Subcommittee on Higher Education of the Education Committee of the House of Representatives shall be chairman of the select committee, that committee vacancies not affect the power of the remaining members to execute committee functions and that committee vacancies be filled in the same manner as the original appointment; and be it further

RESOLVED, That the committee may hold hearings, take testimony and conduct investigations within this Commonwealth as necessary; and be it further

RESOLVED, THAT IF AN INDIVIDUAL MAKES AN ALLEGATION AGAINST A FACULTY MEMBER CLAIMING BIAS, THE FACULTY MEMBER MUST BE GIVEN AT LEAST 48 HOURS' NOTICE OF THE SPECIFICS OF THE ALLEGATION PRIOR TO THE TESTIMONY BEING GIVEN AND BE GIVEN AN OPPORTUNITY TO TESTIFY AT THE SAME HEARING AS THE INDIVIDUAL MAKING THE ALLEGATION; AND BE IT FURTHER

RESOLVED, That the Chief Clerk, with the Speaker's approval, pay for the reasonable, appropriate and proper expenses incurred by the committee; and be it further

RESOLVED, That the committee make a report of its findings and any recommendations for remedial legislation and other appropriate action by June 30, 2006, and that the committee may extend the investigation for additional time, if necessary, but no later than November 30, 2006.

# Notes

## Chapter 1

1. A partial list of the antidiscrimination statutes that apply to universities includes Title VII of the Civil Rights Act of 1964 (outlawing discrimination in employment based on race, color, religion, sex, national origin), Title VI of the Civil Rights Act of 1964 (nondiscrimination in federally funded educational programs), Title IX of the 1972 Higher Education Amendments (discrimination based on sex in federally funded education programs, traditionally interpreted to mean athletic programs), the Rehabilitation Act of 1973 (discrimination and accommodation for individuals with disabilities in federally funded programs), the Americans with Disabilities Act of 1990, the Age Discrimination in Employment Act, the Age Discrimination Act, and Executive Order 11246 (establishing affirmative action for federal contractors). In addition, universities also face a host of state laws and regulations relating to human rights, immigration, and nondiscrimination.

## Chapter 2

1. A well-known indictment of this kind is Dinesh D'Souza, *Illiberal Education: The Politics of Race and Sex on Campus* (New York: Free Press, 1991).

2. Richard Hofstadter, *Anti-Intellectualism in American Life* (New York: Alfred A. Knopf, 1963).

3. Ibid.

4. Herbert Storing, *Essays on the Scientific Study of Politics* (University of Chicago Press, 1962). His critique drew a critical commentary from John H. Schaar and Shelden

S. Wolin, "Essays on the Scientific Study of Politics: A Critique," *American Political Science Review,* vol. 57 (March 1963): 125–50.

5. Allan Bloom, *The Closing of the American Mind: How Higher Education Has Failed Democracy and Impoverished the Souls of Today's Students* (New York: Simon and Schuster, 1987).

6. The story is told in Gerald Graff, *Beyond the Culture Wars: How Teaching the Conflicts Can Revitalize American Education* (New York: W. W. Norton, 1992), chap. 2.

7. Ibid., p. 7.

8. Lynne V. Cheney, director of the National Endowment for the Humanities, later extended the argument and explicitly linked curriculum politics to real-world politics, asserting that "treating humanities texts as though they were primarily political documents is the most noticeable trend in the study of the humanities today. Truth and beauty and excellence are regarded as irrelevant."

9. James D. Hunter, *Culture Wars: The Struggle to Define America* (New York: Basic Books, 1991).

10. James D. Hunter, "The Enduring Culture War," in *Is There a Cultural War? A Dialogue on Values and American Public Life,* edited by James D. Hunter and Alan Wolfe (Brookings, 2006). The discussion of traditionalists and orthodoxy is in Hunter, *Culture Wars,* p. 44.

11. Hunter and Wolfe, eds., *Is There a Cultural War?* p. 15.

12. Graff, *Beyond the Culture Wars,* p. 7.

13. Ibid.

14. Ibid., p. 8.

15. Mark Lilla, "Only Disconnect...," in *Our Country, Our Culture: The Politics of Political Correctness,* edited by Edith Kurzweil and William Phillips (Boston: Partisan Review Press, 1994), p. 131. Lilla did not, however, take his own advice, rejoining the fray with an eloquent new book, *The Stillborn God: Religion, Politics, and the Modern World* (New York: Alfred A. Knopf, 2007).

16. Thomas Bender, "Politics, Intellect, and the American University," in *American Academic Culture in Transformation,* edited by Thomas Bender and Carl E. Schorske (Princeton University Press, 1998), p. 40.

17. Ibid.

18. See, among others, John Searle, "Is There a Crisis in American Higher Education?" in *Our Country, Our Culture,* edited by Kurzweil and Phillips, pp. 227–43; C. Vann Woodward, "Political Fallacies in the Academy," in *Our Country, Our Culture,* edited by Kurzweil and Phillips, pp. 292–98; Louis Menand, "The Limits of Academic Freedom," in *The Future of Academic Freedom,* edited by Louis Menand (University of Chicago Press, 1996), chap. 1; Louis Menand, "Marketing Postmodernism," in *The Condition of American Liberal Education: Pragmatism and a Changing Tradition,* edited by Robert O'Neill (New York: The College Board, 1995), pp. 140–44.

19. Woodward, "Political Fallacies in the Academy," p. 297.

20. One of the present authors (Smith), then a junior faculty member at Columbia, was secretary of the organization, which was most active in the 1968–73 period. The diverse nature of the membership made for some difficulties, and national differences

prevented a cohesive definition of the organization's mission. Even though most of the colleagues were cultural conservatives, they fractured on how strongly they should oppose such policies as affirmative action and how much government interference should be "normal" and even desirable in the management and support of universities. The council was exclusively a membership organization composed of individual professors. Administrators were barred (unless they were temporarily on leave from their teaching duties), and no government official of any kind could belong.

21. Andrew Delbanco, "The Politics of Separatism," in *Our Country, Our Culture,* edited by Kurzweil and Phillips, pp. 34–41.

22. Gertrude Himmelfarb, "Comment: The Other Culture War," in *Is There a Cultural War?* edited by Hunter and Wolfe, p. 7.

23. Alan Wolfe, *One Nation, After All* (New York: Viking, 1998).

24. Ibid.

25. Ibid.

26. Morris P. Fiorina, Samuel J. Abrams, and Jeremy C. Pope, *Culture War? The Myth of a Polarized America* (New York: Longman, 2005).

27. A Pew survey in 2005 found that President Bush's popularity among scientists had plunged 6 percent, in part reflecting a perceived "anti-science" attitude on the administration's part and partly mirroring general public discontent with the Iraq War. For our own survey, see chapter 5.

28. The major recent studies have included Daniel Klein and Charlotta Stern, "Political Diversity in Six Disciplines," *Academic Questions,* vol. 18 (2004–05): 40–52; Daniel Klein and Charlotta Stein, "Professors and Their Politics: The Policy Views of Social Scientists," *Critical Review,* vol. 17, no. 3-4 (2005): 257–303; Stanley Rothman, S. Robert Lichter, and Neil Nevitte, "Politics and Professional Advancement among College Faculty," *The Forum,* vol. 3, no. 1 (2005): art. 2; Gary A. Tobin and Aryeh Weinberg, *A Profile of American College Faculty: Political Beliefs and Behavior* (San Francisco: Institute for Jewish and Community Research, 2006). Neil Gross and Solon Simmons have characterized these studies as "second-wave" studies, with Paul Lazarsfeld, Everett Ladd, Seymour Martin Lipset, and other pioneers of empirical research on faculty political attitudes being the "first wave" of efforts to study systematically faculty political attitudes. Gross and Simmons criticize the second-wave studies as being tendentious and fault-seeking, that is, as efforts to identify liberal bias. See Neil Gross and Solon Simmons, "The Social and Political Views of American Professors," Working Paper (Harvard University and George Mason University, September 24, 2007).

29. Rothman, Lichter, and Nevitte, "Politics and Professional Advancement among College Faculty."

30. ACTA student survey. The survey was conducted by the Roper Center of the University of Connecticut and published in 2005. It is available on the ACTA website, www.goacta.org.

31. Gross and Simmons, "The Social and Political Views of American Professors," p. 12.

32. Cited in "Survey of Higher Education," *The Economist,* September 10–16, 2005, p. 8. For the full survey, go to the *Economist* website (www.economist.com).

33. Matthew Woessner and April Kelly-Woessner, "Left Pipeline: Why Conservatives Don't Get Doctorates," paper prepared for the conference Reforming the Politically Correct University, American Enterprise Institute, Washington, November 14, 2007.

34. Ibid.

35. The extraordinarily high cost of college in America, which contrasts with the free or deeply discounted education available to college students in OECD countries, may account partly for the much lower retention rate among U.S. students, whose resources may run out.

## Chapter 3

1. David A. Hollinger, *Science, Jews, and Secular Culture: Studies in Mid-Twentieth-Century American Intellectual History* (Princeton University Press, 1996).

2. Daniel Kevles, "The Physics, Mathematics, and Chemistry Communities: A Comparative Study," in *The Organization of Knowledge in Modern America, 1860–1920,* edited by Alexandra Oleson and John Voss (Johns Hopkins University Press, 1979). For the social sciences, see Ira Katznelson, *Political Science: The State of the Discipline* (New York: W. W. Norton, 2003). See also Robert V. Bruce, *The Launching of Modern American Science, 1846 to 1876* (New York: Alfred A. Knopf, 1987).

3. James Piereson, "The Left University: How It Was Born, How It Grew, How to Overcome It," *Weekly Standard,* September 27, 2005, presents a lucid account of this phase in the development of American universities. On the founding fathers generally, see Gordon S. Wood, *Revolutionary Characters: What Made the Founders Different* (New York: Penguin Press, 2006). Jefferson's conception of what a university should be in America is eloquently suggested in his letter to Joseph Priestley in 1800. The letter is reproduced in Richard Hofstadter, ed., *American Higher Education: A Documentary History,* vol. 1 (University of Chicago Press, 1961), p. 175.

4. See Gary Wills, *Inventing America: Jefferson's Declaration of Independence* (New York: Vintage Books, 1979), on how a "national identity" was forged during Jefferson's presidency, even though the nation's early leaders did not agree wholly on political premises or on how higher learning should serve the nation. On the general opposition of other founding fathers to Jefferson's and Rush's idea of a federal university, see A. Lee Fritschler, Paul Weissberg, and Philip Magness, *Changing Relationships with Governments in Europe and the U.S: Balancing Quality Concerns with the Desire for Intellectual Independence in the University* (Hauppauge, N.Y.: NOVA Science Publishers, forthcoming), chap. 4.1. On Jefferson's ideas on education and citizenship, see Benjamin R. Barber, "Education and Democracy: Summary and Comment," in *Thomas Jefferson and the Education of a Citizen,* edited by James Gilreath (Washington: U.S. Library of Congress, 1999), pp. 134–52.

5. Fritschler, Weissberg, and Magness, *Changing Relationships with Governments.*

6. Henry Wheaton, "*Trustees of Dartmouth College* v. *Woodward,*" in *Reports of Cases Argued and Adjudged in the Supreme Court of the United States. February Term 1819* (R. Donaldson, 1819). For a full analysis of the Dartmouth College case, see Daniel Walker

Howe, *What Hath God Wrought: The Transformation of America, 1815–1848*, Oxford History of the United States (Oxford University Press, 2007), especially pp. 457–59.

7. See the letter of William G. Durden, president of Dickinson College, in the *Weekly Standard*, October 6, 2005, in reaction to James Piereson's article, "The Left University." Dr. Durden regarded Piereson as having neglected the "republican" and more American vision of higher education of Dr. Rush, citing *Proceedings of the American Revolutionary College Conference on the Liberal Arts and Education for Citizenship in the Twenty-First Century* (Carlisle, Pa.: Dickinson College, March 1998), for an explication of Rush's views.

8. Piereson, "The Left University." For an engrossing and learned account of the whole history of pre–Civil War higher education, see Daniel Walker Howe, *What Hath God Wrought*, ch. 12, "Reason and Revelation." On pp. 460–61, table 4 lists the more than 100 colleges founded in the United States before 1848.

9. Laurence R. Veysey, *The Emergence of the American University* (University of Chicago Press, 1965). See also Richard C. Atkinson and William A. Blanpied, "Research Universities: Core of the U.S. Science and Technology System," *Technology in Society* 30 (2008): 30–48.

10. Earle D. Ross, *Democracy's Colleges: The Land Grant Movement in Its Formative Stage* (Iowa State College Press, 1942); Allan Nevins, *The State Universities and Democracy* (University of Illinois Press, 1962); Edward D. Eddy Jr., *Colleges for Our Land and Time: The Land Grant Movement in the Formative Stage* (New York: Harper and Row, 1956).

11. Atkinson and Blanpied, "Research Universities: Core of the U.S. Science and Technology System," p. 33.

12. Burton J. Bledstein, *The Culture of Professionalism: The Middle Class and the Development of Higher Education in America* (New York: W. W. Norton, 1976) p. 297. See also the sources cited in Bledstein's note 16 on p. 297.

13. Nathan Leites, *Operational Code of the Politboro* (New York: McGraw-Hill, 1951).

14. See Richard Hofstadter and W. P. Metzger, *The Development of Academic Freedom in the United States* (Indianapolis: John Wiley, 1955). Also see Louis Menand, ed., *The Future of Academic Freedom* (University of Chicago Press, 1996).

15. Upton Sinclair, *The Goose-Step: A Study of American Education* (Kissinger Publishing, 2004). Our page numbers in the quotations are from the original 1922 edition. A commentary is Abraham Bladaman, "Upton Sinclair's Criticism of Higher Education in America: A Study of the Goose Step, Its Sources, Critical History," PhD dissertation, New York University School of Education, 1963.

16. Sinclair, *Goose-Step*, p. 347.

17. Ibid., p. 346.

18. Ibid., pp. 400–01.

19. Ibid., p. 104.

20. Ibid, p. 23.

21. Ross, 1914, quoted in Sinclair, *Goose-Step*, p. 402.

22. Sinclair, *Goose-Step*, p. 87.

23. See Sinclair *Goose-Step*, pp. 15–17.

24. Stanley O. Ikenberry, *Beyond Academic Departments: The Story of Institutes and Centers* (San Francisco: Jossey-Bass, 1972).

25. See David A. Hollinger, "The Disciplines and the Identity Debates, 1970–1990," in *American Academic Culture in Transformation: Fifty Years, Four Disciplines*, edited by Thomas Bender and Carl E. Schorske (Princeton University Press, 1998), pp. 363–71.

26. Veysey, *Emergence of the American University*, p. 411.

27. Ibid., p. 279.

28. Ibid., and see the sources cited in Veysey's note 49.

29. "The Typical Undergraduate," *Harvard Graduates Magazine*, vol. 17 (1909): 647.

30. Veysey, *Emergence of the American University*, p. 279 and the work cited in the footnote.

31. Raymond E. Callahan, *Education and the Cult of Efficiency: A Study of the Social Forces That Have Shaped the Administration of the Public Schools* (University of Chicago Press, 1962).

32. Lionel Trilling, *The Liberal Imagination* (New York: Harcourt Brace Jovanovich, 1946, 1950), p. 2.

33. Thorsten Veblen, *The Higher Learning in America: A Memorandum on the Conduct of Universities by Business Men* (New York: B. W. Huebsch, 1918).

34. A. Hunter Dupree, *Science in the Federal Government: A History of Policies and Activities to 1940* (Harvard University Press, 1980).

35. Irwin Stewart, *Organizing Scientific Research for War* (Boston: Little Brown, 1948).

36. Bruce L. R. Smith, *American Science Policy since World War II* (Brookings, 1990).

37. See "The Brains Business: A Survey of Higher Education," *The Economist*, September 10, 2005.

38. An excellent overall study is Roger G. Noll, *Challenges to Research Universities* (Brookings, 1998).

39. As discussed in an important 1997 conference convened under the auspices of the American Academy of Arts and Sciences, many humanities and social science fields in the 1945–60 period displayed a marked tendency to emulate the hard sciences. See Bender and Schorske, cited in note 25 above.

## Chapter 4

1. Richard Freeland, *Academia's Golden Age: Universities in Massachusetts, 1945–70* (Oxford University Press, 1992). See also Roger Geiger, *Research and Relevant Knowledge: American Research Universities since World War II* (Oxford University Press, 1993), and Hugh Davis Graham and Nancy Diamond, *The Rise of the American Research University* (Johns Hopkins University Press, 1996).

2. Thomas Bender, "Politics, Intellect, and the American University, 1945–1995," in *American Academic Culture in Transformation: Fifty Years, Four Disciplines*, edited by Thomas Bender and Carl E. Schorske (Princeton University Press, 1998) p. 17, and David Damrosch, *We Scholars: Changing the Culture of the University* (Harvard University Press, 1995), p. 51.

3. Bender, "Politics, Intellect, and the American University," p. 18, note 6. The Emergency Committee in Aid of Displaced Foreign Scholars, between 1933 and 1943, helped to find 269 academic positions in the United States for foreign scholars fleeing from totalitarianism. See also Mark Lilla, "Only Disconnect . . .," in *Our Country, Our Culture,* edited by Edith Kurzweil and William Phillips (Boston: Partisan Review Press, 1994), pp. 126–31, and Marjorie Lamberti, "The Reception of Refugee Scholars from Nazi Germany in America: Philanthropy and Social Change in Higher Education," *Jewish Social Studies,* vol. 12, no. 3 (Spring-Summer 2006): 157–92.

4. From 1946 to 1958, foundation support for social science amounted to more than $85 million, nearly half of which went to three institutions (Harvard, Columbia, and Berkeley). Between 1959 and 1964, the three biggest foundations awarded some $100 million in grants to political science alone at the same three universities. See Bender and Schorske, eds., *American Academic Culture in Transformation,* pp. 23–24; Geiger, *Recent and Relevant Knowledge,* pp. 105–06; Albert Somit and Joseph Tanenhaus, *The Development of American Political Science* (Boston: Allyn and Bacon, 1967), pp. 168–69.

5. President's Scientific Research Board, *Science and Public Policy: Administration for Research* [the Steelman report], 3 vols. (Washington: Government Printing Office, 1947), vol. 1, p. 26. See also Vannevar Bush, *Science: The Endless Frontier* (Arlington, Va.: National Science Foundation, 1960 [1945]), p. 12. For the debate over the National Science Foundation, see Daniel Kevles, "The National Science Foundation and the Debate over Postwar Research Policy, 1942–1945," *Isis,* vol. 68, no. 1 (1977): 6, and Don K. Price, *Government and Science* (New York University Press, 1954).

6. See Bruce L. R. Smith, *American Science Policy since World War II* (Brookings, 1990).

7. Bender, "Politics, Intellect, and the American University," p. 17.

8. Ibid.

9. Richard Freeland, quoted in Bender and Schorske, eds., *American Academic Culture in Transformation,* p. 22.

10. Paul F. Lazarsfeld and Walter Thielens, *The Academic Mind: Social Scientists in a Time of Crisis* (Manchester, N.H.: Ayer Publishing, 1977).

11. See James B. Conant, *On Understanding Science* (Oxford University Press, 1947). For an excellent critique of Conant's work, see David A. Hollinger, *Science, Jews, and Secular Culture: A Mid-Twentieth Century Intellectual History* (Princeton University Press, 1998), especially chap. 8.

12. Christopher Jencks and David Riessman, *The Academic Revolution* (Edison, N.J.: Transaction Publications, 2001, originally published in 1968).

13. See Edward Shils, *The Calling of Sociology and Other Essays on the Pursuit of Learning* (University of Chicago Press, 1980), and Edward Shils, *The Constitution of Society* (University of Chicago Press, 1982). Also see note 2 of chapter 3 for further sources on the individual disciplines.

14. Hollinger, *Science, Jews, and Secular Culture,* chaps. 1–3.

15. Jerome Karabel, *The Chosen: The Hidden History of Admission and Exclusion at Harvard, Yale, and Princeton* (Boston: Houghton Mifflin, 2006).

16. Quoted in Bender, "Politics, Intellect, and the American University," p. 21.

17. Panel members Compton and Freeland objected to the emphasis on diversity.

18. David Potter, *People of Plenty: Economic Abundance and the American Character* (University of Chicago Press, 1954), and John Kenneth Galbraith, *The Affluent Society* (Boston: Houghton Mifflin, 1958).

19. See Daniel Bell, *The Social Sciences since the Second World War* (New Brunswick, N.J.: Transaction Books, 1982), and the commentary on this work by Charles E. Lindblom, "Political Science in the 1940s and 1950s," in *American Academic Culture in Transformation*, edited by Bender and Schorske, pp. 243–70.

20. Bender and Schorske, eds., *American Academic Culture in Transformation*, p. 23.

21. Thomas Kuhn, *The Structure of Scientific Revolutions* (University of Chicago Press, 1962). There have been nineteen editions of this book, and it has spawned a massive secondary literature.

22. Rogers M. Smith, "Still Blowing in the Wind: The American Quest for a Democratic, Scientific Political Science," in *American Academic Culture in Transformation*, edited by Bender and Schorske, pp. 271–305.

23. See Robert E. Calvert, ed., *To Restore American Democracy: Political Education and the Modern University* (Lanham, Md.: Rowman and Littlefield, 2006), especially the essays by Galston, Barber, Gitlin, Sandel, Walzer, and Calvert.

24. Quoted in Bender and Schorske, eds., *American Academic Culture in Transformation*, p. 30. The full discussion is in David Easton, "Political Science in the United States and Europe," in *Divided Knowledge: Across Disciplines, Across Cultures*, edited by David Easton and Corinne S. Schelling (Beverly Hills: Sage Publications, 1991).

25. David M. Ricci, *The Tragedy of Political Science* (Yale University Press, 1984), characterizes political science as a discipline in flight from itself.

26. Bender, "Politics, Intellect, and the American University," p. 22.

27. Edward S. Flash Jr., *Economic Advice and Presidential Leadership: The Council of Economic Advisors* (Columbia University Press, 1965).

28. See William J. Barber, "Reconfigurations in American Academic Economics: A General Practitioner's Perspective," in *American Academic Culture in Transformation*, edited by Bender and Schorske, pp. 105–22.

29. Bender, "Politics, Intellect, and American University," p. 23, note 19.

30. Shils, *The Calling of Sociology and Other Essays*.

31. Quoted in Bender, "Politics, Intellect, and the American University," p. 23, note 20, citing Terence Halliday, "Sociology's Fragile Professionalism," in *Sociology and Its Publics: The Forms and Fates of Disciplinary Organization*, edited by Terence Halliday and Morris Janowitz (University of Chicago Press, 1992), p. 6. Bender calls attention to an interesting comparison between the professionalism of Parsons and the more civic professionalism of Morris Janowitz in this work, as discussed in Halliday and Janowitz, eds., *Sociology and Its Publics*, pp. 3–12.

32. Robert K. Merton, "A Note on Science and Democracy," *Journal of Legal and Political Sociology*, vol. 1, no. 1-2 (1942): 116; Robert K. Merton, *Social Theory and Social Structure: Toward the Codification of Theory and Research* (Glencoe, Ill.: Free Press, 1968), pp. 604–15; Robert K. Merton in *The Sociology of Science: Theoretical and Empirical Inves-*

*tigations,* edited by Norman Storer (University of Chicago Press, 1973), pp. 267–78; Robert K. Merton, "The Sociology of Science: An Episodic Memoir," in *The Sociology of Science in Europe,* edited by Robert K. Merton and Jerry Gaston (Southern Illinois University Press, 1977), pp. 48–50. For a discussion of how Merton's formulation changed from its initial emphasis on science's relation to democracy to a more "scientific" theory of the sociology of science, see Hollinger, *Science, Jews, and Secular Culture,* chap. 5. For a discussion of the flare-up between scientists and the observers belonging to the post-Mertonian "constructionist" science of science school in the mid-1990s, see Evelyn Fox Keller, "Science and Its Critics," in *The Future of Academic Freedom,* edited by Louis Menand (University of Chicago Press, 1996). Keller is critical of her scientific colleagues for what she regards as their hostility to feminist studies of science and society and theorizes as to why scientists suddenly took exception to science of science studies (the reason being, she argues, that scientists had grown fearful that such studies would jeopardize funding for science).

33. Seymour Martin Lipset, presidential address to the American Sociological Association, April 2, 1993, published as "The State of Sociology," *Sociological Forum,* vol. 9, no. 2 (June 1994): 2; and also Seymour Martin Lipset, "The Academic Mind at the Top: The Political Behavior of Faculty Elites," *Public Opinion Quarterly,* vol. 46, no. 2 (Summer 1982): 143–68.

34. Alvin W. Gouldner, *The Coming Crisis of Western Sociology* (New York: Basic Books, 1970).

35. Daniel Bell, *The End of Ideology* (New York: Simon and Schuster, 1965).

36. Arthur Schlesinger Jr., *The Vital Center: The Politics of Freedom* (Boston: Houghton Mifflin, 1949).

37. Alan Brinkley, "The Problem of American Conservatism," *American Historical Review,* vol. 99, no. 2 (April 1994): 409–29.

38. Louis Hartz, *The Liberal Tradition in America* (New York: Harcourt Brace, 1955).

39. Everett C. Ladd and Seymour Martin Lipset, *The Divided Academy* (New York: McGraw-Hill, 1975).

40. Lionel Trilling, *The Liberal Imagination: Essays on Literature and Society* (New York: Viking Press, 1950).

41. Richard Hofstadter, *The Progressive Historians* (New York: Cape Publishing, 1969).

42. Julie A. Reuben, *The Making of the Modern University* (University of Chicago Press, 1996).

43. See M. H. Abrams, "The Transformation of English Studies: 1930–1995," in *American Academic Culture in Transformation,* edited by Bender and Schorske.

44. Denis Donoghue, *The Old Moderns* (New York: Knopf, 1994).

45. See the enlightening essay by Paul A. Cantor of the University of Virginia, "When Is Diversity Not Diversity: A Brief History of the English Department," Paper prepared for the American Enterprise Conference, Washington, D.C., November 14, 2007.

46. See Bender, "Politics, Intellect, and the American University." Also see Linda K. Kerber, "Diversity and the Transformation of American Studies," *American Quarterly,* vol. 41 (March 1989): 415–31; Michael Geyer, "Multiculturalism and the Politics of General Education," *Critical Inquiry,* vol. 19, no. 3 (1993): 507–08; David Bromwich, *Politics by Other Means* (Yale University Press, 1992).

47. See Connor Cruise O'Brien, "Enlightenment under Threat," in *History and the Idea of Progress*, edited by Peter Burke and others (New York: John Wiley, 1997); Peter Burke, "Of Critical Theory and Its Theorists; Cultural Studies and Beyond: Fragments of Empire; Fantasy, and Reality in History; and History and the Idea of Progress," *Journal of the History of the Behavioral Sciences*, vol. 33, no. 4 (Fall 1997): 428–30.

48. See E. J. Dionne, "The State of the Union: Why the Culture War Is the Wrong War," *Atlantic Monthly*, January-February 2006, pp. 130–35.

49. Bender, "Politics, Intellect, and the American University," p. 41. Also see Ira Katznelson, "From the Streets to the Lecture Hall: The 1960s," in *American Academic Culture in Transformation*, edited by Bender and Schorske; William Galston, "Political Theory in the 1980s: Perplexity amidst Diversity," in *Political Science: The State of the Discipline*, edited by Ada Finifter (Washington: American Political Science Association, 1983).

50. See David A. Hollinger, "The Disciplines and the Identity Debate, 1870–1995," in *American Academic Culture in Transformation*, edited by Bender and Schorske, pp. 353–71.

51. Ibid., p. 356.

52. Ibid., p. 358.

53. On the Berkeley incidents and the role of activist Mario Savio, see Donald A. Downs, *Restoring Free Speech and Liberty on Campus* (Cambridge University Press, 2005), chaps. 1–4.

54. Students for a Democratic Society, "The Port Huron Statement," New York, 1962.

55. Bruce L. R. Smith, "The Politics of Protest: How Effective Is Violence?" *Proceedings of the Academy of Political Science*, vol. 29 (March 1968): 115–33.

56. See Cox Commission Report, *Crisis at Columbia* (Columbia University Press, 1968), also published by Vintage Press in 1969. For an institutional history of Columbia, see Robert S. McCaughey, *Stand, Columbia: A History of Columbia University* (Columbia University Press, 2003), which provides a careful account of the 1968 crisis and its aftermath.

57. David Horowitz, *The Professors: The 101 Most Dangerous Academics in America.* (Washington: Regnery, 2006).

58. Bender, "Politics, Intellect, and the American University," p. 40.

59. Ibid.

60. Bruce L. R. Smith and Joseph J. Karlesky, *The State of Academic Science: The Universities in the Nation's Research* (New York: Change Magazine Press, 1977).

61. Quoted in Colleen J. Shogan, "Anti-intellectualism in the Modern Presidency: A Republican Populism," *Perspectives on Politics*, vol. 5, no. 2 (June 2007): 298.

62. See Hollinger, *Science, Jews, and Secular Culture*, chap. 7, with reference to the University of Michigan; Craig Kaplan and Ellen Schrecker, eds., *Regulating the Intellectuals: Perspectives on Academic Freedom in the 1980s* (New York: Praeger, 1983), chap. 2, and, more broadly, Ellen Schrecker, *The Age of McCarthyism: A Brief History with Documents* (New York: Palgrave McMillan, 2002). The biggest single instance of faculty dismissals occurred at City University of New York in the late 1940s. Most of the pro-

fessors dismissed were natural scientists whose professional conduct in the classroom was not questioned but who had previously had or still had affiliations with communist or communist-front organizations.

63. Association of American Universities, "The Rights and Responsibilities of Universities and Their Faculties," March 24, 1953.

64. See Ellen Schrecker, *The Age of McCarthyism: A Brief History with Documents* (Boston: Bedford Books of St. Martin's Press, 1994).

65. Derek C. Bok, *Beyond the Ivory Tower: Social Responsibilities of the Modern University* (Harvard University Press, 1982), p. 21.

66. American Anthropological Association, *Annual Report* (Washington, 1972), p. 39.

67. John Rawls, *A Theory of Justice* (Belknap Press of Harvard University Press, 1971), and Robert Nozick, *Anarchy, State, and Utopia* (New York: Basic Books, 1974).

68. See Ricci, *The Tragedy of Political Science*, pp. 320–23.

69. Ladd and Lipset, *The Divided Academy*.

70. Ibid.

## Chapter 5

1. Dinesh D'Souza, *Illiberal Education: The Politics of Race and Sex on Campus* (New York: Free Press, 1991), p. 2.

2. Quoted in Ibid., p. 227.

3. Patrick Coyle and Ron Robinson, *The Conservative Guide to Campus Activism* (Herndon, Va.: Young Americas Foundation, 2005), p. 5.

4. Ibid., p. 3.

5. James Glazov, "Purging Conservatives from College Faculties," *Frontpagemagazine.com*, May 23, 2005.

6. David Horowitz, *Indoctrination U: The Left's War against Academic Freedom* (Milwaukee: Encounter Books, 2007); Ben Shapiro, *Brainwashed: How Universities Indoctrinate America's Youth* (Nashville: Thomas Nelson, 2004); Roger Kimball, *Tenured Radicals, Revised: How Politics Has Corrupted Our Higher Education* (New York: HarperCollins, 1990); Jim Nelson Black, *Freefall of the American University: How Our Colleges Are Corrupting the Minds and Morals of the Next Generation* (Nashville: Thomas Nelson, 2004).

7. Stanley Rothman, S. Robert Lichter, and Neil Nevitte, "Politics and Professorial Advancement among College Faculty," *The Forum*, vol. 3, no. 1 (2005): art. 2.

8. Committee on Maximizing the Potential of Women in Academic Science and Engineering of the National Academies, *Beyond Bias and Barriers: Fulfilling the Potential of Women in Academic Science and Engineering* (Washington, D.C.: National Academies Press, 2007); Christina Hoff Somers, "Why Can't a Woman Be More Like a Man? Women Earn Most of America's PhDs but Lag Physical Sciences; Beware of Plans to Fix the 'Problem,'" *The American* (March-April 2008), available online at www.american.com/archive/2008/march-april-magazine-contents/why-can2019t-a-woman-be-more-like-a-man (March 31, 2008).

9. Derek Bok, *Universities in the Marketplace: The Commercialization of Higher Education* (Princeton University Press, 2004); Shelia Gallagher and Larry L. Leslie, *Academic Capitalism: Politics, Policies, and the Entrepreneurial University* (Johns Hopkins University Press, 1999).

10. The Carnegie studies are a series of studies done for Carnegie by Everett Ladd and Seymour Lipset, starting with *Divided Academy*, which contained data for 1969. See Everett C. Ladd Jr. and Seymour Martin Lipset, *Divided Academy: Professors and Politics* (New York: McGraw-Hill, 1975). Studies for the other years—for 1997, for example—were by other authors, but they were all under the Carnegie auspices and are referred to as such hereafter. Except where we mention the Rothman-Lichter recantation and confession of computational error of 2007, all references are to Rothman, Lichter, and Nevitte, "Politics and Professorial Advancement among College Faculty."

11. Ibid.

12. Stanley Rothman and S. Robert Lichter, "The Vanishing Conservative: Is There a Glass Ceiling?" paper presented at the conference Reforming the Politically Correct University, American Enterprise Institute, Washington, November 14, 2007, p. 7. We use their revised figure in tables 5-2 and 5-3.

13. The Rothman and Lichter study asked questions in terms of the categories left, liberal, middle of the road, conservative, and strongly conservative. We consider this formulation dated, since the distinction between left and liberal has blurred over time. One might judge that the categories used in the Rothman study are not entirely one-dimensional. So we have used the categories strongly liberal, moderately liberal, middle of the road, moderately conservative, and strongly conservative.

14. A further explanation of the distinctiveness of Rothman study's is that its measure produced a much higher refusal rate than did the traditional measure of ideology used in Lipset and other Carnegie studies. An analysis of a subset of their data, which included the vast majority of their cases, showed that more than 35 percent of faculty opted not to place themselves on the ten-point scale. This level of nonresponse to a single question raises questions about the validity of their findings on this key point, as does their failure to inform the wide discrepancy in response. This error was the one that resulted in their corrected 2007 numbers.

15. Ladd and Lipset, *Divided Academy*, p. 73.

16. Ibid.

17. Klein and Western found a higher percentage of Democrats than Republicans using voter registration rolls of faculty in six counties adjacent to Stanford and University of California, Berkeley. See Daniel Klein and Andrew Western, "Voter Registration of Berkeley and Stanford Faculty," *Academic Questions*, vol. 18, no. 1 (Winter 2005): 53–65. Klein and Stern reported varying ratios of Democrats to Republicans in different disciplines, ranging from 3:1 in economics to as high as 18:1 in sociology. See Daniel Klein and Charlotta Stern, "Political Diversity in Six Disciplines," *Academic Questions*, vol. 18, no. 1 (Winter 2005): 40–52. Gross and Simmons found that their faculty respondents in the 2000 presidential election voted Republican, 23.5 percent; Democratic, 68.6 percent; and other, 9.9 percent. They concluded, "It is worth noting

that while the percentage of professors voting Republican has declined by about 12 percentage points since 1984, the percentage voting Republican in 2004, according to our data, was actually higher than the percentage voting Republican in 1992 and 1996—a fact that calls into question claims that the professoriate is growing more Democratic by the year." Neil Gross and Solon Simmons, "The Social and Political Views of American Professors," Working Paper (Harvard University and George Mason University, September 24, 2007), pp. 38–39.

18. Misperception could still explain why faculty lean left, but perceive their campuses and departments as being more balanced. Suppose that liberals and conservatives are both more likely to be hired by departments that reflect either liberal or conservative ideological viewpoints. Then, imagine that this effect is masked by the tendency to misperceive reality so that liberal faculty on liberal campuses see the climate as middle of the road and conservative faculty on conservative campuses are influenced by their misperceptions as well. Our data do not offer any clear resolution of such surmises about faculty misperception.

19. Gross and Simmons, "The Social and Political Views of American Professors," p. 69.

20. Ibid.

21. See chapter 8 for our discussion of student attitudes.

22. This complaint was made by a number of our survey respondents, all saying in one way or another, "I have no way of knowing what goes on in my colleagues' classroom!" While this is often true, the third-party assessment remains one way of measuring at least the perception of classroom bias among faculty. For more comments from our respondents, see appendix B on sampling methodology.

23. R. Eugene Rice, "Religious Diversity and the Making of Meaning: Implications for the Classroom," *Diversity and Democracy*, vol. 11, no. 1 (Winter 2008): 1–3. Rice also notes that the Higher Education Research Institute of UCLA study found that students have a "strong interest and involvement in spirituality and religion, but that faculty and institutions do little to foster student interest in questions of meaning and purpose."

24. Rothman, Lichter, and Nevitte, "Politics and Professional Advancement among College Faculty."

## Chapter 6

1. Theodore J. Lowi, *The End of the Republican Era* (University of Oklahoma Press, 1995), chap. 1, struggles with a definition of "public philosophy" and tries to distinguish old liberalism from new liberalism and old conservatism from new conservatism.

2. The core values of this social (or cultural) liberalism are summed up in the formulation of Michael Berube, *What's Liberal about the Liberal Arts? Classroom Politics and "Bias" in Higher Education* (New York: W. W. Norton, 2006), pp. 23–24: "I never speak ill of Christianity, Judaism, Islam, or any organized religion so there is no sense in which a religious student should feel that he or she has to argue twice in my class-

room. But on race and sexuality, invariably, my syllabus, my comments, and my very character cannot help but cue students that some forms of social conservatism will indeed have to make their case twice in order to be heard." See also Andrew Delbanco, "The Politics of Separatism," in *Our Country, Our Culture: The Politics of Political Correctness,* edited by Edith Kurzweil and William Phillips (Boston: Partisan Review Press, 1994), p. 40.

3. Empirical evidence of a shift toward a more conservative politics is found in Cass R. Sunstein, David Schkade, Lisa M. Ellman, and Andres Sawicki, *Are Judges Political? An Empirical Analysis of the Federal Judiciary* (Brookings, 2006).

4. The political party affiliations of the University of Minnesota's Political Science Department in 1953–57 were approximately two-thirds Democratic and one-third Republican, with one consistent third-party identifier. The distribution today might be 75 percent, Democratic; 15 percent, Republican or Libertarian; and 10 percent, third party or other independent.

5. See John W. Kingdon, *Agendas, Alternatives, and Public Policies,* 2d ed. (Boston: Pearson Education, 1997).

6. See, for example, Gary Nelson and Michael Berube, eds., *Higher Education under Fire* (New York: Rutledge, 1995).

7. Bruce L. R. Smith and David Korn, "Is There a Crisis of Accountability in America's Research Universities?" *Minerva,* vol. 38, no. 2 (2000): 129–45.

8. See C. Wright Mills, *The Power Elite* (Oxford University Press, 1957), as an example of the old left. Mill's power elite, amazingly few in number, were said to dominate American society and all aspects of government from the Pentagon to the Department of Agriculture. The moneyed interests of the Northeast were the chief culprits, according to Mills. Noam Chomsky, *Failed States: The Abuse of Power and the Assault on Democracy* (New York: Metropolitan Book/Henry Holt, 2006), is a contemporary version of an American power elite thesis. Mathew A. Crenson, *The Un-Politics of Air Pollution: A Study of Non-Decisionmaking in the Cities* (Johns Hopkins University Press, 1971), illustrates a new left approach of a generation ago. Crenson argues that concerns about air quality could not be seriously addressed for a long time because economic interests benefiting from pollution structured the political agenda so as to block serious attempts to control pollution.

9. A Florida measure was tabled and did not receive a vote. South Dakota adopted a reporting requirement in February 2006 in the state's House of Representatives, but the proposal was killed in the South Dakota Senate by a vote of 18-15 in March 2006. Georgia adopted a nonbinding resolution calling for balance and openness on campus. Colorado and Ohio dropped legislative consideration of versions of the academic bill of rights in exchange for a pledge by university officials to review their internal procedures protecting academic freedom, including student rights. The Commonwealth of Pennsylvania adopted HR 177 in the House of Representatives by a party-line vote of 110-90 to conduct hearings on academic freedom (the hearings are discussed in chapter 7 of this volume). An illustration of the kind of measure that has been introduced is House Bill 1643 of the Virginia State Legislature in January 2007. The bill would have

required every public college or university in the state to "report annually on the steps it is taking to ensure intellectual diversity and free exchange of ideas." A list of things to be prohibited included the "heckling of speakers"; on the positive side, the universities were to "encourage balance [on] panels." This bill was blocked almost immediately and became a dead letter when it was strongly opposed by the Democrats in the chamber. Governor Tim Kaine indicated that he would veto it.

10. ACTA has taken up the challenge of pushing such measures at the state level and on its website reports progress in six or seven states toward securing passage of intellectual diversity bills. See ACTA's website www.goacta.org [March 31, 2008] for further information.

11. The reasons why Arthur Lovejoy and John Dewey originally did not include *Lehrfreiheit* in the American ideas of academic freedom were practical. The German notion of *Lehrfreiheit* presumed a uniform system of universities, which gave students the right to attend any university in the country and to take their final exam at the end of four years at a university of their choosing. For a succinct account of the American ideal of academic freedom, see Robert Post, "The Structure of Academic Freedom," in *Academic Freedom after September 11*, edited by Beshara Doumani (New York: Zone Books, 2006), pp. 61–106.

12. Horowitz sometimes goes over the top in his critiques, especially on matters having to do with Israel and Middle East policy. For example, he has accused liberals of aiding the Iraq insurgency: "Progressive America—most of progressive America—has not wanted us to win the [Iraq] war but has done everything it could to help the enemy and encourage his war against us." See David Horowitz, "Why Progressives Love Water-Boarding," Frontpagemagazine.com, November 20, 2007.

13. See Amy Newhall, "The Unraveling of the Devil's Bargain: The History of Politics and Language Acquisition," and Joel Beinin, "The New McCarthyism: Policing Thought about the Middle East," in *Academic Freedom after September 11*, edited by Doumani.

14. Interview, Washington, January 2008.

15. For a commentary, see Sara Hebel, "Higher Education Groups Issue Statement on Academic Rights and Intellectual Diversity on Campuses," *Chronicle of Higher Education*, July 1, 2005, and "Détente with David Horowitz," Insidehighered.com, June 23, 2005. According to David Ward, president of the ACE, the idea was to embrace part, but not all, of Horowitz's message: "What was happening was that individuals who were critics of higher education were making, to my mind, perfectly reasonable statements that universities should be places of intellectual pluralism, civility, and fairness. . . . I might quibble about details, but I found myself saying, 'They have a point.'" Apropos of student complaints about being discriminated against because of their political views, Ward added, "Some of our institutions don't have procedures in place [for student grievances], and they should."

16. William F. Buckley Jr., *God and Man at Yale* (Chicago: Henry Regnery, 1951).

17. Ibid.

18. According to Daniel Klein and Charlotta Stern, economics is more ideologically

diverse but at the same time more methodologically unified than other social science disciplines. Sociology, in contrast, is methodologically disunited but ideologically united. See Daniel B. Klein and Charlotta Stern, "Professors and Their Politics: The Policy Views of Social Scientists," *Critical Review,* vol. 17, no. 3–4 (2005): 257–303.

19. See William J. Barber, "Reconfigurations in American Academic Economics: A General Practitioner's Perspective," in *American Academic Culture in Transformation: Fifty Years, Four Disciplines,* edited by Thomas Bender and Carl E. Schorske (Princeton University Press, 1998), pp. 105–22.

20. In addition to Buckley's better-known roles in the media, he also played a pivotal role in creating the first major conservative organization devoted to organizing campus activities and focusing attention on the cause of freedom. Buckley served as first president of the Intercollegiate Studies Institute, a large membership organization founded in 1953 that provides scholarships to undergraduates and sponsors events on campus. See Lee Edwards, *Educating for Liberty: The First Half-Century of the Intercollegiate Studies Institute* (Chicago: Henry Regenery, 2005).

21. Robert E. Calvert, ed., *To Restore American Democracy: Political Education and the Modern University* (Lanham, Md.: Rowman and Littlefield, 2006).

22. Jon Wiener, *Historians in Trouble: Plagiarism, Fraud, and Politics in the Ivory Tower* (New York: New Press, 2005).

23. Some liberals on campus see this penchant for appealing to the media as grounds for not hiring or not promoting conservatives. Jon Lott, an economist now with the American Enterprise Institute, was denied tenure at the Wharton School partly on the grounds that many of his publications were "popular" and thus showed a lack of interest in true scholarship. Juan Cole of Michigan, who could not be called a conservative, was disinvited to come to Yale and accept a chair partly on the grounds that he was an inveterate blogger and thus lacked a certain gravitas necessary for a true scholar and Yale professor. One never knows from the outside (and sometimes not even from the inside) the grounds for any particular appointment.

24. Doumani, ed., *Academic Freedom after September 11,* p. 13.

25. Doumani's analysis reflects his perspective of what is happening in Middle East studies. He sees "right-wing pro-Israel" forces as threatening free expression in the classroom. Right-wing and anti-Islam (the two terms are apparently interchangeable) forces comprise a far-reaching conspiracy or at least an organized campaign. He sees Harvard president Laurence Summers's criticism of proposals to divest investments in firms doing business with Israel as having a chilling effect on academic discourse. He notes conspiratorially that Summers's criticism "coincided with the appointment of a professor of Israeli studies at Harvard." Doumani, ed., *Academic Freedom after September 11,* chap. 1.

26. Ibid., p. 14.

27. Ellen Schrecker, "Worse than McCarthy," *Chronicle of Higher Education: Colloquay,* vol. 52, no. 3 (February 20, 2006): 8. Schrecker is careful to add that she regards the danger as "potential."

28. Neil Gross found that one-third of professors now compared to about one-fifth

in the previous survey felt such threats. See "Political Views on Academic Freedom," Insidehighered.com, August 15, 2007.

29. Morris P. Fiorina, Samuel J. Abrams, and Jeremy C. Pope, eds., *Culture War? The Myth of a Polarized America* (Harvard University Press, 2005).

30. Ibid., p. 5.

31. See Timothy C. Shiell, *Campus Hate Speech on Trial* (University Press of Kansas, 1998); Jon B. Gould, *Speak No Evil: The Triumph of Hate Speech Regulation* (University of Chicago Press, 2005); Donald A. Downs, *Restoring Free Speech and Liberty on Campus* (Cambridge University Press; Oakland, Calif.: Independent Institute, 2005); and Cass R. Sunstein, "Academic Freedom and the Law: Liberalism, Speech Codes, and Related Problems," in *The Future of Academic Freedom,* edited by Louis Menand (University of Chicago Press, 1996), pp. 93–118.

32. See Gould, *Speak No Evil.*

33. See, for example, Sunstein, "Academic Freedom and the Law." Another approach relies on a different legal strategy analogous to the working environment standards operative in the corporate world to supplant Sunstein's "narrow code" argument.

34. Alan C. Kors and Harvey A. Silverglade, *The Shadow University: The Betrayal of Liberty on America's Campuses* (New York: Free Press, 1998).

35. For a brief history of ACTA, see its newsletter, *Inside Academy*, vol. 10, no. 3 (Spring 2005): 1–4, 9.

36. Jerry L. Martin and Anne D. Neal, *Defending Civilization: How Our Universities Are Failing America and What Can Be Done about It* (Washington: American Council of Trustees and Alumni, 2002).

37. Edwin Meese, ACTA member and a trustee of George Mason University, spoke at ACTA's tenth anniversary conference and pointed with pride to curricular changes made by George Mason's History Department. The department, apparently with the trustees' prodding, revised its offerings in the direction of a more traditional curriculum (for example, more American constitutional history, more survey courses, and fewer "identity" courses).

38. See Richard Hofstadter, *The Paranoid Style in American Politics and Other Essays* (Harvard University Press, 1996).

39. The June 23, 2005, ACE statement on academic rights and responsibilities signed by the nearly thirty higher educational associations was on the delegates' minds. It was viewed as an important step and commented on favorably by a number of the speakers and participants. The ACE statement had endorsed "intellectual pluralism and academic freedom [as] central principles of American higher education. . . . Colleges and universities should welcome intellectual pluralism and the free exchange of ideas." ACTA considered the ACE statement as a victory for its principles, and trustees were urged to work with their presidents and provosts to get the ACE statement incorporated into university policies. A subsequent ACTA report found, however, that the universities themselves had done little or nothing to adopt the principles agreed to by their Washington associations. See ACTA, *Intellectual Diversity: Time for Action* (Washington, D.C., 2005). For a forceful statement of ACTA's views, see also Anne D. Neal's testimony before the Commonwealth of Pennsylvania, House of Representatives, Select

Committee on Academic Freedom in Higher Education, January 10, 2006, official transcript, hearings held at Temple University in Philadelphia.

## Chapter 7

1. Neil Gross and Solon Simmons, "Americans' Views of Political Bias in the Academy and Academic Freedom," Working Paper (Harvard University and George Mason University, May 22, 2006), pp. 12, 23.

2. See Michael Berube, *What's Liberal about the Liberal Arts? Classroom Politics and "Bias" in Higher Education* (New York: W. W. Norton, 2006), chap. 6 for a useful exposition.

3. On the notion of whether certain philosophies undermine rationalist thought and objective scholarship, see the illuminating essay by Richard Rorty, "Does Academic Freedom Have Philosophical Presuppositions?" in *The Future of Academic Freedom*, edited by Louis Menand (University of Chicago Press, 1996), pp. 21–42.

4. Cass R. Sunstein, Davide Schkade, Lisa M. Ellman, and Andres Sawicki, *Are Judges Political? An Empirical Analysis of the Federal Judiciary* (Brookings, 2006), point to this kind of effect among judges. Three-judge circuit court panels made up of all Democrats or all Republicans accentuate their liberal or conservative leanings. On mixed-party panels, Republican judges voted 38 percent liberal, compared to Democrats, who voted 51 percent liberal, but on all-Republican panels, they voted 31 percent liberal, whereas all-Democrat panels voted 66 percent liberal. The inference might be that if a department is made up of all liberals, they will move to the extreme left and vice versa.

5. Horowitz himself has diagnosed his own problem in such terms. His main problem, he commented, is with conservatives. "The liberals know they are in a war . . . ; it's our side that doesn't recognize the problem." Quoted in Valerie Richardson, "Academic Manifesto Takes Root," *Washington Times*, July 3, 2006.

6. For a useful short history of government funding for Middle East studies and language programs, see Amy Newhall, "The Unraveling of the Devil's Bargain: The History and Politics of Language Acquisition," in *Academic Freedom after September 11*, edited by Beshara Doumani (New York: Zone Books, 2006), pp. 203–36. The feud in Middle East studies began in the 1950s when older scholars who worked under the framework of "Near East studies" were challenged by a newer breed who attacked what they deemed an excessively philological approach. The newer breed of scholars favored more attention to the political, social, and economic realities of the Middle East. Programs of Middle East languages and culture gradually supplanted the Near East departments at most elite universities, spurred by government funding for language study after the National Defense Education Act of 1958 and Title VI of the Higher Education Act of 1965. A bitter personal feud between Columbia's Edward Said and Princeton's Bernard Lewis erupted in 1982, which reflected some of the central differences between the older generation of Near Eastern linguistic scholars and the newer generation of scholars (and exacerbated by Said's championing of postcolonial theory). Lewis saw Said's criticism of Orientalism as a personal attack. The personal animus between the two hardened after a confrontation at a conference in 1986. What started

as a personal feud became in time a battle between warring ideological camps in the field of Middle East studies. Martin S. Kramer, *Ivory Towers on Sand: The Future of Middle East Studies in America* (Washington: Institute for Near East Policy, 2001), assailed the main practitioners of Middle East studies in the universities and heated up the ideological feud. The events of September 11, 2001, did not precipitate, but did exacerbate, the complex, bitter ideological-methodological disputes within Middle Eastern studies. The scholarly dispute became intermingled with pro-Israel and anti-Israel politics. For an account of the history of this dispute, written from the point of view of someone who sees Zionist influences at work, see Joel Beinin, "The New McCarthyism: Policing Thought about the Middle East," in *Academic Freedom after September 11*, edited by Doumani, pp. 237–66. John Voll analyzes how "advocacy" has affected the field over many years but can be coped with in a thoughtful essay, "Advocacy and Explanation: The Problems of Explaining Adversaries," in *Advocacy in the Classroom*, edited by Patricia Meyer Spacks (New York: St. Martin's Press, 1996), pp. 171–83.

7. Quoted in Beinin, "The New McCarthyism," p. 253.

8. Ibid.

9. The measure was watered down before it reached the Senate to limit the board's powers to that of merely suggesting improvements in programs, not vetoing funding altogether.

10. See Amy Newhall, "The Unraveling of the Devil's Bargain," in *Academic Freedom after September 11*, edited by Doumani, pp. 220–21.

11. Timothy Starks, "The Universities Resist Efforts to Require Intellectual Diversity," *New York Sun*, April 15, 2003, cited in Beinin, "The New McCarthyism," p. 266.

12. For the text of HR 177 of the Commonwealth of Pennsylvania, see appendix E.

13. Buoyed by the Pennsylvania developments, South Dakota in February 2006 passed House Bill 1222 in the House of Representatives, which called for the state's public universities to issue an annual intellectual diversity report. The report would require each university to note progress during the preceding year toward the goal of greater intellectual diversity. The South Dakota Senate, however, after intense lobbying efforts by university officials, defeated the measure on February 23, 2006, by a vote of 13-10. In Colorado and Ohio, the Horowitz forces claimed small victories in 2005. State legislators in Colorado dropped consideration of a diversity measure when the presidents of the state's major colleges and universities agreed to a memorandum of understanding to seek intellectual diversity as a goal. In Colorado the flagship Boulder campus was in such turmoil that any measure to secure peace with the legislature seemed highly desirable. The Boulder campus had been rocked by the Ward Churchill controversy, the football team scandal, the firing of campus president Elizabeth Hoffman, and the deaths of two students in a dormitory drinking incident. In Ohio, state Senator Larry A. Mumper proposed an academic bill of rights, Senate Bill 24, in the 2005–06 session, which was the most intrusive of its kind. Mumper withdrew the bill when the state's public college and university presidents agreed informally to look into the issues of diversity of views.

14. Official transcript, Commonwealth of Pennsylvania, House of Representatives, Select Committee on Academic Freedom in Higher Education, January 9, 2006, p. 6.

15. Ibid., pp. 40–43.

16. Official transcript, January 10, 2006, pp. 146–47.

17. Ibid., pp. 101, 161, 167.

18. Ibid., p. 171.

19. *Final Report of the Select Committee on Academic Freedom in Higher Education Pursuant to House Resolution 177* (Commonwealth of Pennsylvania, House of Representatives, Harrisburg, Pa., November 21, 2006).

20. See http://dangerousprofessors.net/ [April 3, 2008]. Horowitz suggests that Curry persuaded two Republicans to embrace his (Curry's) view of HR 177.

21. See Spacks, ed., *Advocacy in the Classroom*.

22. The American Council on Education in November 2007 issued an eight-page memorandum, "Political Campaign-Related Activities of and at Colleges and Universities," in which it sought to clarify for its member institutions what is and is not a permissible political activity on campus. The memorandum, prepared by the Washington law firm of Hogan & Hartson, LLP, was directed at activities during "campaigns," but there was no definition of the point at which a campaign or campaign season begins. The document was both highly detailed and highly general, an artful composition, but one that probably went straight into the files of a university's general counsel and was seldom referred to or even read by the institution's operating officers. Examples of permitted activities include voter education programs and nonpartisan voter registration activities, institution-sponsored public forums, invitations asking candidates to appear "in a non-candidate capacity," and public statements by faculty provided they are clearly identified as "personal." Examples of prohibited activities include undertaking certain kinds of voter registration drives, combining voter registration drives with campaign events, endorsing a candidate for public office, commenting on specific actions or positions taken by a candidate, sponsoring events to advance the candidacy of a particular candidate, issuing public statements by institutional officials on behalf of specific candidates, and providing a forum for one candidate without providing similar venues for other candidates.

## Chapter 8

1. Louis Menand, "Culture and Advocacy," in *Advocacy in the Classroom: Problems and Possibilities,* edited by Patricia Meyer Spacks (New York: St. Martin's Press, 1996), p. 122.

2. Jeremy D. Mayer and Heather M. Schmidt, "Gendered Political Socialization in Four Contexts: Political Interest and Values among Junior High School Students in China, Japan, Mexico, and the United States," *Social Science Journal*, vol. 41, no. 3 (2004): 393–407.

3. Geert Hofstede and Gert Jan Hofstede, *Cultures and Organizations: Software of the Mind* (New York: McGraw-Hill, 2005), pp. 6–9, 21–22, 208–12.

4. Gordon Hewett and Mack Mariani, an article forthcoming in *PS: Political Science,* in 2008. An article giving some of the study's findings is available at http://

spotlight.encarta.msn.com/Features/encnet_Departments_eLearning_default_article_ProfessorPolitics.html?GT1=27001 [April 18, 2008].

5. See Todd Gitlin, "The Values of Media, the Values of Citizenship, and the Values of Higher Education," in *To Restore American Democracy: Political Education and the Modern University,* edited by Robert E. Calvert (Lanhan, Md.: Rowman and Littlefield, 2006), pp. 79–94.

6. John Zaller, *The Nature and Origins of Mass Opinion* (Cambridge University Press, 1992).

7. April Kelly-Woessner and Matthew Woessner, "My Professor Is a Partisan Hack: How Perceptions of a Professor's Political Views Affect Student Course Evaluations," *PS: Political Science & Politics,* vol. 39, no. 3 (2006): 495–501, at p. 498.

8. Ibid., p. 500.

9. Molly S. Andolina and Jeremy D. Mayer, "Demographic Shifts and Racial Attitudes: How Tolerant Are Whites in the Most Diverse Generation?" *Social Science Journal,* vol. 40, no. 1 (2003): 19–31.

10. See *Final Report of the Select Committee on Academic Freedom in Higher Education Pursuant to House Resolution 177* (House of Representatives, Commonwealth of Pennsylvania, Harrisburg, Pa., November 21, 2006), pp. 11–12.

11. Official transcript, Commonwealth of Pennsylvania, House of Representatives, Select Committee on Academic Freedom in Higher Education, January 9, 2006, Testimony of Robert M. O'Neil, p. 67.

12. Ibid., pp. 65–66.

13. Cass R. Sunstein, "Public Spaces and MyUniversity.com," in *To Restore American Democracy,* edited by Calvert, pp. 95–116.

14. *Washington Post,* December 21, 2006.

15. Ibid.

16. Ibid.

17. R. Eugene Rice, "Religious Diversity and the Making of Meaning: Implications for the Classroom," *Democracy and Diversity,* vol. 1, no. 1 (Winter 2008): 1.

18. Roper Center, Politics in the Classroom: A Survey of Students at the Top 50 Colleges and Universities, conducted by the Center for Survey Research and Analysis, University of Connecticut, 2005.

19. American Council of Trustees and Alumni (ACTA), "Analysis and Commentary: Executive Summary" (Center for Survey Research and Analysis, University of Connecticut, 2005), p. 2.

20. Ibid., p. 9.

21. Ibid., p. 12.

22. Ibid.

23. Ibid., p. 13.

24. Ibid.

25. Neil Gross and Solon Simmons, "The Social and Political Views of American Professors," Working Paper (Harvard University and George Mason University, September 24, 2007), p. 29. They find that community colleges have 37.1 percent liberal professors; bachelor of arts–granting, nonliberal arts colleges, 38.8 percent; liberal arts

colleges, 61 percent; non-elite PhD-granting universities, 44.3 percent; and elite PhD-granting universities, 56.6 percent. The figures, respectively, for conservative faculty members at these categories of schools are 19.0, 12.7, 3.9, 3.8, and 10.2 percent.

26. The number of students in the survey who identified themselves as conservative—only three out of the 658 total respondents—is too small to have any significance.

27. Woessner and Woessner, "My Professor Is a Partisan Hack," pp. 10–11.

28. Ibid.

29. Ibid., p. 15.

30. Stuart Taylor and K. C. Johnson, "Guilty in the Duke Case," *Washington Post,* September 11, 2007, p. A21, and Stuart Taylor and K. C. Johnson, *Until Proven Innocent: Political Correctness and the Shameful Injustices of the Duke Lacrosse Rape Case* (New York: Thomas Dunne Books/St. Martin's Press, 2007).

31. Neil Gross and Solon Simmons, "Americans' Attitudes toward Academic Freedom and Liberal 'Bias' in Higher Education," Working Paper (Harvard University and George Mason University, May 22, 2006).

32. Ibid., p. 12.

33. Ibid., p. 20.

34. Ibid., p. 22.

35. ACE Statement on Academic Rights and Responsibilities, June 23, 2005, para. 2. See chapter 6 of this volume for a discussion of how this statement came about.

36. Gross and Simmons, "Americans' Attitudes toward Academic Freedom," p. 12.

37. Frederick Randolph, *American Colleges and Universities* (Georgia University Press, 1962), pp. 159–60.

38. William A. Galston, "Between Resignation and Utopia: Political Education in the Modern American University," in *To Restore American Democracy,* edited by Calvert, p. 37.

39. Robert E. Calvert, "Utopias Gone Wrong: The Antipolitical Culture of the Modern University and How to Change It," in *To Restore American Democracy,* edited by Calvert, p. 250.

40. Ibid.

41. Gross and Simmons, "Americans' Attitudes toward Academic Freedom," p. 15; Walter Russell Mead, "God's Country," *Foreign Affairs,* vol. 85, no. 5 (September-October 2006): 24–43.

42. Gross and Simmons, "Americans' Attitudes toward Academic Freedom," p. 12.

## Chapter 9

1. Gary A. Tobin and Aryeh K. Weinberg, *A Profile of American College Faculty,* vol. 1: *Political Beliefs and Behavior* (San Francisco: Institute for Jewish and Community Research, 2006), p. 2.

2. Andrew Delbanco, for example, points to "vestiges of male chauvinism in university life, especially in certain scientific fields that have been slow to recruit and promote

qualified women." See his review essay, "Higher Education Scandals," *New York Review of Books*, March 29, 2007, p. 45.

3. Sarah E. Turner and William G. Bowen, "The Flight from the Arts and Sciences: Trends in Degrees Conferred," *Science*, October 26, 1990, pp. 517–21.

4. Jerome Karabel, *The Chosen: The Hidden History of Admission and Exclusion at Harvard, Yale, and Princeton* (Boston: Houghton Mifflin, 2005).

5. By contrast, today places are allocated by lot.

6. There had been an issue in the 1950s over Harvard's alleged collaboration with the investigation by the Un-American Activities Committee of the U.S. House of Representatives dealing with the issue of communists in higher education. In particular, McGeorge Bundy as dean of the College of Arts and Sciences was criticized for his role in the firing of Sigmund Diamond, who had been a communist in the late 1930s. See David A. Hollinger, *Science, Jews, and the Secular Culture: Studies in Mid-Twentieth-Century American Intellectual History* (Princeton University Press, 1998), chap. 7, and Sigmund Diamond, *Compromised Campus: The Collaboration of Universities with the Intelligence Community, 1945–55* (Oxford University Press, 1992), chaps. 2–5. Robert Bellah, sociologist, also left Harvard for Berkeley because of pressures he experienced and his displeasure at Harvard's response to McCarthyism.

7. Daniel Bell, *The End of Ideology* (New York: Free Press, 1960).

8. John B. Williams, *Race Discrimination in Public Higher Education: Interpreting Federal Civil Rights Enforcement, 1964–1996* (New York: Praeger, 1997).

9. John R. Thelin, *A History of American Higher Education* (Johns Hopkins University Press, 2004), p. 305.

10. On the current status of women, see Judith Glazer-Raymond, *Shattering the Myths: Women in Academe* (Johns Hopkins University Press, 2001), and Lynn H. Collins, Joan C. Chrisler, and Kathryn Quina, eds., *Career Strategies for Women in Academia: Arming Athena* (Thousand Oaks, Calif.: Sage Publications, 1998).

11. Joanne Moody, *Faculty Diversity: Problems and Solutions* (New York: Routledge, 2004).

12. Gross and Simmons found sharp disagreements among faculty on questions of affirmative action. See Neil Gross and Solon Simmons, "The Social and Political Views of American Professors," Working Paper (Harvard University and George Mason University, September 24, 2007).

13. Matthew Woessner and April Kelly-Woessner, "Left Pipeline: Why Conservatives Don't Get Doctorates," paper prepared for the conference Reforming the Politically Correct University, American Enterprise Institute, Washington, November 14, 2007.

14. For an example, consider the "opportunity hire" programs at the University of Southern Maine (http://www.usm.maine.edu/eeo/diversity/lac.html [April 18, 2008]) and Trinity College (http://www.trincoll.edu/prog/facman/doc0018.html [April 18, 2008]). The same or similar terms are also used to describe spousal hires and some senior hires made in an accelerated and opportunistic fashion. They are rarely used to hire a white male junior faculty member, however. The legality of such programs has been challenged and, to the extent that they focus exclusively on race, are illegal in the public university system in states that have banned racial preferences, such as California,

Texas, and Florida. See Roger Clegg, "Faculty Hiring Preferences and the Law," *Chronicle of Higher Education*, May 19, 2006.

15. See Derek Bok, *Beyond the Ivory Tower: Social Responsibilities of the Modern University* (Harvard University Press, 1982), p. 21.

16. "Comparative Politics Section," *Newsletter of the American Political Science Association*, vol. 18, no. 1 (Winter 2007).

17. Ibid.

18. David Horowitz, *The Professors: The 101 Most Dangerous Academics in America* (Washington: Regnery, 2006).

19. Jennifer Howard, "DePaul U. Turns Norman Finkelstein Down for Tenure," *Chronicle of Higher Education*, April 5, 2007.

20. "Comparative Politics Section," p. 13.

21. Ibid., p. 14. Dan Olson, *Joining the Club: A History of Jews at Yale* (Yale University Press, 2000).

22. See Michael Walzer, "Moral Education and Democratic Citizenship," in *To Restore American Democracy: Political Education and the Modern University*, edited by Robert E. Calvert (Lanhan, Md.: Rowman and Littlefield, 2006); see also the essay by William Galston, "Between Resignation and Utopia: Political Education and the Modern University," in that volume, especially pp. 40–42, for practical suggestions on how to improve civic education in the contemporary university. Calvert in his concluding chapter, "Utopias Gone Wrong: The Anti-Political Culture of the Modern University and How to Change," calls for issues to be taught, Galston, "Between Resignation and Utopia," calls for internships, and Steven Holmes, "Plato's Dogs: Reflections on the University after 9/11," calls for a return to a language requirement. Consult their chapters in *To Restore American Democracy*, edited by Calvert.

23. Galston, "Between Resignation and Utopia," pp. 40–42.

24. Quoted in *To Restore American Democracy*, edited by Calvert, p. 2, and see the accompanying discussion by Calvert. Holmes, "Plato's Dogs," gives a critique of participation alone without wider intellectual engagement as inadequate and as a holdover from 1960s radicalism. Calvert, however, in his concluding chapter, "Utopias Gone Wrong," considers civic republicanism as requiring citizen involvement and disavows Holmes's equating of participation with 1960s radicalism.

25. "Comparative Politics Section."

26. Ibid.

27. See Rogers M. Smith, "Still Blowing in the Wind: The American Quest for a Democratic, Scientific Political Science," in *American Academic Culture in Transformation*, edited by Thomas Bender and Carl E. Schorske, pp. 271–308 (Princeton University Press, 1997); Ira Katznelson, "From the Street to the Lecture: The Sixties," in *American Academic Culture in Transformation*, edited by Bender and Schorske, pp. 331–52.

28. Stanley Rothman, S. Robert Lichter, and Neil Nevitte, "Politics and Professional Advancement among College Faculty," *The Forum*, vol. 3, no. 1 (2005): art. 2.

29. Their measure of religion is interactive. Bivariate comparisons of religious faith and institutional quality showed no relationship, however: when denomination plus frequency of attendance at worship services were combined, a bivariate relationship was

observed. Thus "practicing Christian" and "practicing Jew" were included as dummy variables in the multivariate analysis. Their article does not indicate what level of attendance distinguished those practicing religion from those merely averring it. Thus, even if their data were publicly available, this would be another obstacle to replication.

30. Rothman, Lichter, and Nevitte, "Politics and Professional Advancement," p. 13.

31. Howard Kurtz, "College Faculties a Most Liberal Lot, Study Finds," *Washington Post*, March 29, 2005, p. C1.

32. Jamie Glazov, "Purging Conservatives from College Faculties," *Front-PageMagazine.com,* May 23, 2005.

33. Everette C. Ladd Jr. and Seymour Martin Lipset, *The Divided Academy: Professors and Politics* (New York: McGraw-Hill, 1975), p. 141.

34. Jeremy D. Mayer, *Running on Race: Racial Politics in Presidential Campaigns* (New York: Random House, 2002).

35. Ibid., p. 163.

36. Paul Lazarsfeld and Walter Thielens, *The Academic Mind* (Glencoe, Ill.: Free Press, 1958), p. 188.

37. One supposes that this may be the case with some leading scholars of religion. They could teach at many institutions ranked well above their current affiliations but choose to belong to a faith-based institution despite its ranking.

38. Michael Berube, *What's Liberal about the Liberal Arts? Classroom Politics and "Bias" in Higher Education* (New York: W. W. Norton, 2006), pp. 284–85. Stephen Holmes, "Plato's Dogs: Reflections on the University after 9/11," in *To Restore American Democracy,* edited by Calvert, pp. 200–01. Berube and Holmes, both admirable scholars who have written interesting works, reflect a trace of "we" against "they" in their analyses, finding it almost inconceivable that any fair-minded individual could hold conservative views.

39. Walter Benn Michaels, *The Trouble with Diversity: How We Learned to Love Identity and Ignore Inequality* (New York: Metropolitan, 2006). For a useful commentary, see Delbanco, "Higher Education Scandals."

40. In 2004 in a series of lectures at the University of Virginia, William Bowen came out in favor of "a thumb on the scale," that is, class-based affirmative action to help poor and working-class students gain admission to college. See William G. Bowen, Marian A. Kurzweil, and Eugene M. Tobin, in collaboration with Suzanne C. Pichler, *Equity and Excellence in American Higher Education* (University of Virginia Press, 2005).

## Chapter 10

1. See Anthony T. Kronman, "Colleges Ignore Life's Biggest Questions, and We All Pay the Price," *Boston Globe*, September 16, 2007, and Anthony T. Kronman, *Education's End: Why Our Colleges and Universities Have Given up on the Meaning of Life* (Yale University Press, 2007), especially chapter 3.

2. Benjamin Rush, "To the Citizens of Pennsylvania," *Pennsylvania Pocket,* February 17, 1785, quoted in A. Lee Fritschler, "Welcoming Remarks," in *Proceedings of the Amer-*

*ican Revolutionary College Conference on the Liberal Arts and Education for Citizenship in the Twenty-First Century* (Carlisle, Pa.: Dickinson College, March 1998), p. 69.

3. For a discussion of the formation and then the breakdown of the postwar consensus of science policy, see Bruce L. R. Smith, *American Science Policy since World War II* (Brookings, 1990).

4. Quoted in Theodore J. Lowi, *The Politics of Disorder* (New York: Basic Books, 1971), p. 127.

5. The "Sokol hoax" of 1995 is an illustration of scientists joining the culture wars. In this case, a New York University physicist duped the editors of *Critical Theory*, a leading journal of the new interdisciplinary scholarship in the humanities and social sciences, into publishing a parody of the genre. The article purported to offer a new theory of science and was laden with jargon and pompous terminology. The editors were acutely embarrassed but accused the perpetrator of malice.

6. Thomas L. Haskell, "Justifying the Rights of Academic Freedom in the Age of 'Power/Knowledge,'" in *The Future of Academic Freedom*, edited by Louis Menand (University of Chicago Press, 1996), p. 43.

7. Hannah Rosen, *God's Harvard: A Christian College on a Mission to Save America* (New York: Harcourt Brace Jovanovich, 2007).

8. See Russell K. Nieli, *The Decline and Revival of Liberal Learning at Duke*, Series on Higher Education Policy (Raleigh, N.C.: John William Pope Center for Higher Education Policy, March 2007), available on the center's website, www.popecenter.org [April 8, 2008].

9. See Cass R. Sunstein, "Public Spaces and MyUniversity.com," in *To Restore American Democracy: Political Education and the Modern University*, edited by Robert E. Calvert (Lanhan, Md.: Rowman and Littlefield, 2006); Cass R. Sunstein, *Republic.com* (Princeton University Press, 2002).

10. William A. Galston, "Between Resignation and Utopia: Political Education in the Modern American University," in *To Restore American Democracy*, edited by Calvert, p. 37.

11. On American attitudes toward government, see Garry Wills, *A Necessary Evil: A History of American Distrust of Government* (New York: Simon and Schuster, 1999).

12. See Sunstein, "Public Spaces and MyUniversity.com," pp. 111–14.

13. See chapter 5 of this volume.

14. Mark Bauerlein, "How Academe Shortchanges Conservative Thinking," *Chronicle of Higher Education*, vol. 55, no. 17 (December 2006): B6.

# Index

269